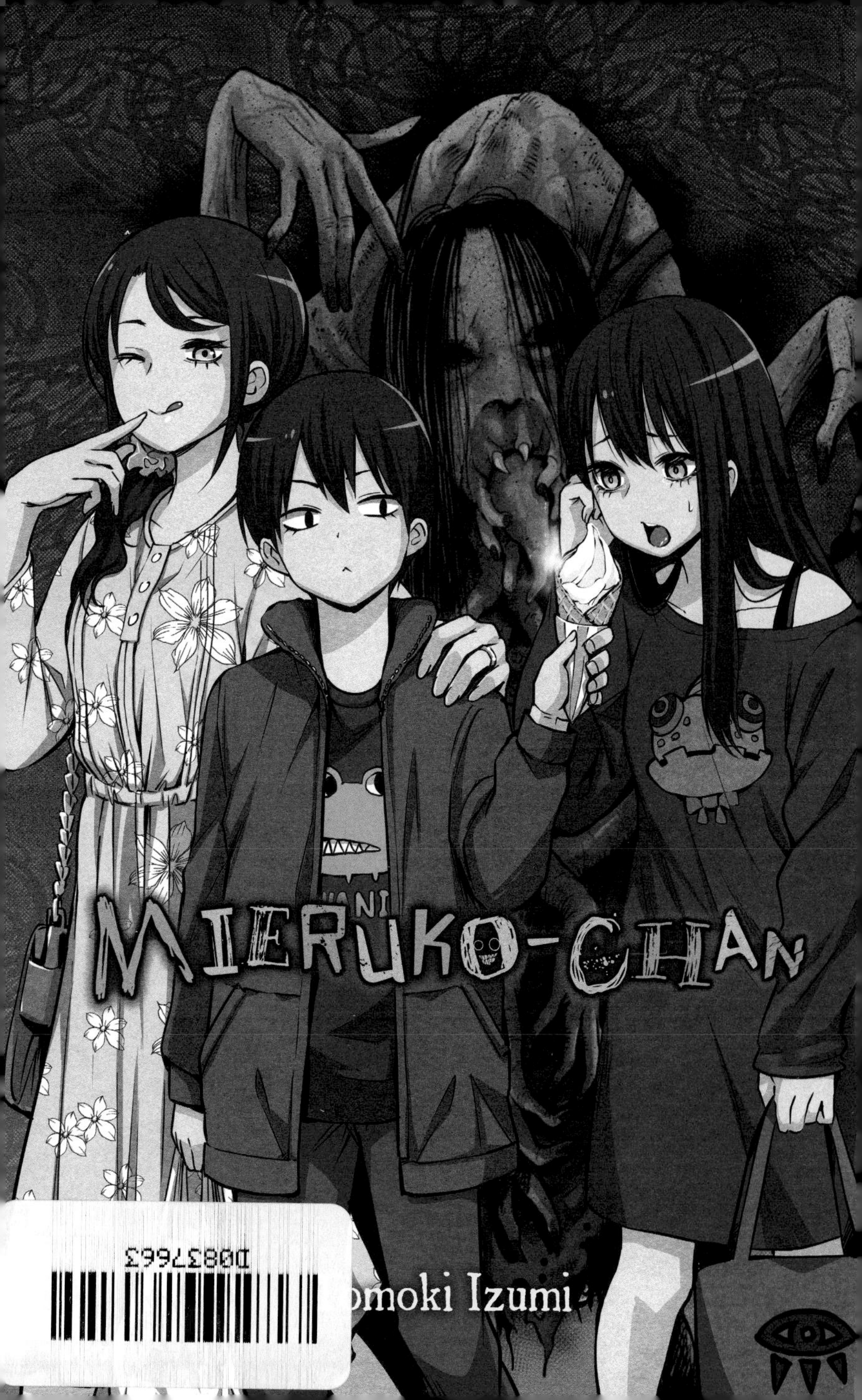
MIERUKO-CHAN
omoki Izumi

CONTENTS

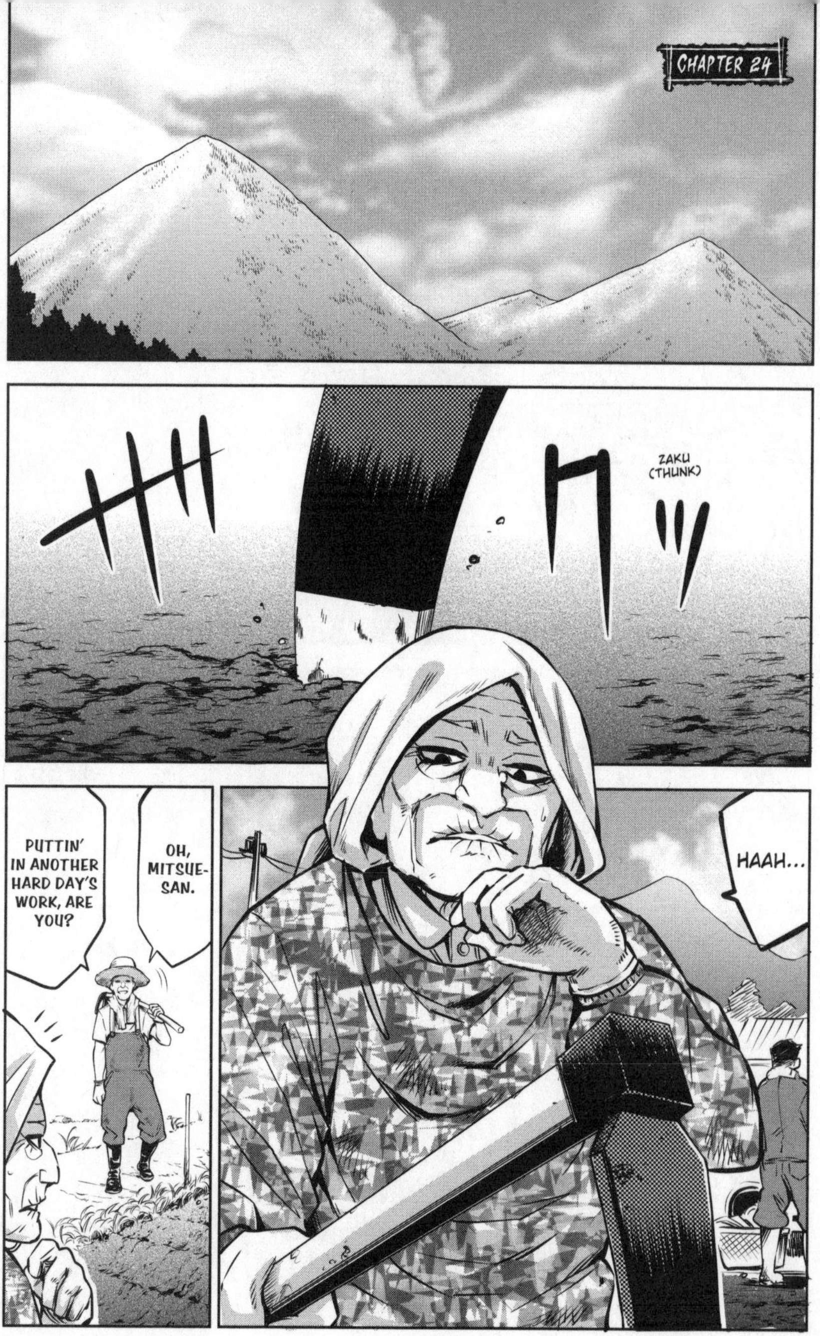
CHAPTER 24
ザクッ
ZAKU (THUNK)
HAAH...
OH, MITSUE-SAN.
PUTTIN' IN ANOTHER HARD DAY'S WORK, ARE YOU?

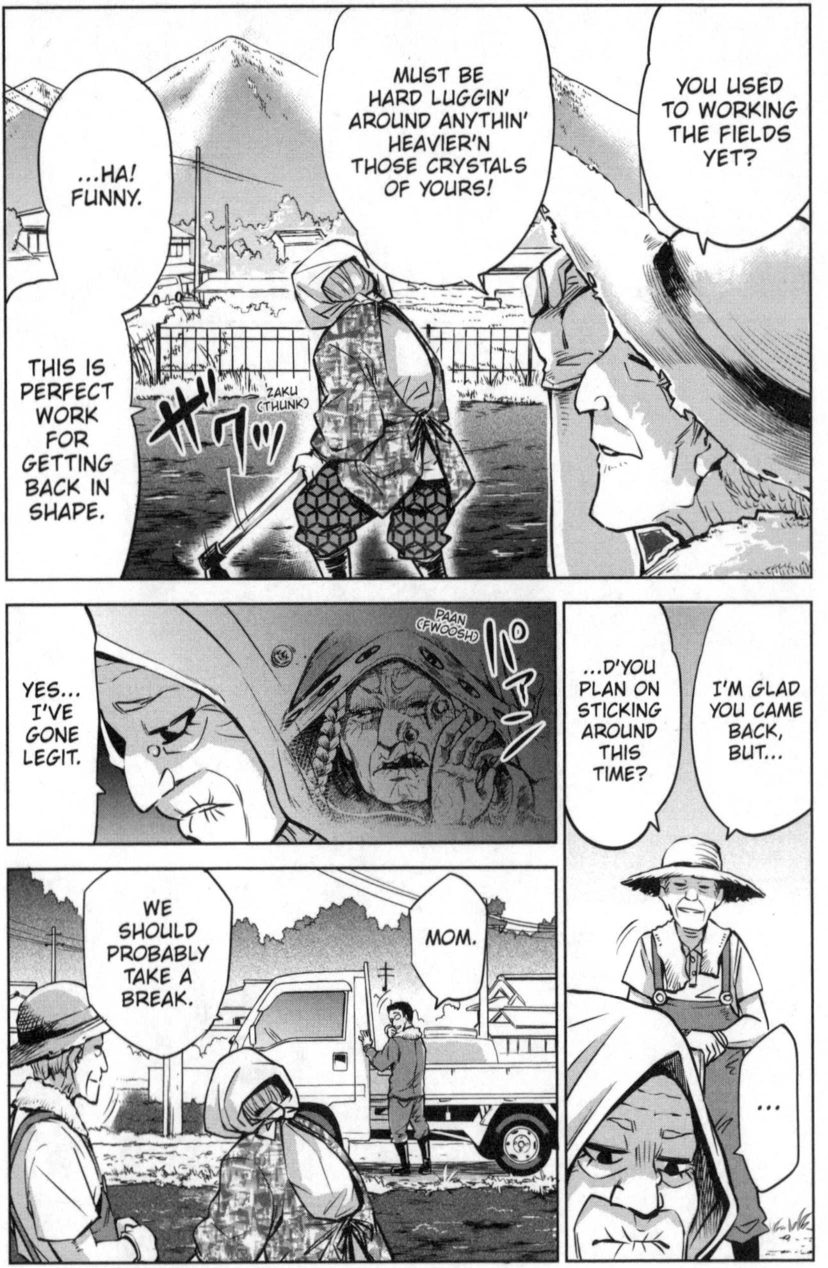
YOU USED TO WORKING THE FIELDS YET?
MUST BE HARD LUGGIN' AROUND ANYTHIN' HEAVIER'N THOSE CRYSTALS OF YOURS!
...HA! FUNNY.
ZAKU (THUNK)
THIS IS PERFECT WORK FOR GETTING BACK IN SHAPE.
I'M GLAD YOU CAME BACK, BUT...
...D'YOU PLAN ON STICKING AROUND THIS TIME?
...
PAAN (FWOOSH)
YES... I'VE GONE LEGIT.
MOM.
WE SHOULD PROBABLY TAKE A BREAK.

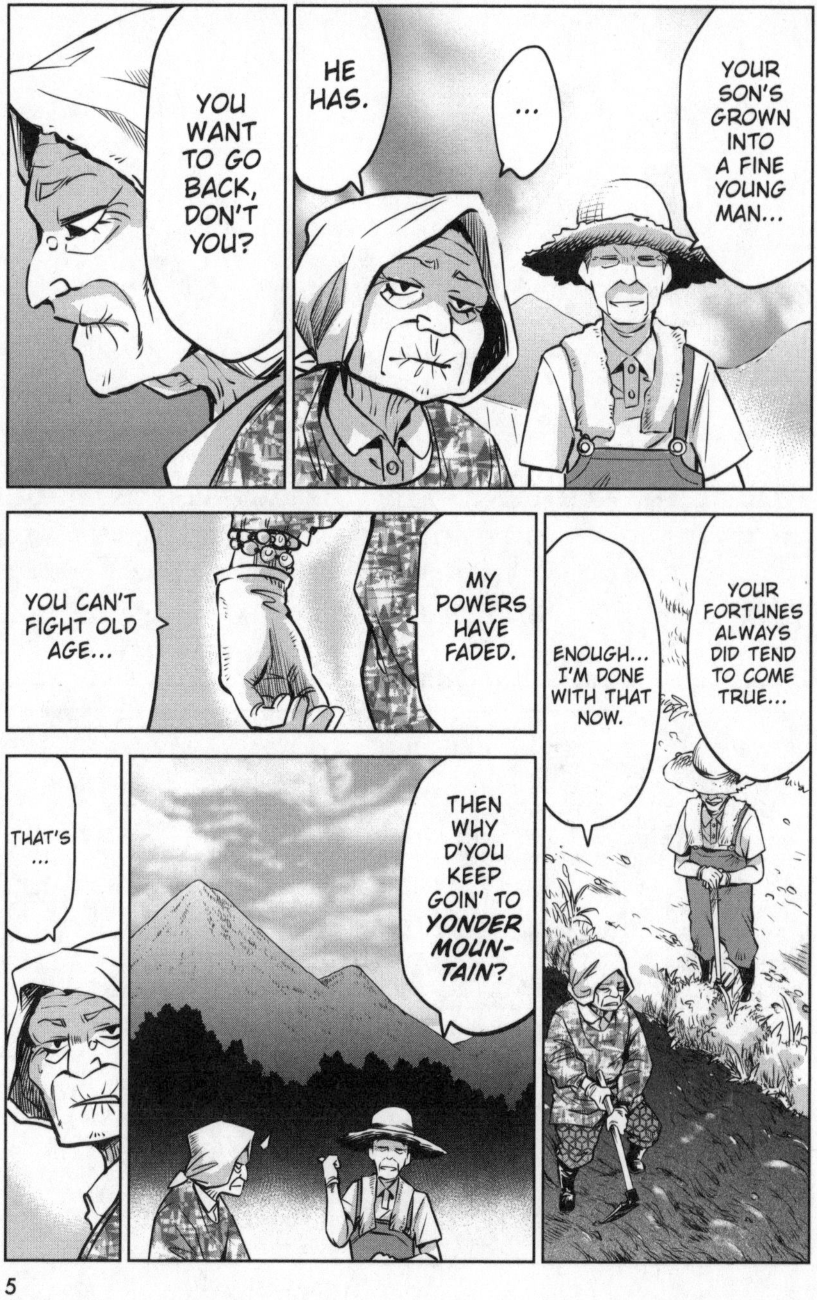
YOUR SON'S GROWN INTO A FINE YOUNG MAN...
...
HE HAS.
YOU WANT TO GO BACK, DON'T YOU?
YOUR FORTUNES ALWAYS DID TEND TO COME TRUE...
ENOUGH... I'M DONE WITH THAT NOW.
MY POWERS HAVE FADED.
YOU CAN'T FIGHT OLD AGE...
THEN WHY D'YOU KEEP GOIN' TO *YONDER MOUNTAIN*?
THAT'S ...

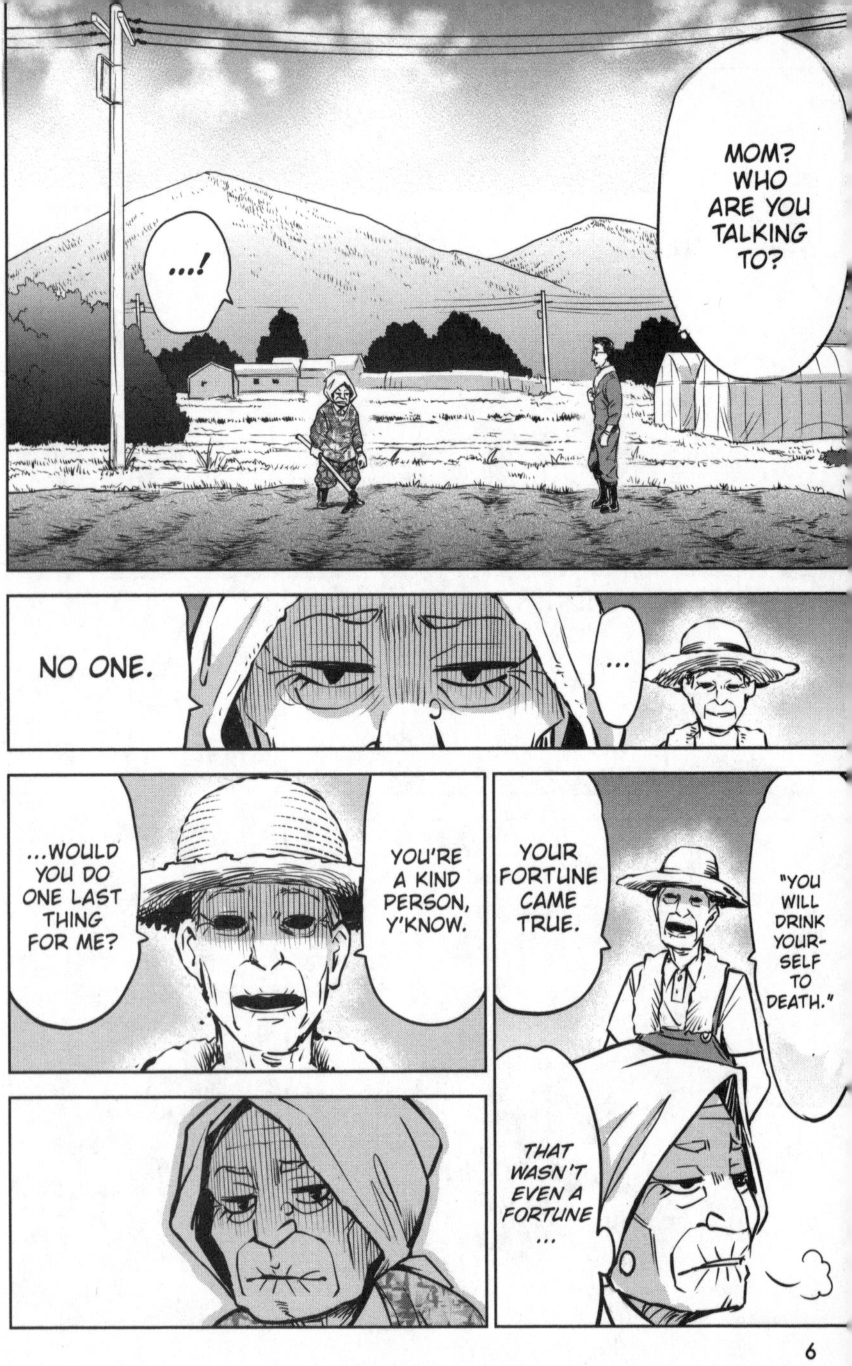
MOM? WHO ARE YOU TALKING TO?
...!
...
NO ONE.
"YOU WILL DRINK YOURSELF TO DEATH."
YOUR FORTUNE CAME TRUE.
THAT WASN'T EVEN A FORTUNE...
YOU'RE A KIND PERSON, Y'KNOW.
...WOULD YOU DO ONE LAST THING FOR ME?

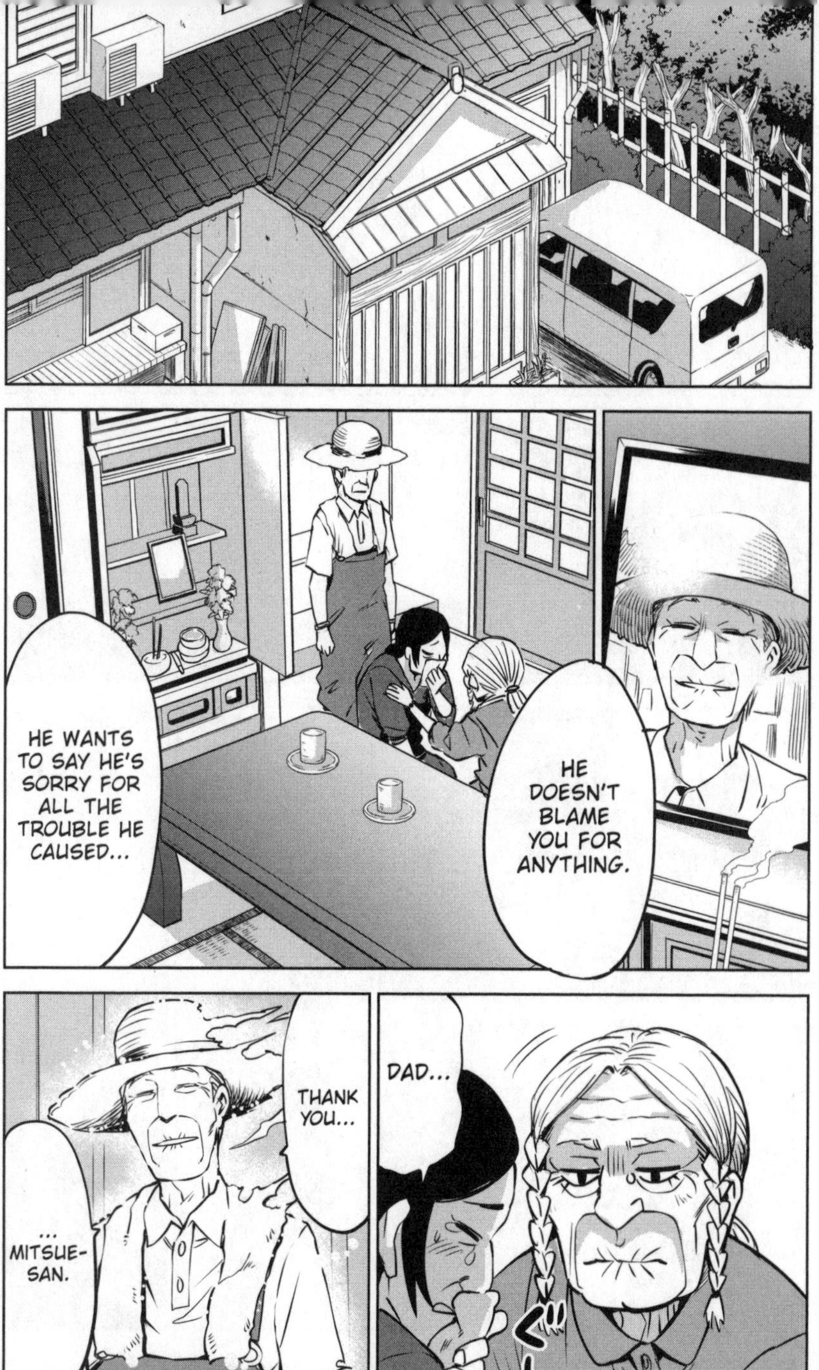
HE DOESN'T BLAME YOU FOR ANYTHING.
HE WANTS TO SAY HE'S SORRY FOR ALL THE TROUBLE HE CAUSED...
DAD...
ぐしっ
GUSHI (SNIFFLE)
THANK YOU...
... MITSUE-SAN.

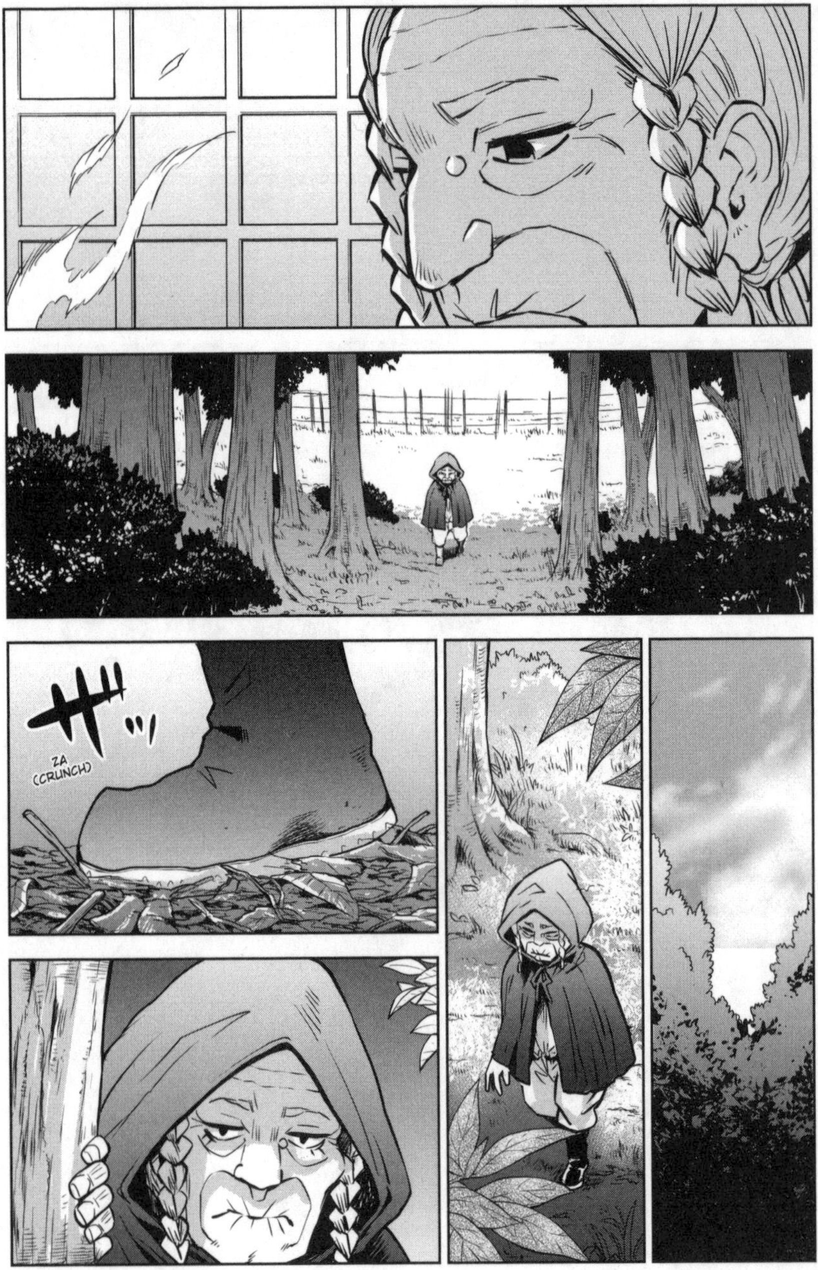
ザッ
ZA (CRUNCH)

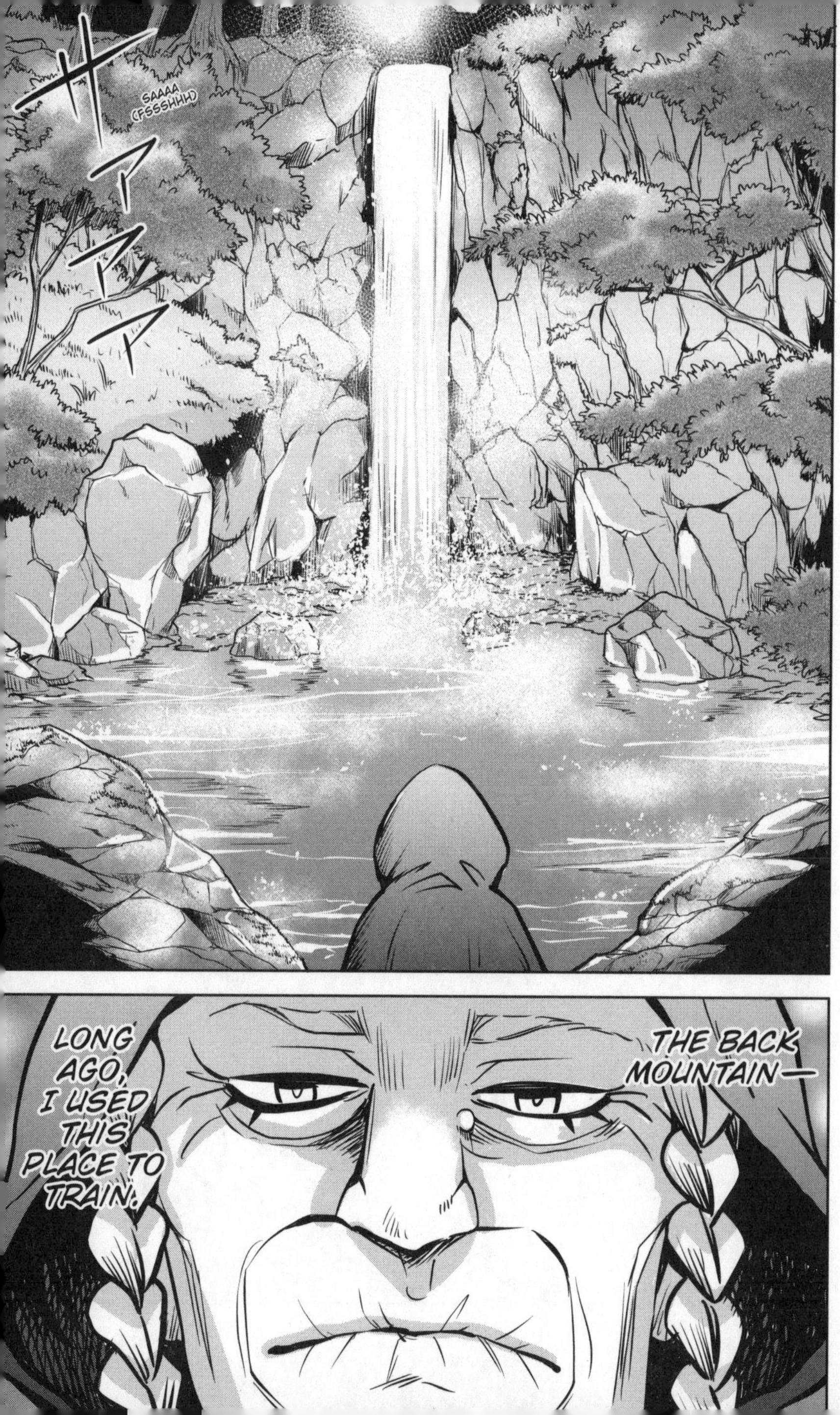
SAAAA (FSSSHHH)
THE BACK MOUNTAIN—
LONG AGO, I USED THIS PLACE TO TRAIN.

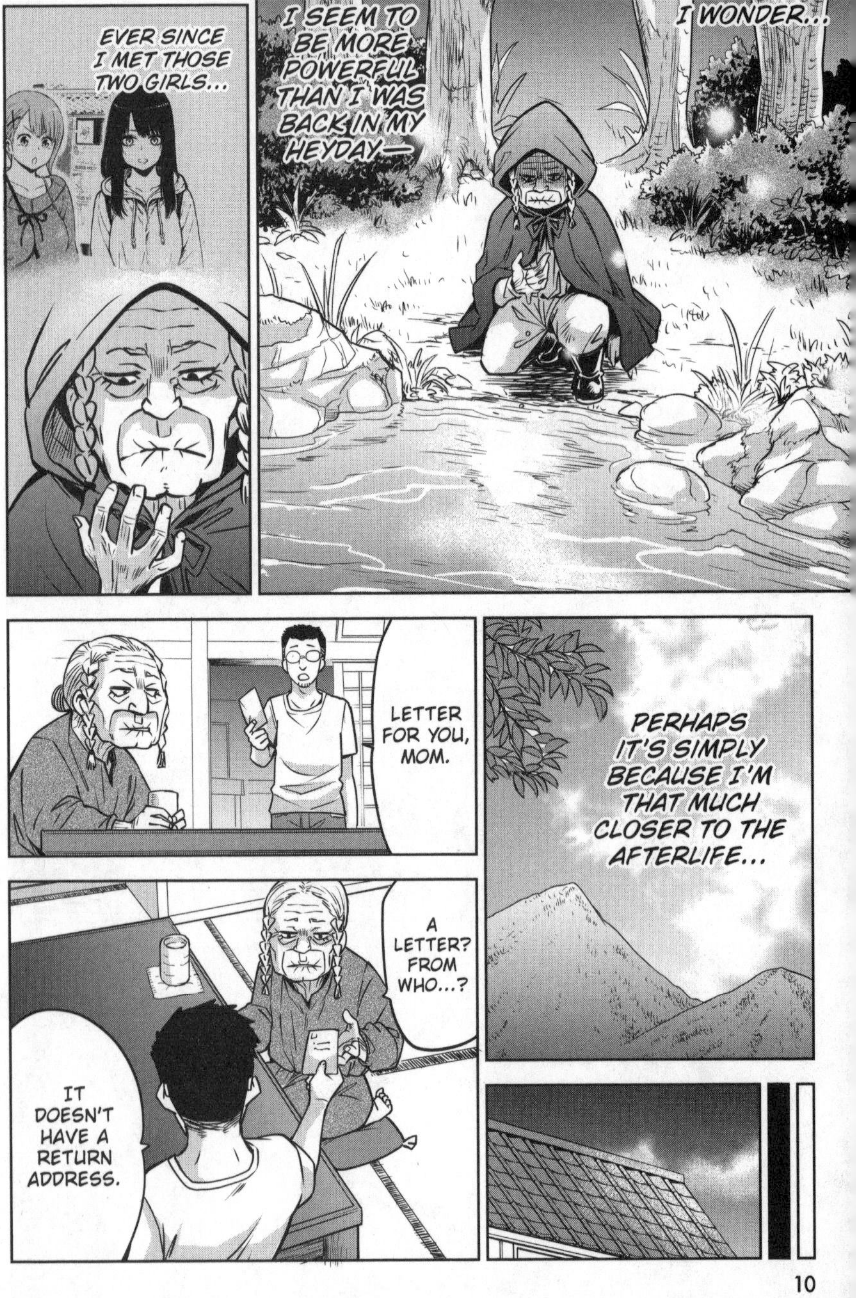
I WONDER...
I SEEM TO BE MORE POWERFUL THAN I WAS BACK IN MY HEYDAY—
EVER SINCE I MET THOSE TWO GIRLS...
PERHAPS IT'S SIMPLY BECAUSE I'M THAT MUCH CLOSER TO THE AFTERLIFE...
LETTER FOR YOU, MOM.
A LETTER? FROM WHO...?
IT DOESN'T HAVE A RETURN ADDRESS.

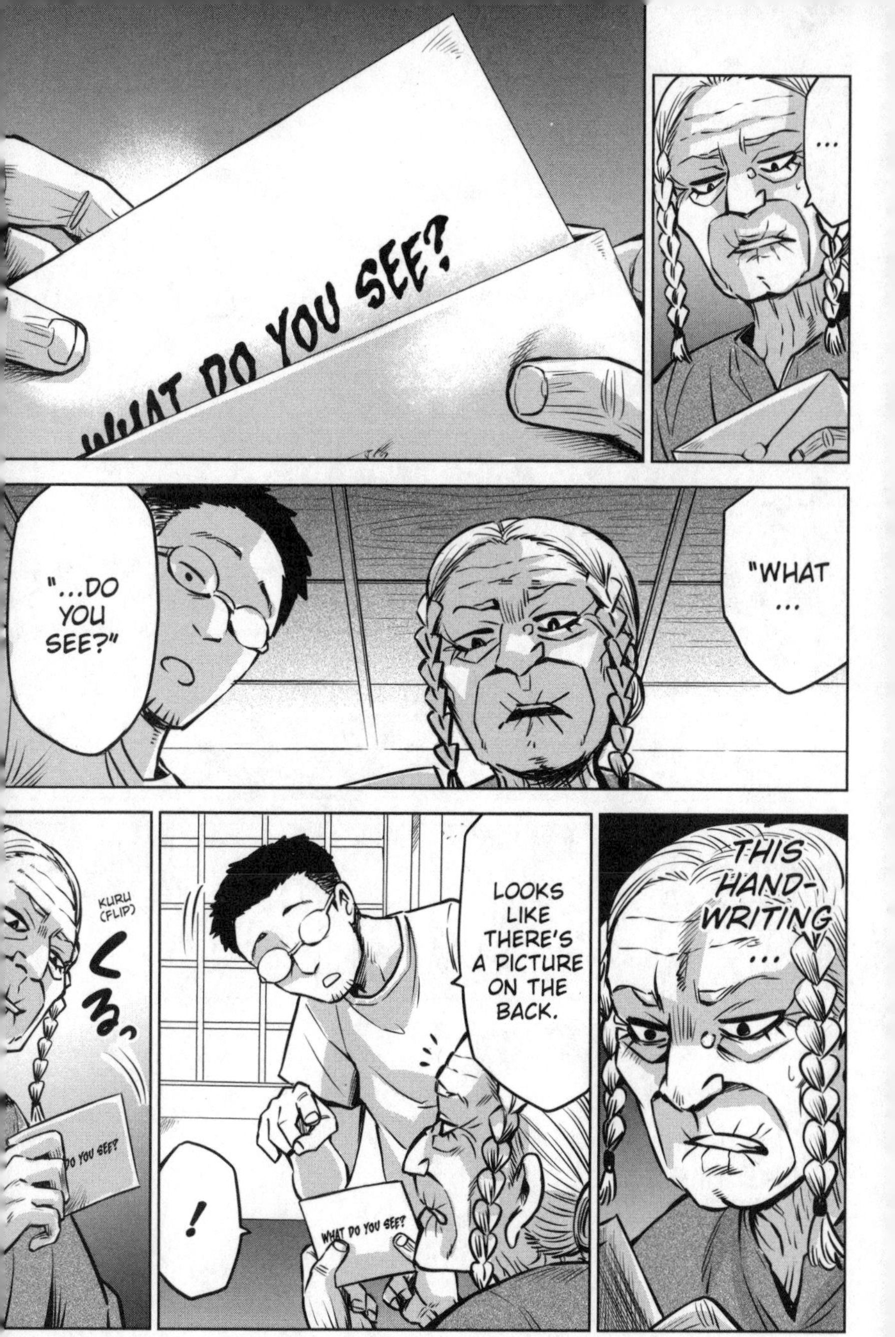
...
WHAT DO YOU SEE?
"WHAT ...
"...DO YOU SEE?"
THIS HAND-WRITING ...
LOOKS LIKE THERE'S A PICTURE ON THE BACK.
WHAT DO YOU SEE?
!
KURU (FLIP)
くる
DO YOU SEE?

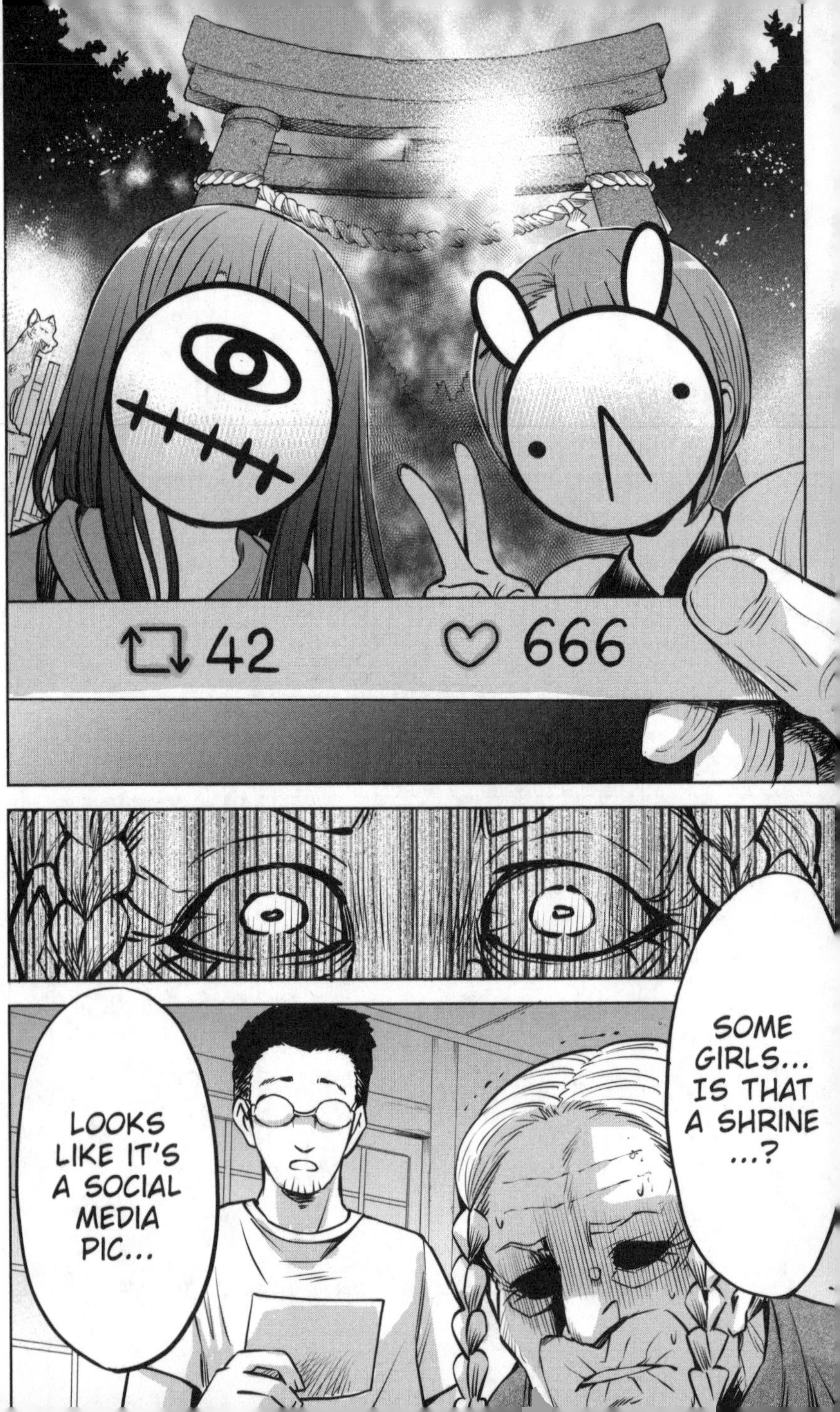
42
666
SOME GIRLS... IS THAT A SHRINE ...?
LOOKS LIKE IT'S A SOCIAL MEDIA PIC...

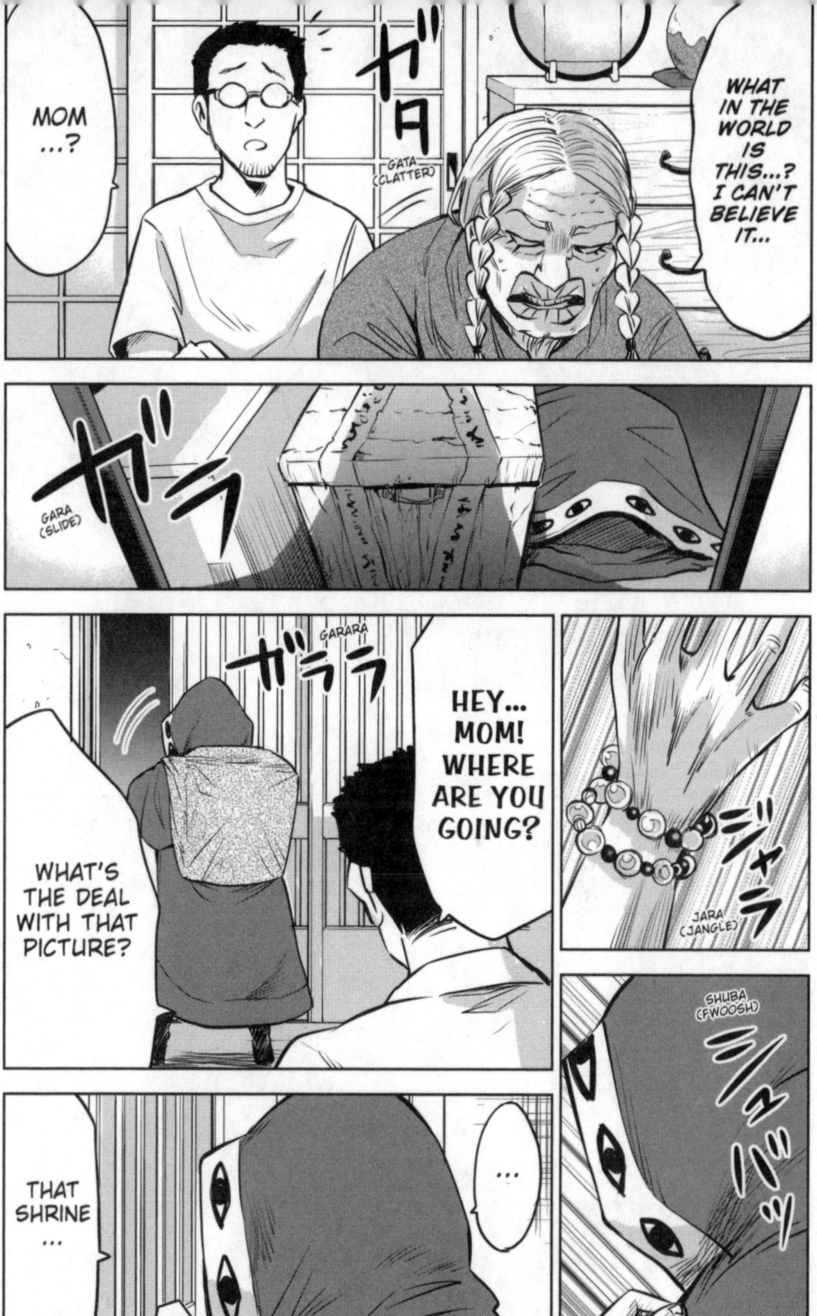
WHAT IN THE WORLD IS THIS...? I CAN'T BELIEVE IT...
ガタ
GATA (CLATTER)
MOM ...?
ガラ
GARA (SLIDE)
ジャラ
JARA (JANGLE)
GARARA
ガララ
HEY... MOM! WHERE ARE YOU GOING?
WHAT'S THE DEAL WITH THAT PICTURE?
SHUBA (FWOOSH)
シュバッ
...
THAT SHRINE ...

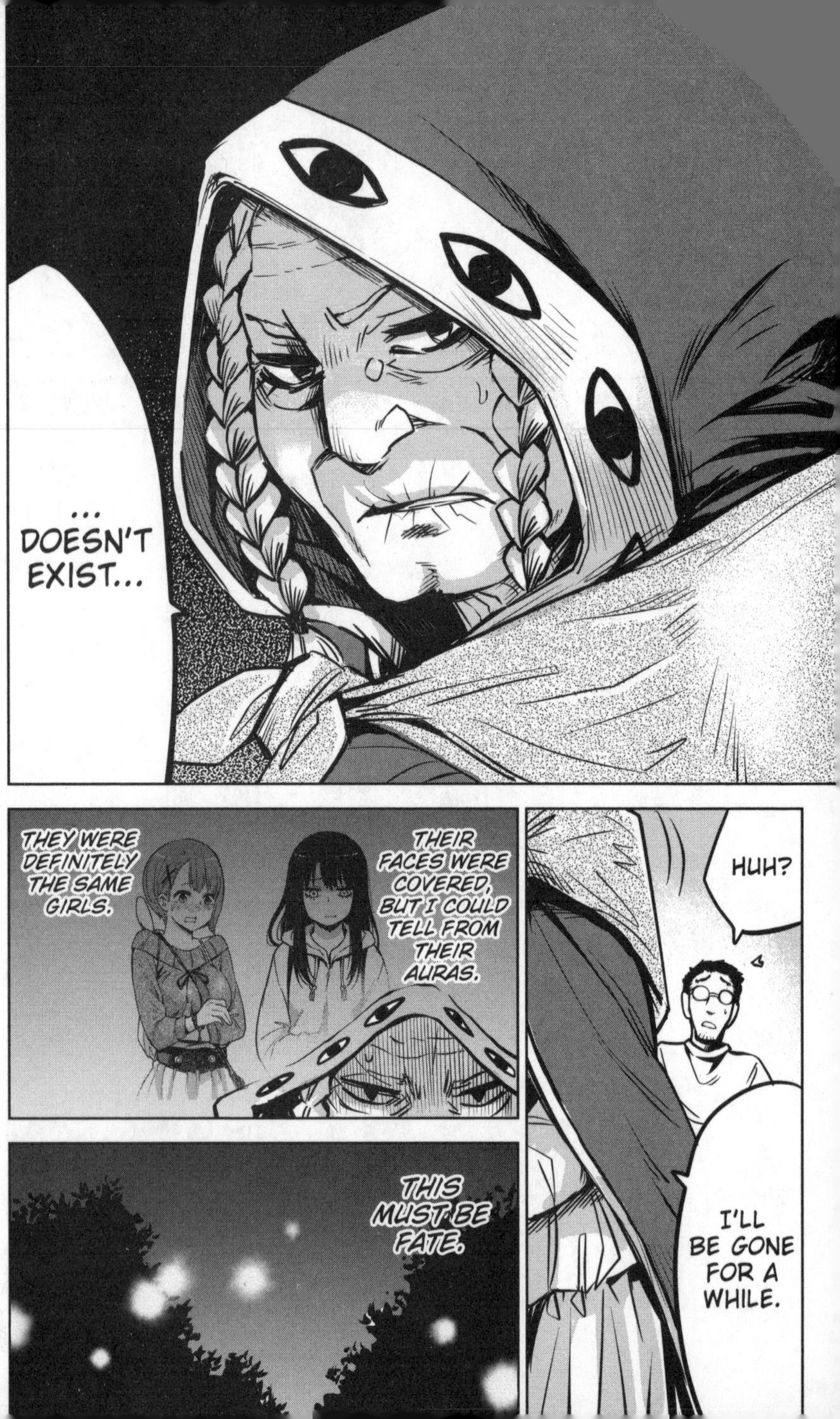
... DOESN'T EXIST...
HUH?
I'LL BE GONE FOR A WHILE.
THEIR FACES WERE COVERED, BUT I COULD TELL FROM THEIR AURAS.
THEY WERE DEFINITELY THE SAME GIRLS.
THIS MUST BE FATE.

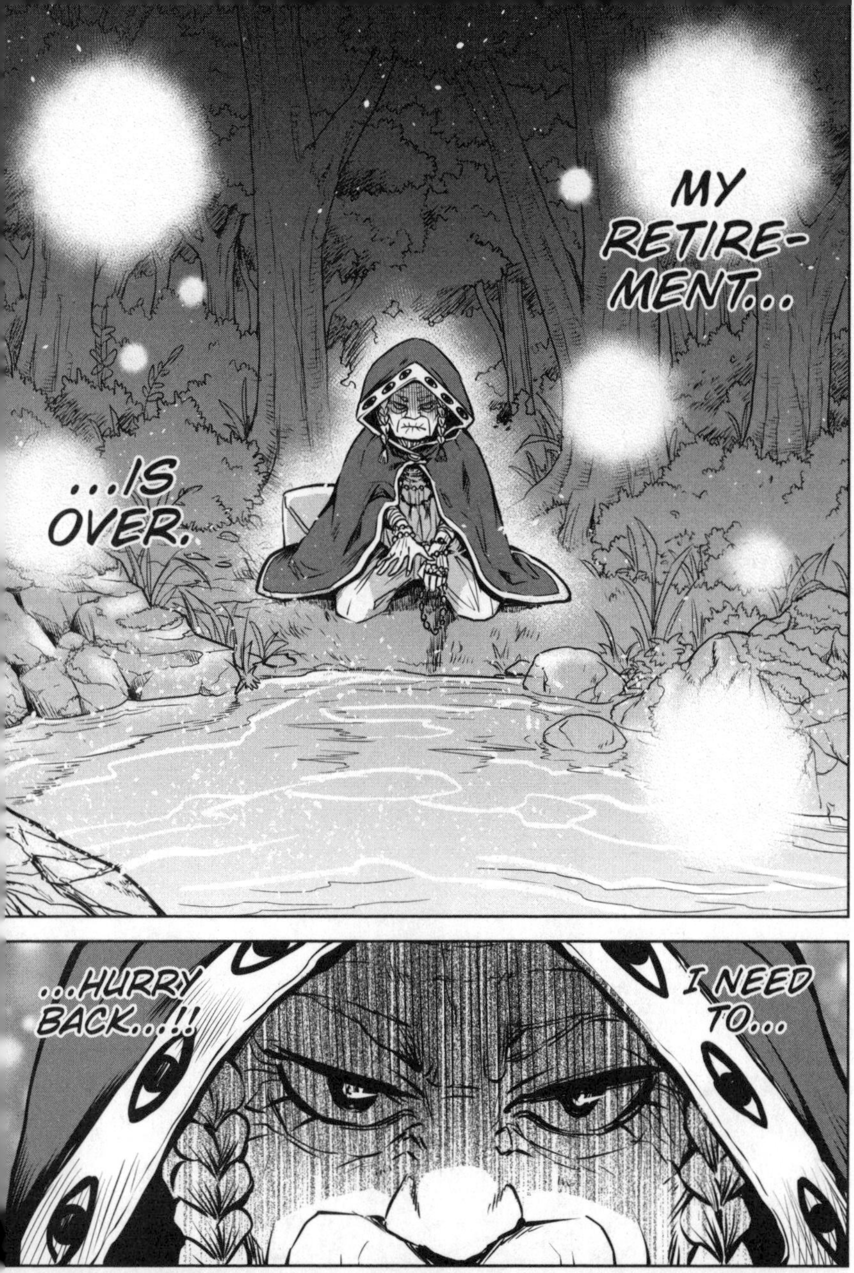
MY RETIRE-MENT...
...IS OVER.
I NEED TO...
...HURRY BACK...!!

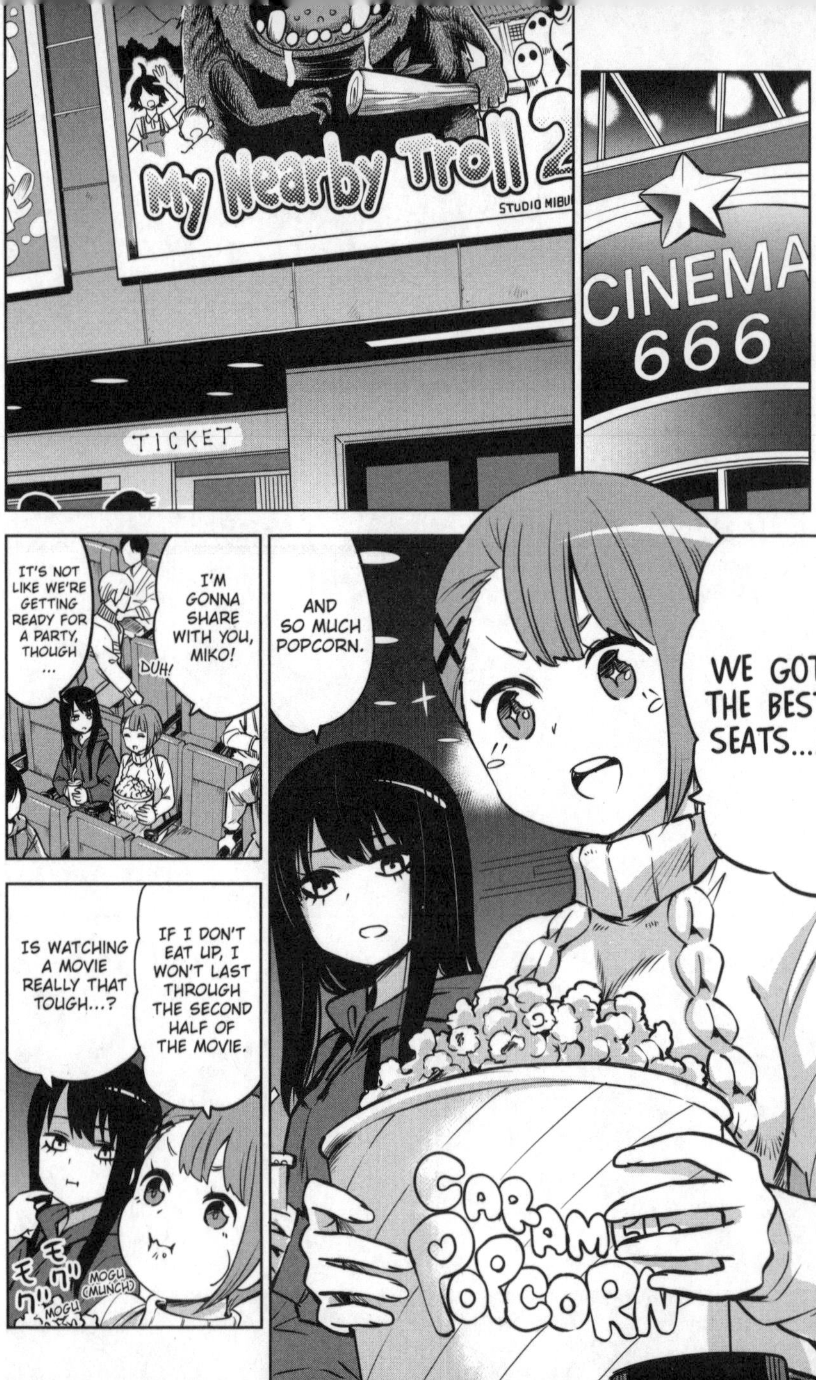
CINEMA 666
My Nearby Troll 2
STUDIO MIBU
TICKET
WE GOT THE BEST SEATS...!
CARAMEL POPCORN
AND SO MUCH POPCORN.
I'M GONNA SHARE WITH YOU, MIKO!
DUH!
IT'S NOT LIKE WE'RE GETTING READY FOR A PARTY, THOUGH ...
IF I DON'T EAT UP, I WON'T LAST THROUGH THE SECOND HALF OF THE MOVIE.
IS WATCHING A MOVIE REALLY THAT TOUGH...?
MOGU (MUNCH)
MOGU

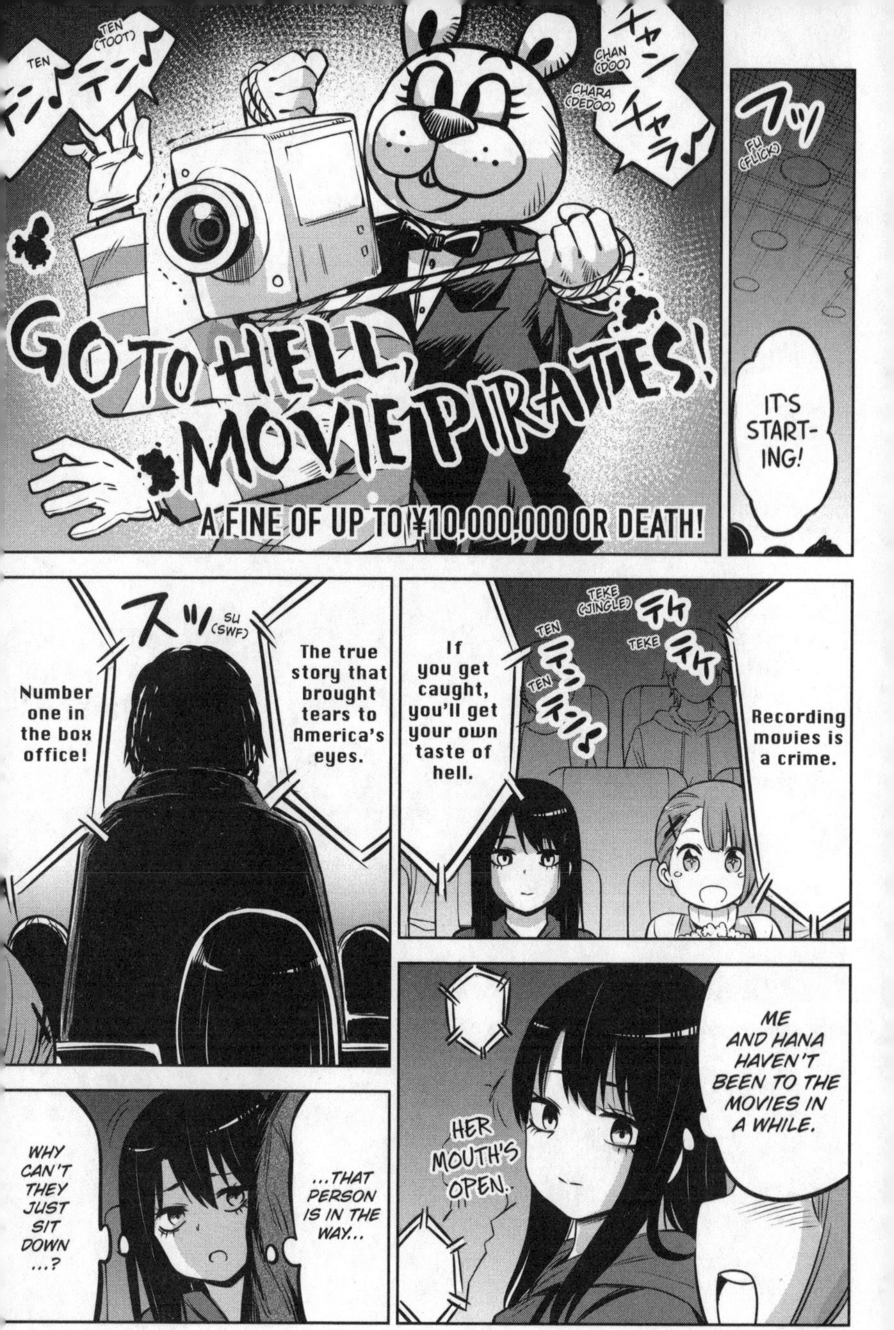
IT'S START-ING!
フッ
FU (FLICK)
チャン
CHAN (DOO)
チャラ♪
CHARA (DEDOO)
テン♪
TEN (TOOT)
テン♪
TEN
GO TO HELL, MOVIE PIRATES!
A FINE OF UP TO ¥10,000,000 OR DEATH!
Recording movies is a crime.
テケ
TEKE (JINGLE)
テケ
TEKE
テン
TEN
テン♪
TEN
If you get caught, you'll get your own taste of hell.
The true story that brought tears to America's eyes.
スッ
SU (SWF)
Number one in the box office!
ME AND HANA HAVEN'T BEEN TO THE MOVIES IN A WHILE.
HER MOUTH'S OPEN.
...THAT PERSON IS IN THE WAY...
WHY CAN'T THEY JUST SIT DOWN ...?

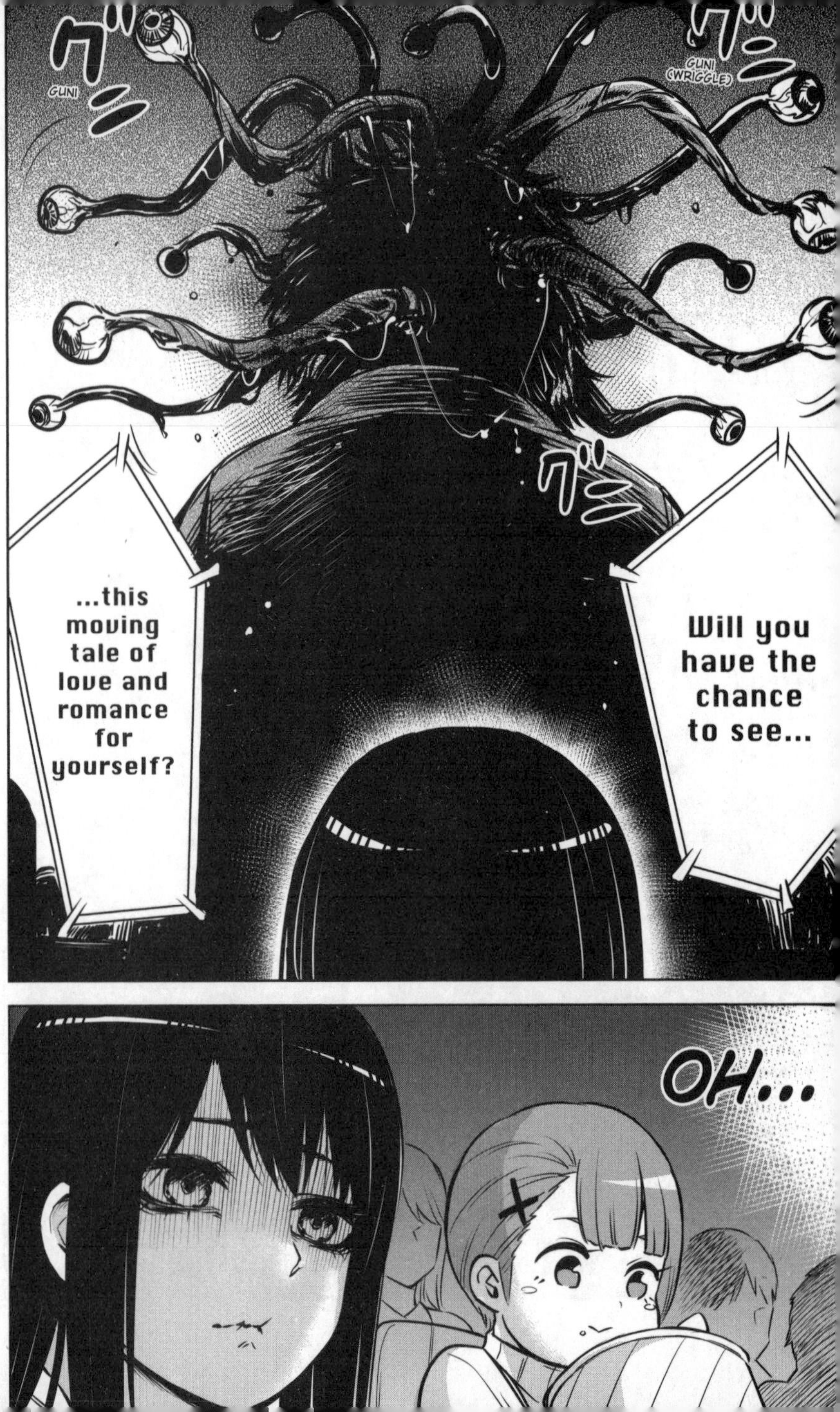
GUNI (WRIGGLE)
GUNI
Will you have the chance to see...
...this moving tale of love and romance for yourself?
OH...

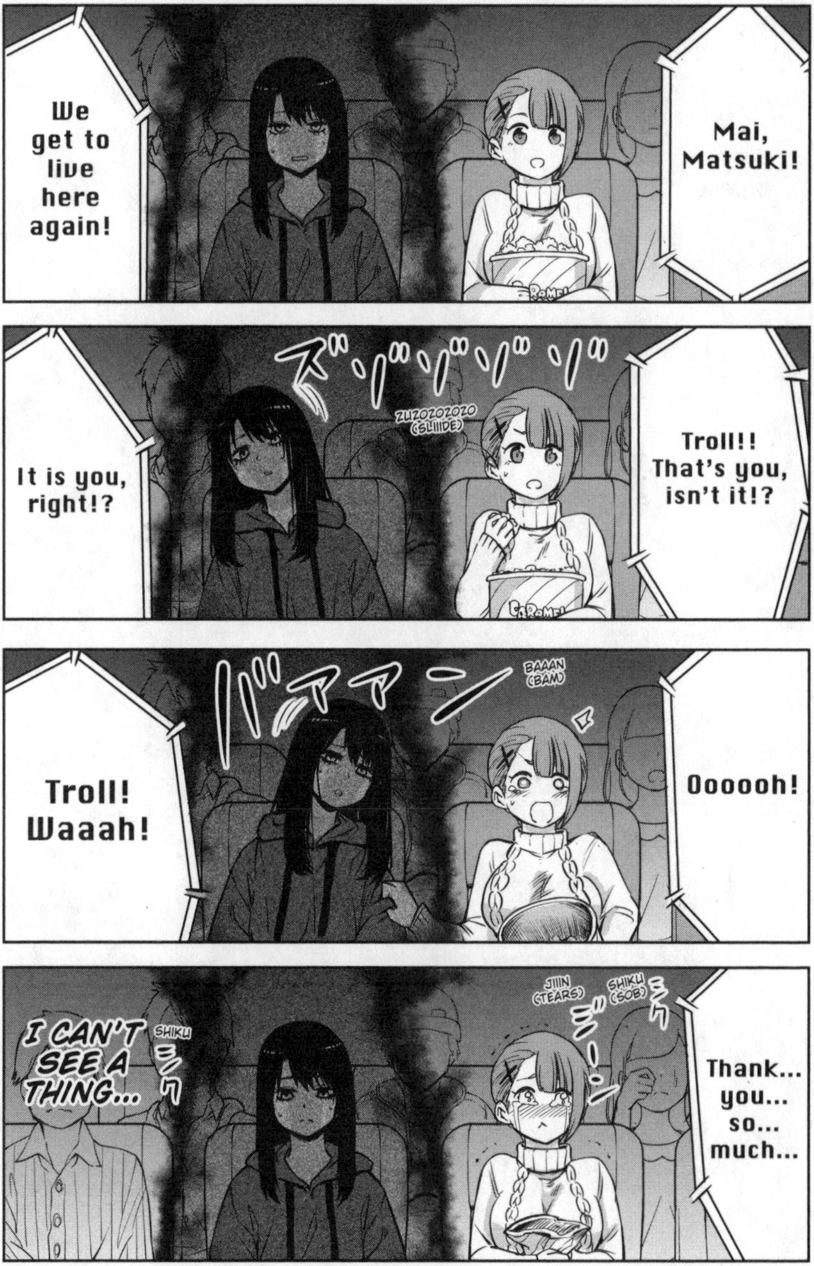
Mai, Matsuki!
We get to live here again!
Troll!! That's you, isn't it!?
ZUZOZOZOZO (SLIIIDE)
It is you, right!?
BAAAN (BAM)
Ooooh!
Troll! Waaah!
SHIKU (SOB)
JIIIN (TEARS)
Thank... you... so... much...
SHIKU
I CAN'T SEE A THING...

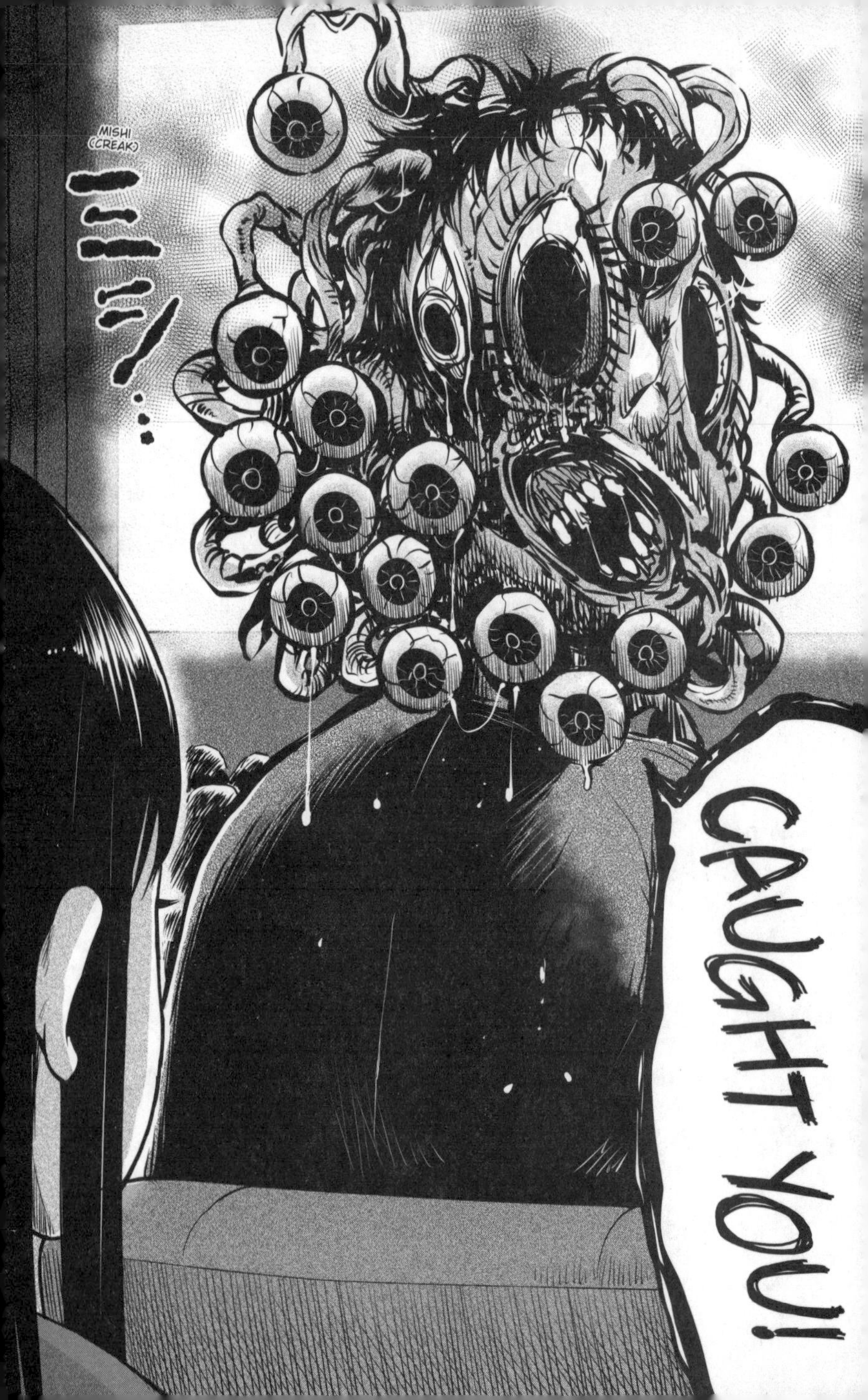
MISHI
(CREAK)
CAUGHT YOU!

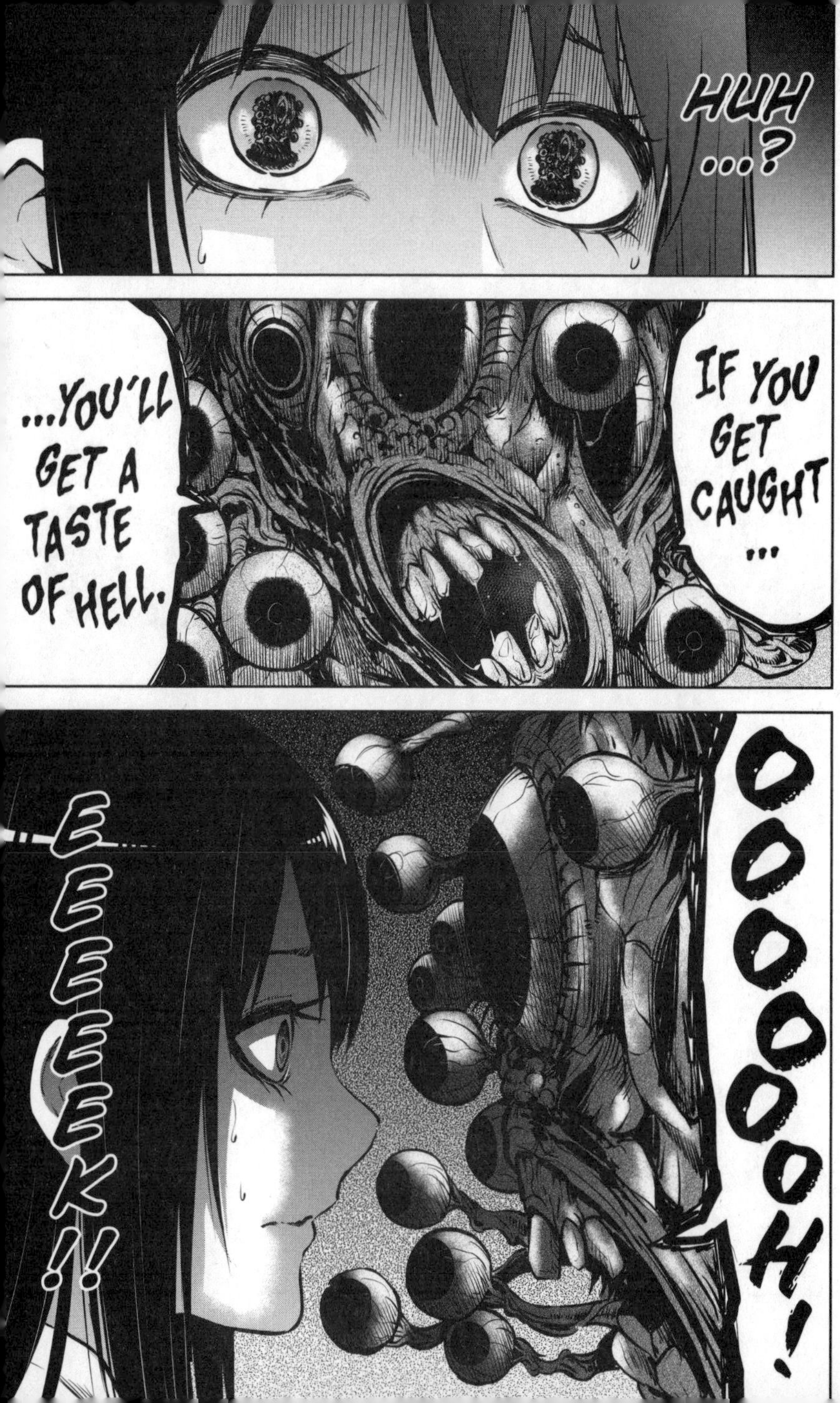
HUH ...?
IF YOU GET CAUGHT ...
...YOU'LL GET A TASTE OF HELL.
OOOOOOOOH!
EEEEEEK!!

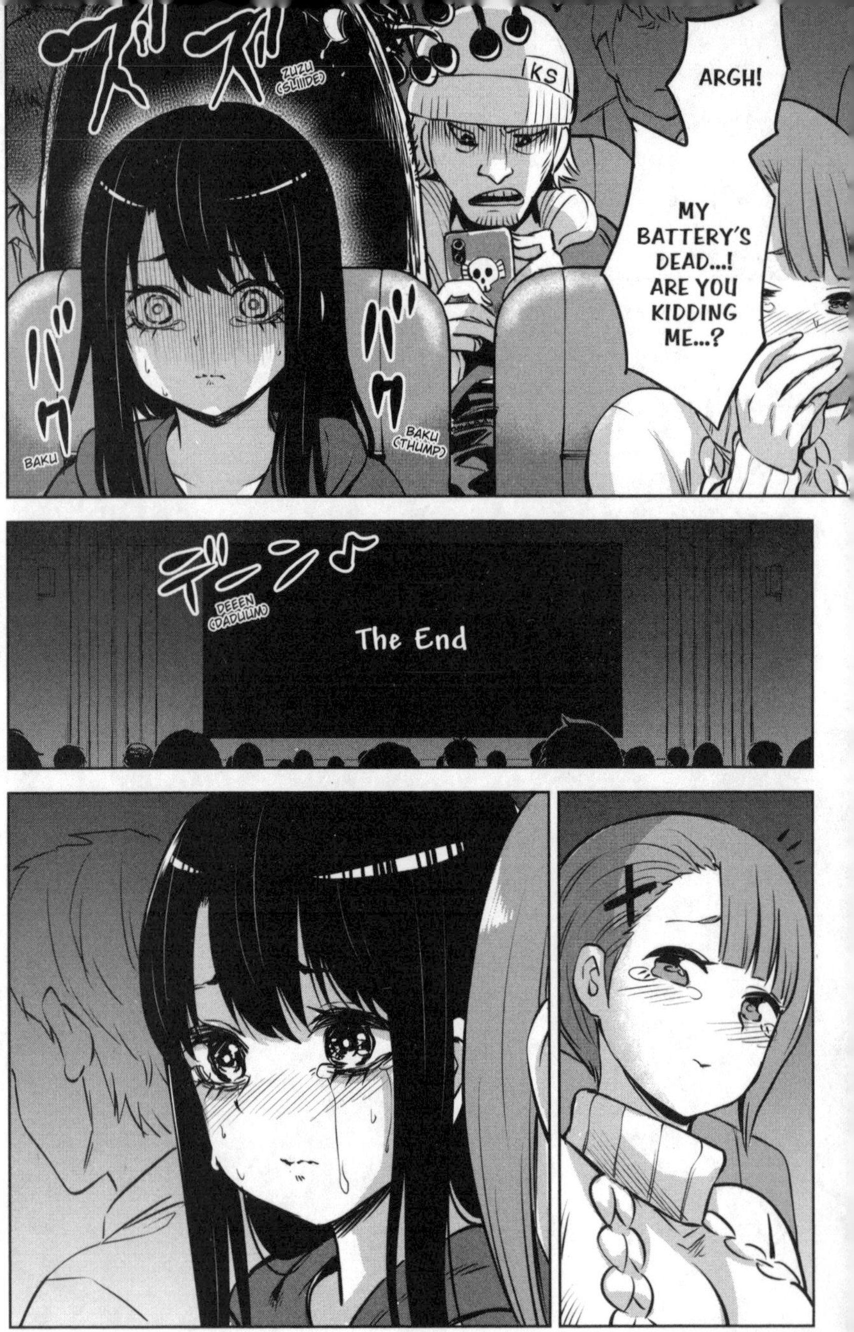
ARGH!
MY BATTERY'S DEAD...! ARE YOU KIDDING ME...?
ZUZU (SLIIIDE)
BAKU (THUMP)
BAKU
DEEEN (DADUUM)
The End

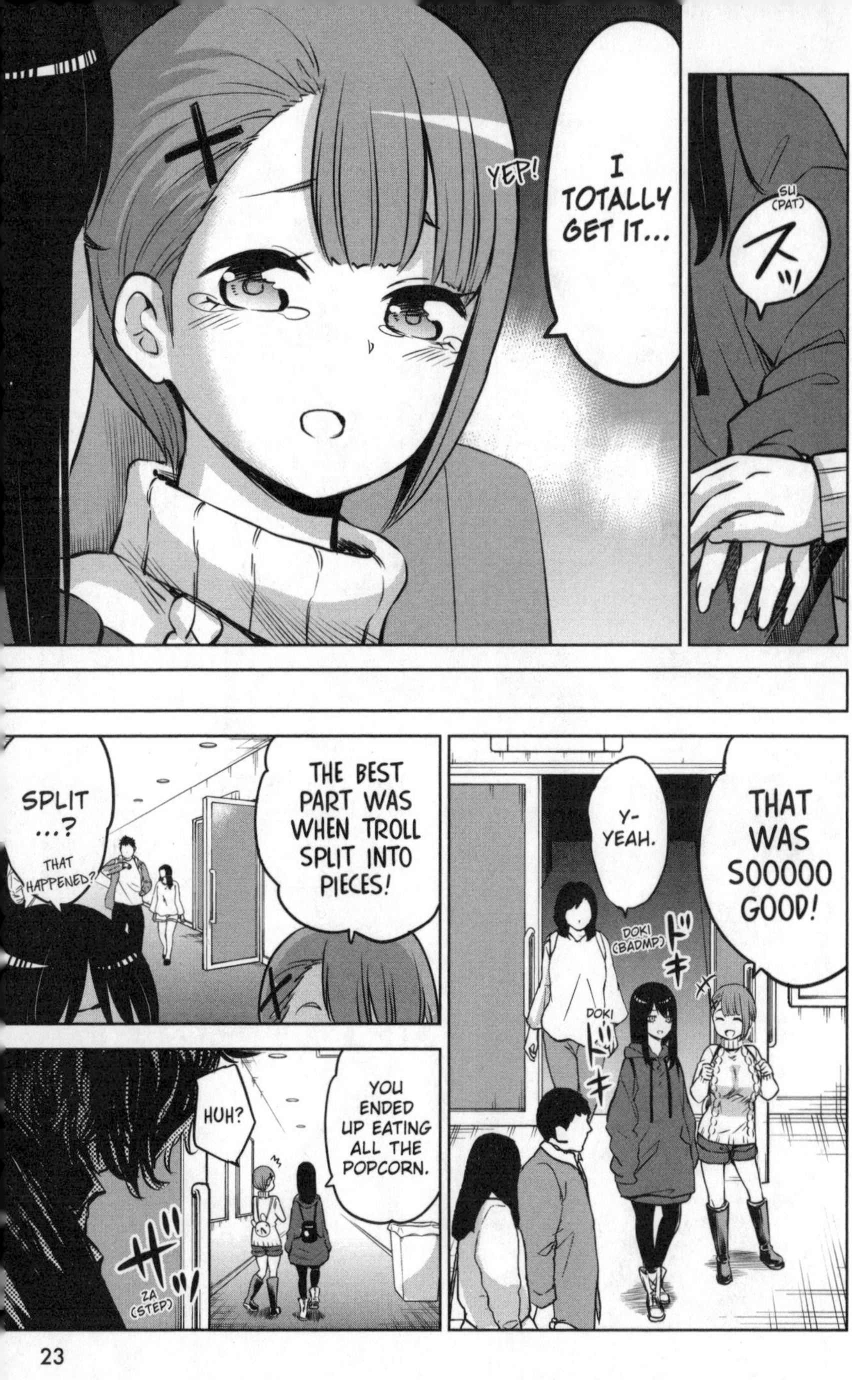
SU (PAT)
スッ
I TOTALLY GET IT...
YEP!
THAT WAS SOOOOO GOOD!
Y-YEAH.
DOKI (BADMP)
ドキ
DOKI
ドキ
THE BEST PART WAS WHEN TROLL SPLIT INTO PIECES!
SPLIT ...?
THAT HAPPENED?
YOU ENDED UP EATING ALL THE POPCORN.
HUH?
ZA (STEP)

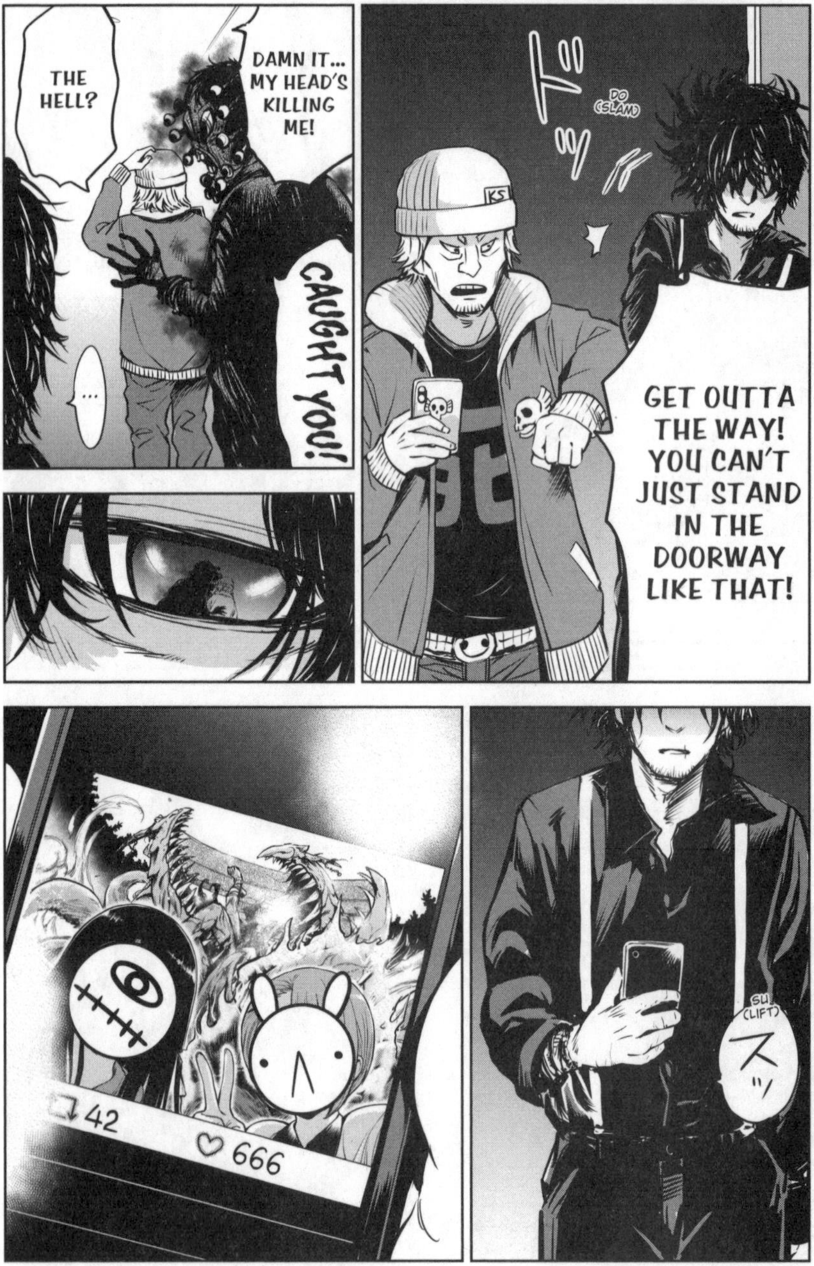
DO (SLAM)
GET OUTTA THE WAY! YOU CAN'T JUST STAND IN THE DOORWAY LIKE THAT!
DAMN IT... MY HEAD'S KILLING ME!
THE HELL?
CAUGHT YOU!
...
SU (LIFT)
42
666

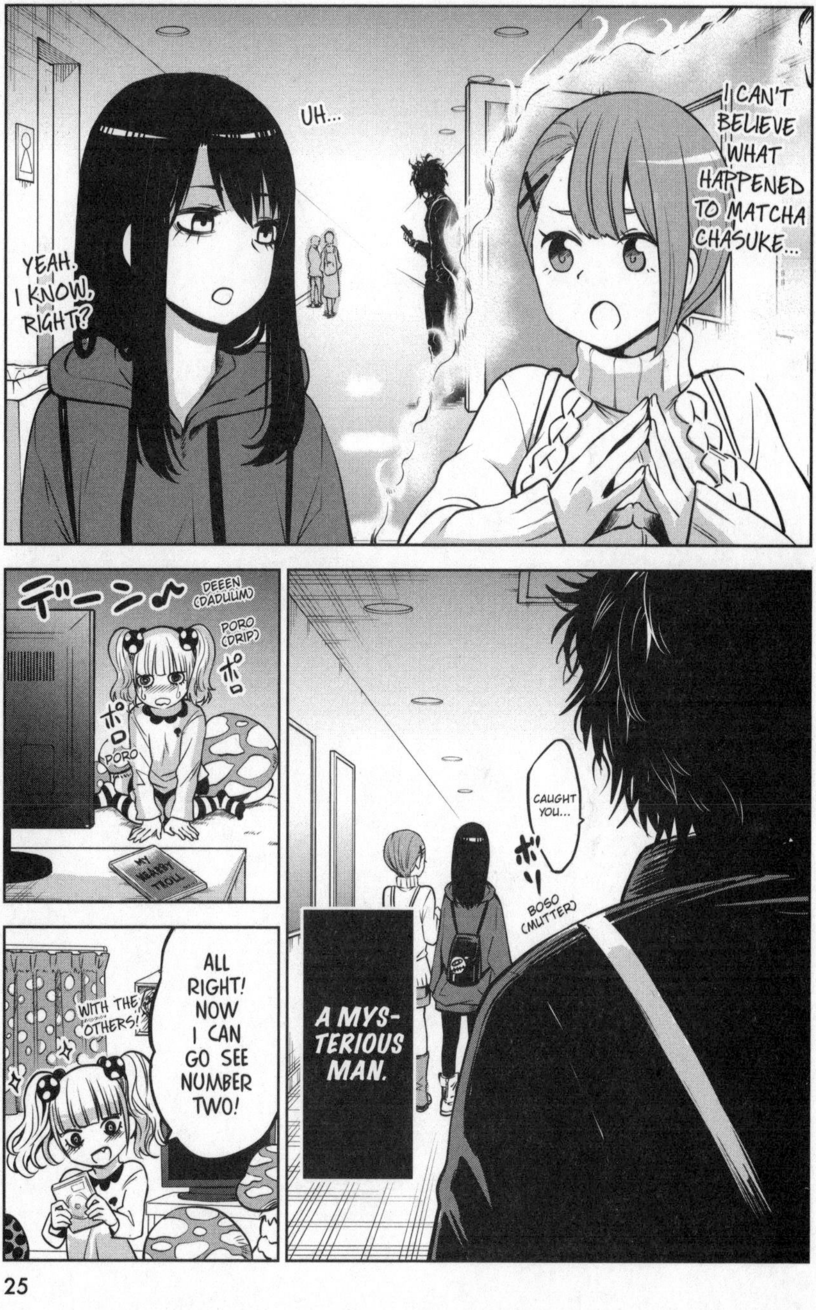

I CAN'T BELIEVE WHAT HAPPENED TO MATCHA CHASUKE...
UH...
YEAH. I KNOW, RIGHT?
CAUGHT YOU...
ボソ
BOSO (MUTTER)
A MYS-TERIOUS MAN.
デーン♪
DEEEN (DADUUM)
PORO (DRIP)
ポロ
ポロ
PORO
MY HEARTY TROLL
ALL RIGHT! NOW I CAN GO SEE NUMBER TWO!
WITH THE OTHERS!

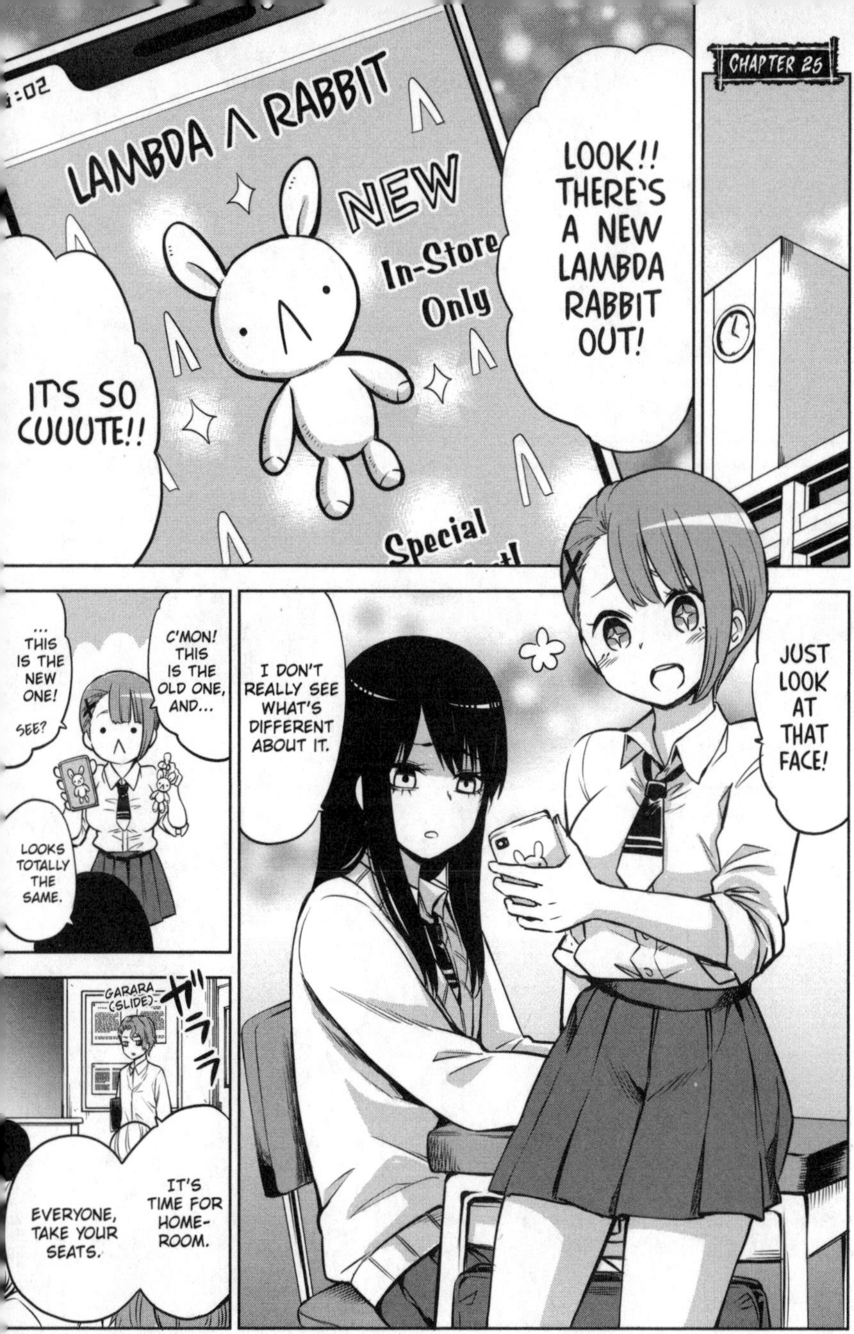
CHAPTER 25
LAMBDA Λ RABBIT
NEW
In-Store Only
Special
LOOK!! THERE'S A NEW LAMBDA RABBIT OUT!
IT'S SO CUUUTE!!
JUST LOOK AT THAT FACE!
I DON'T REALLY SEE WHAT'S DIFFERENT ABOUT IT.
C'MON! THIS IS THE OLD ONE, AND...
... THIS IS THE NEW ONE! SEE?
LOOKS TOTALLY THE SAME.
ガララ
GARARA (SLIDE)
IT'S TIME FOR HOME-ROOM.
EVERYONE, TAKE YOUR SEATS.

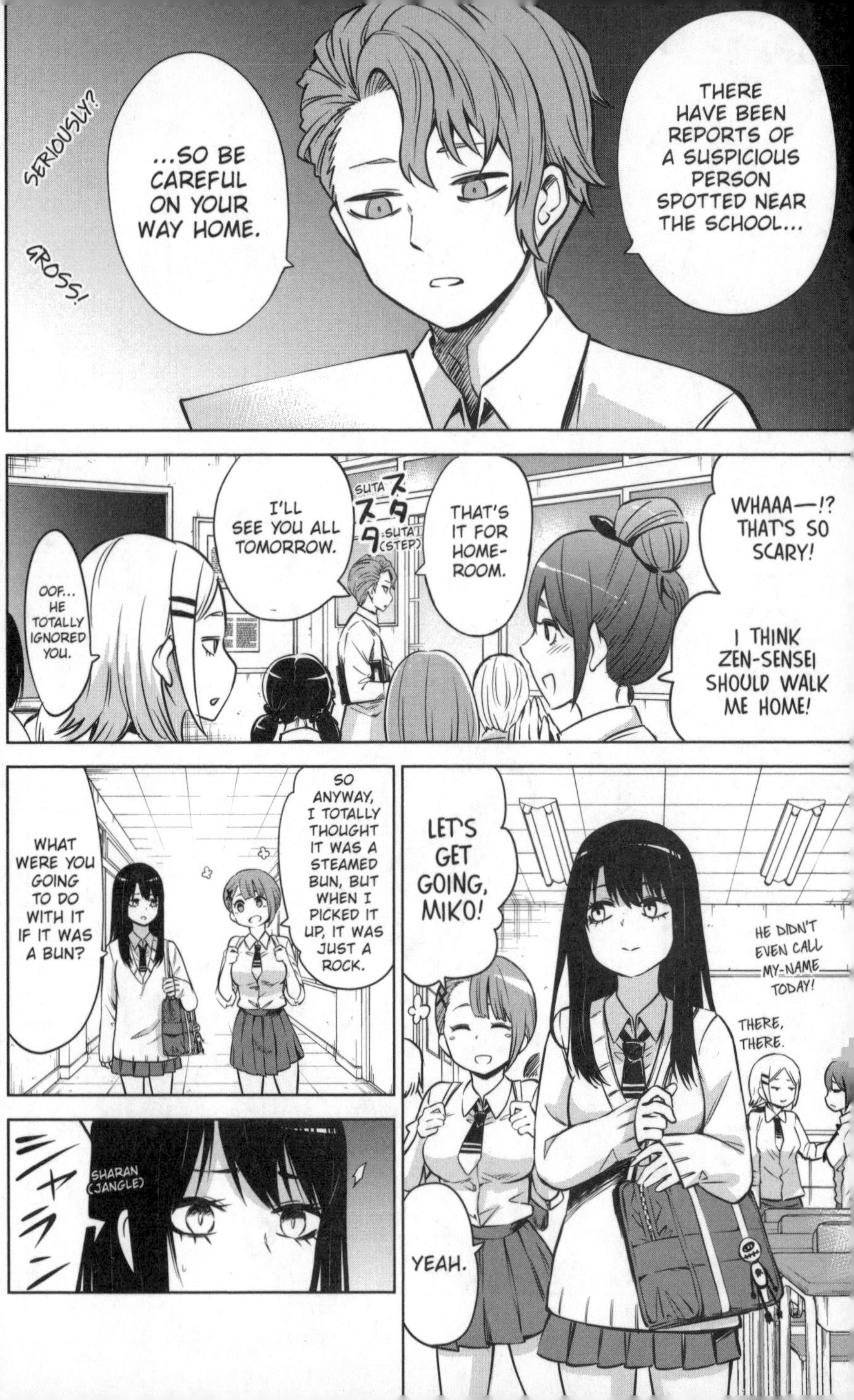
THERE HAVE BEEN REPORTS OF A SUSPICIOUS PERSON SPOTTED NEAR THE SCHOOL...
...SO BE CAREFUL ON YOUR WAY HOME.
SERIOUSLY?
GROSS!
WHAAAA—!? THAT'S SO SCARY!
I THINK ZEN-SENSEI SHOULD WALK ME HOME!
THAT'S IT FOR HOME-ROOM.
スタ
SUTA
スタ
SUTA (STEP)
I'LL SEE YOU ALL TOMORROW.
OOF... HE TOTALLY IGNORED YOU.
HE DIDN'T EVEN CALL MY NAME TODAY!
LET'S GET GOING, MIKO!
THERE, THERE.
YEAH.
SO ANYWAY, I TOTALLY THOUGHT IT WAS A STEAMED BUN, BUT WHEN I PICKED IT UP, IT WAS JUST A ROCK.
WHAT WERE YOU GOING TO DO WITH IT IF IT WAS A BUN?
シャラン
SHARAN (JANGLE)

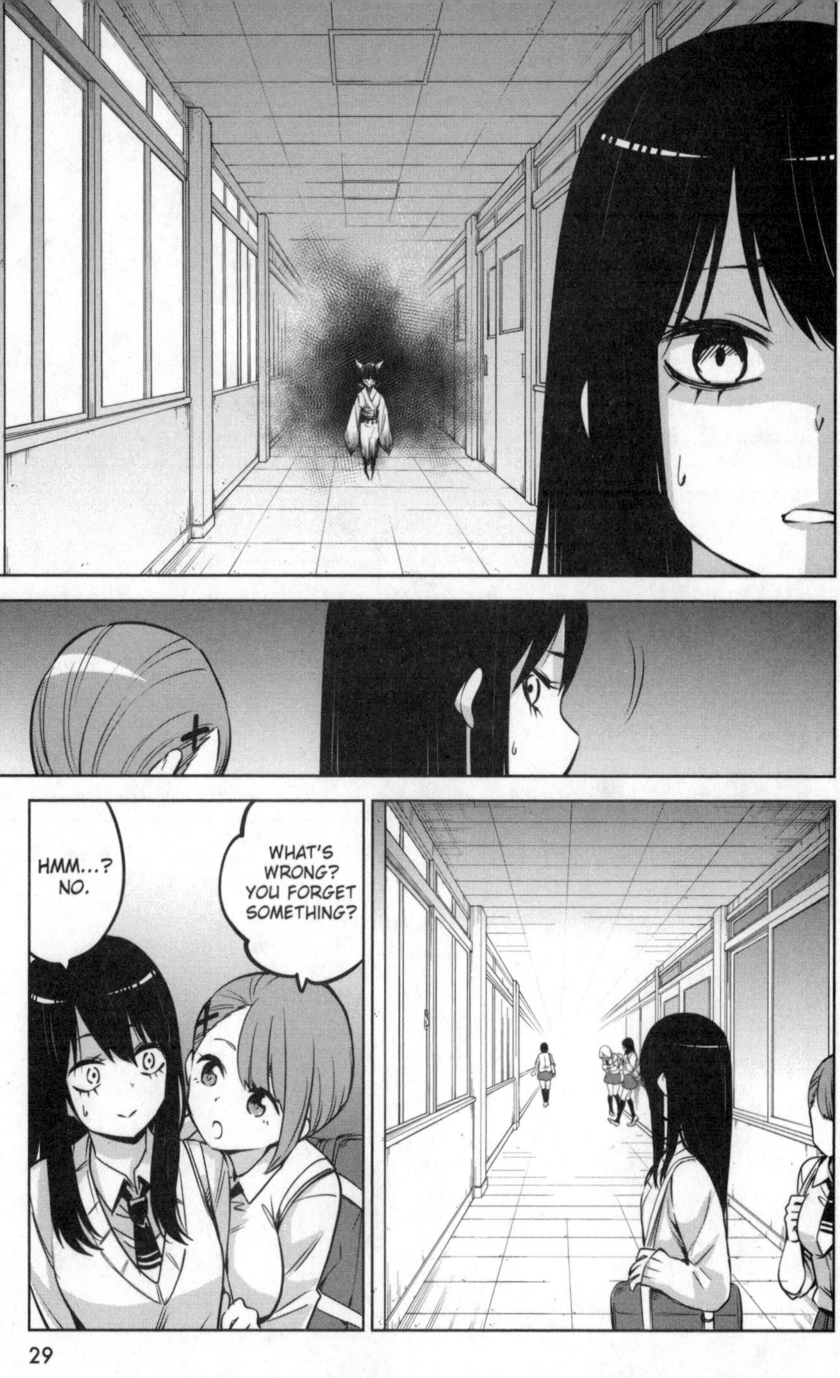
WHAT'S WRONG? YOU FORGET SOMETHING?
HMM...? NO.

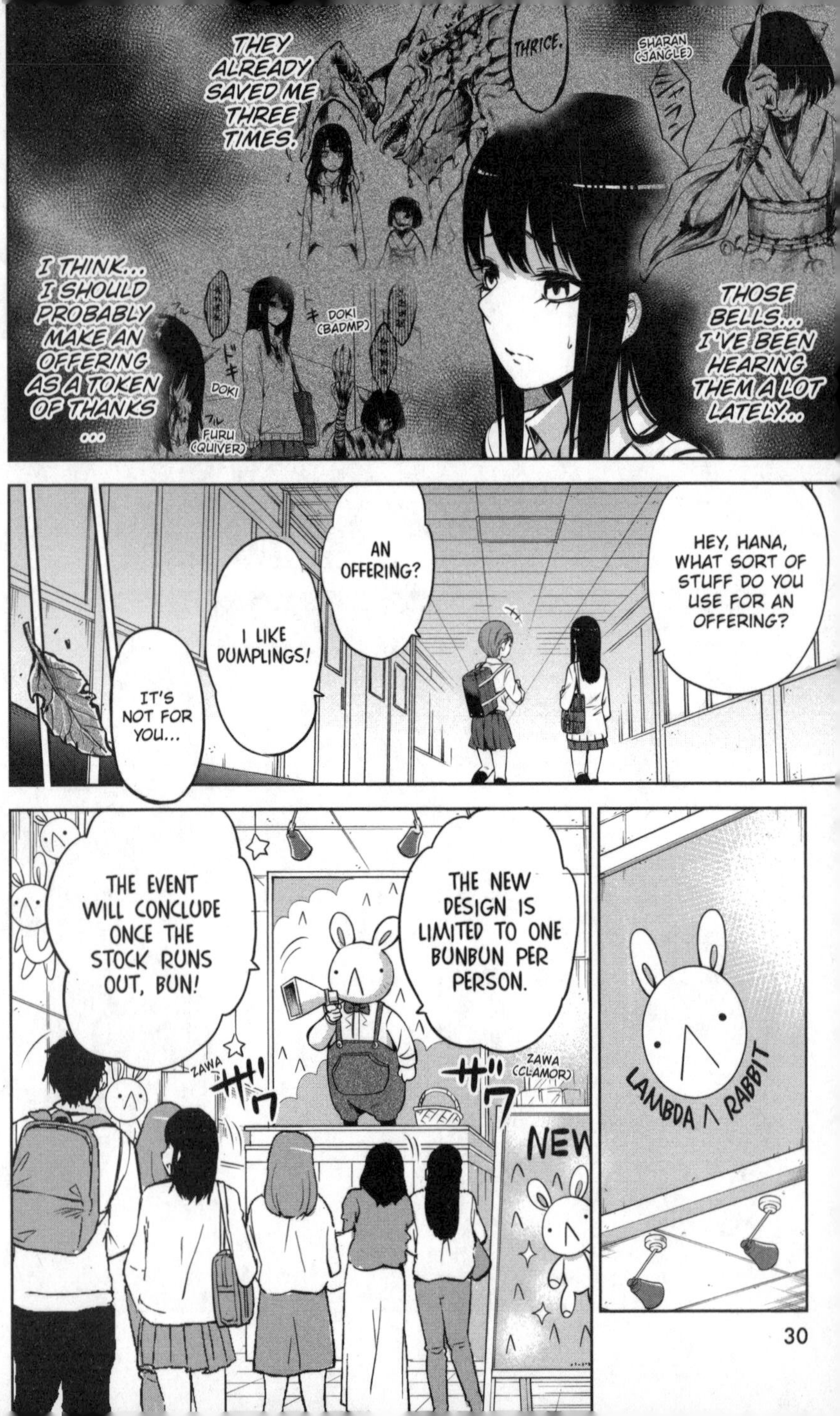
SHARAN (JANGLE)
THRICE.
THEY ALREADY SAVED ME THREE TIMES.
THOSE BELLS... I'VE BEEN HEARING THEM A LOT LATELY...
DOKI (BADMP)
I THINK... I SHOULD PROBABLY MAKE AN OFFERING AS A TOKEN OF THANKS...
DOKI
FURU (QUIVER)
HEY, HANA, WHAT SORT OF STUFF DO YOU USE FOR AN OFFERING?
AN OFFERING?
I LIKE DUMPLINGS!
IT'S NOT FOR YOU...
LAMBDA Λ RABBIT
THE NEW DESIGN IS LIMITED TO ONE BUNBUN PER PERSON.
ZAWA (CLAMOR)
THE EVENT WILL CONCLUDE ONCE THE STOCK RUNS OUT, BUN!
ZAWA
NEW

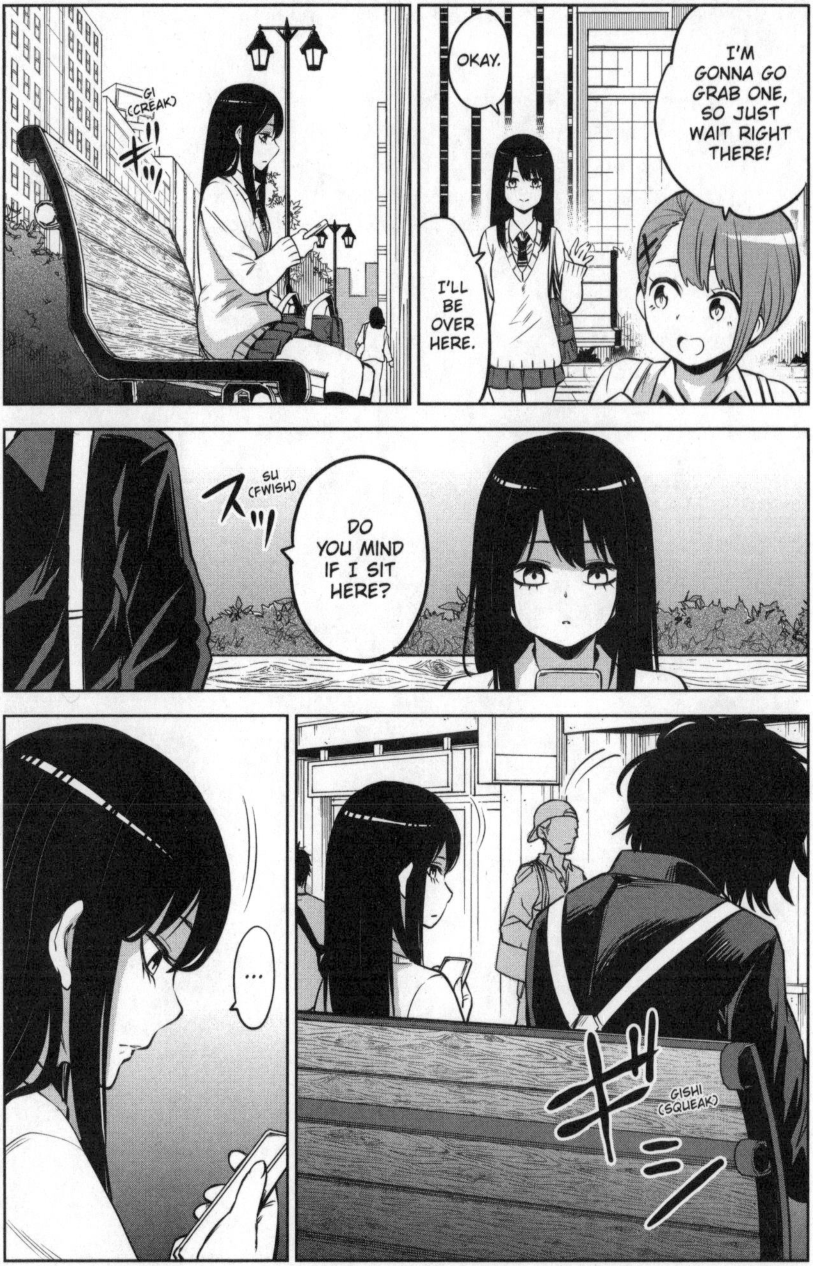
I'M GONNA GO GRAB ONE, SO JUST WAIT RIGHT THERE!
OKAY.
I'LL BE OVER HERE.
GI (CREAK)
DO YOU MIND IF I SIT HERE?
SU (FWISH)
GISHI (SQUEAK)
...

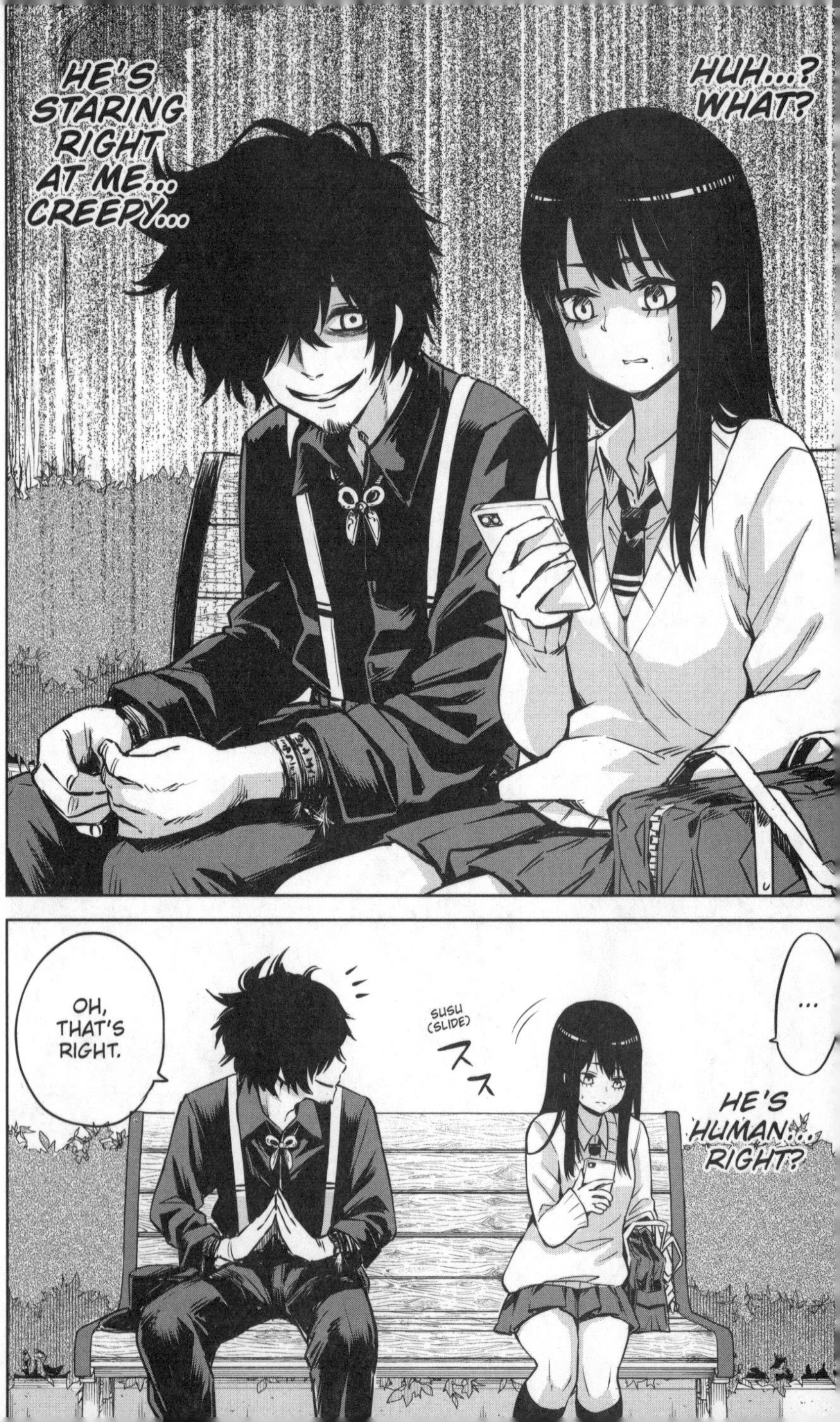
HUH...? WHAT?
HE'S STARING RIGHT AT ME... CREEPY...
...
SUSU (SLIDE)
スス
OH, THAT'S RIGHT.
HE'S HUMAN... RIGHT?

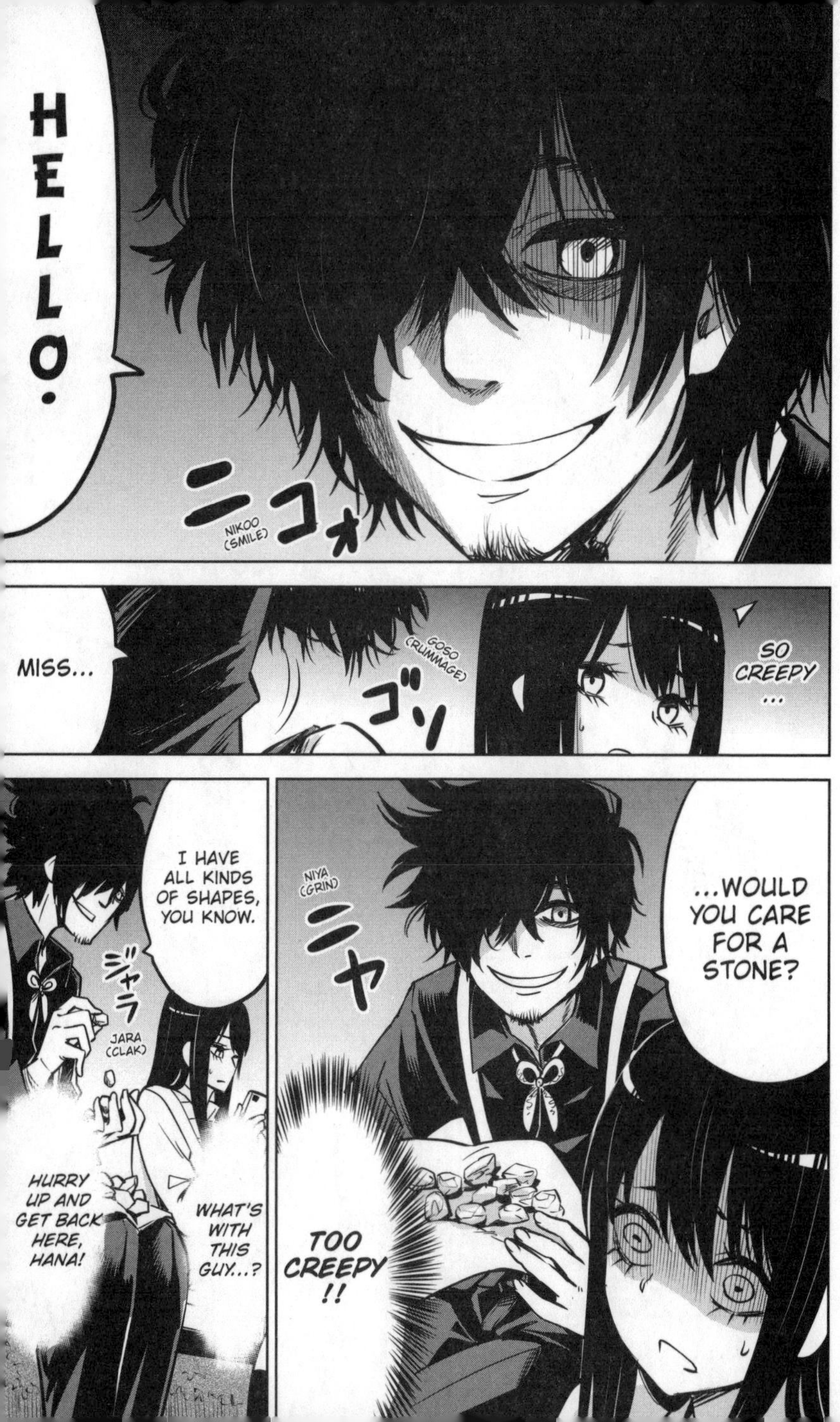
HELLO.
ニコォ
NIKOO (SMILE)
SO CREEPY...
ゴソ
GOSO (RUMMAGE)
MISS...
...WOULD YOU CARE FOR A STONE?
ニヤ
NIYA (GRIN)
TOO CREEPY!!
I HAVE ALL KINDS OF SHAPES, YOU KNOW.
ジャラ
JARA (CLAK)
WHAT'S WITH THIS GUY...?
HURRY UP AND GET BACK HERE, HANA!

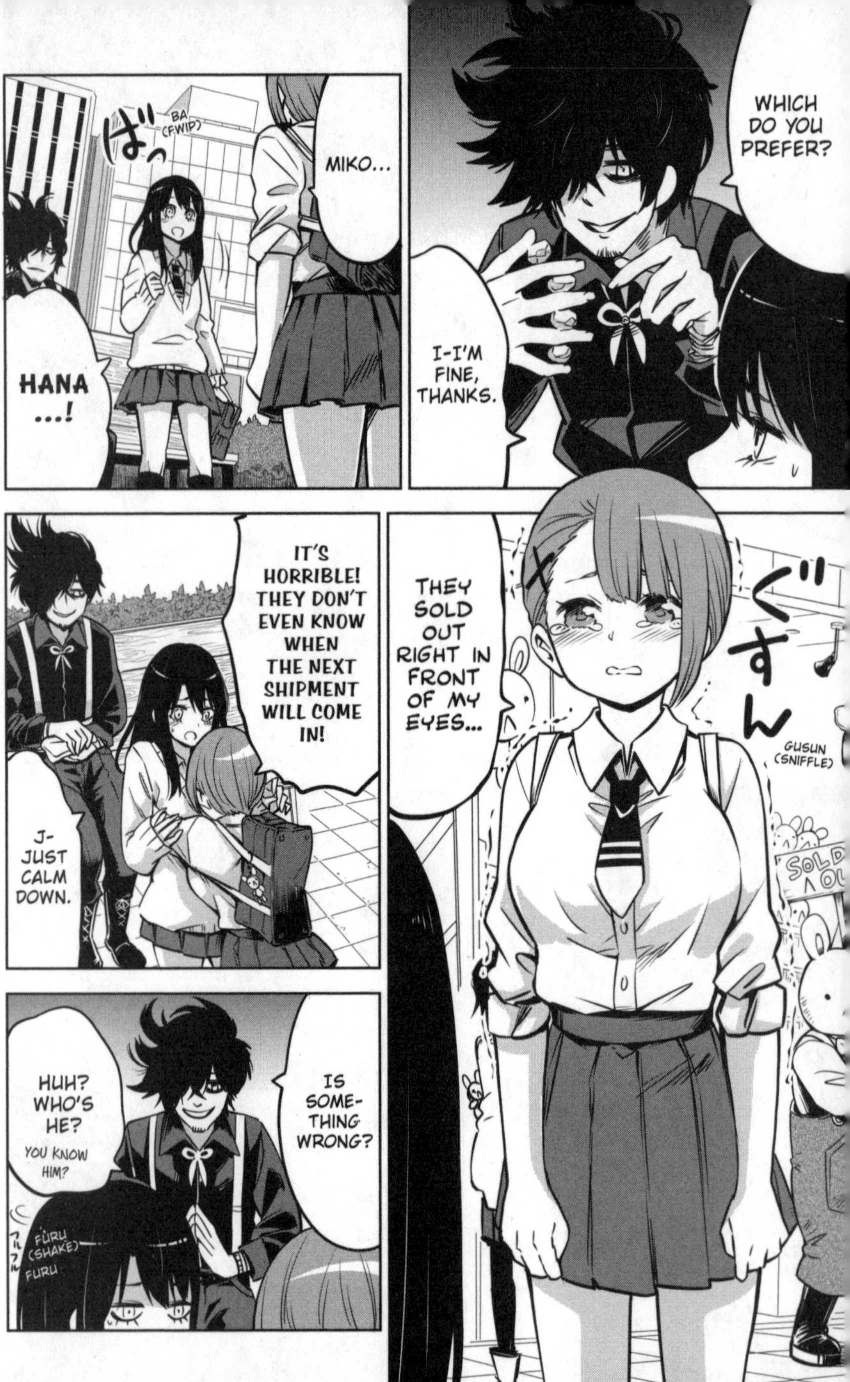
WHICH DO YOU PREFER?
I-I'M FINE, THANKS.
MIKO...
ばっ
BA (FWIP)
HANA ...!
THEY SOLD OUT RIGHT IN FRONT OF MY EYES...
ぐすん
GUSUN (SNIFFLE)
SOLD OU
IT'S HORRIBLE! THEY DON'T EVEN KNOW WHEN THE NEXT SHIPMENT WILL COME IN!
J-JUST CALM DOWN.
IS SOME-THING WRONG?
HUH? WHO'S HE?
YOU KNOW HIM?
FURU (SHAKE) FURU

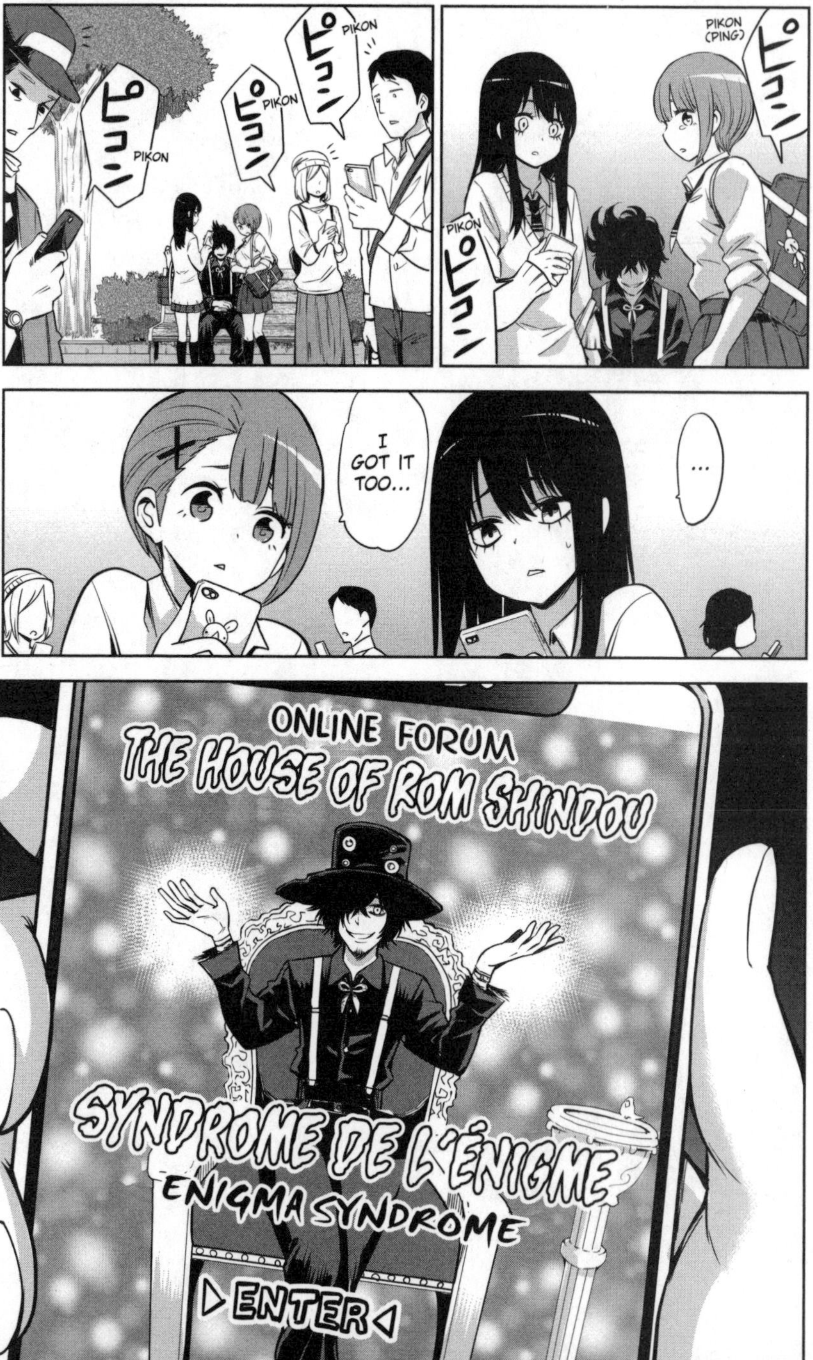

ピコン
PIKON (PING)
ピコン
PIKON
ピコン
PIKON
ピコン
PIKON
ピコン
PIKON
...
I GOT IT TOO...
ONLINE FORUM
THE HOUSE OF ROM SHINDOU
SYNDROME DE L'ÉNIGME
ENIGMA SYNDROME
ENTER

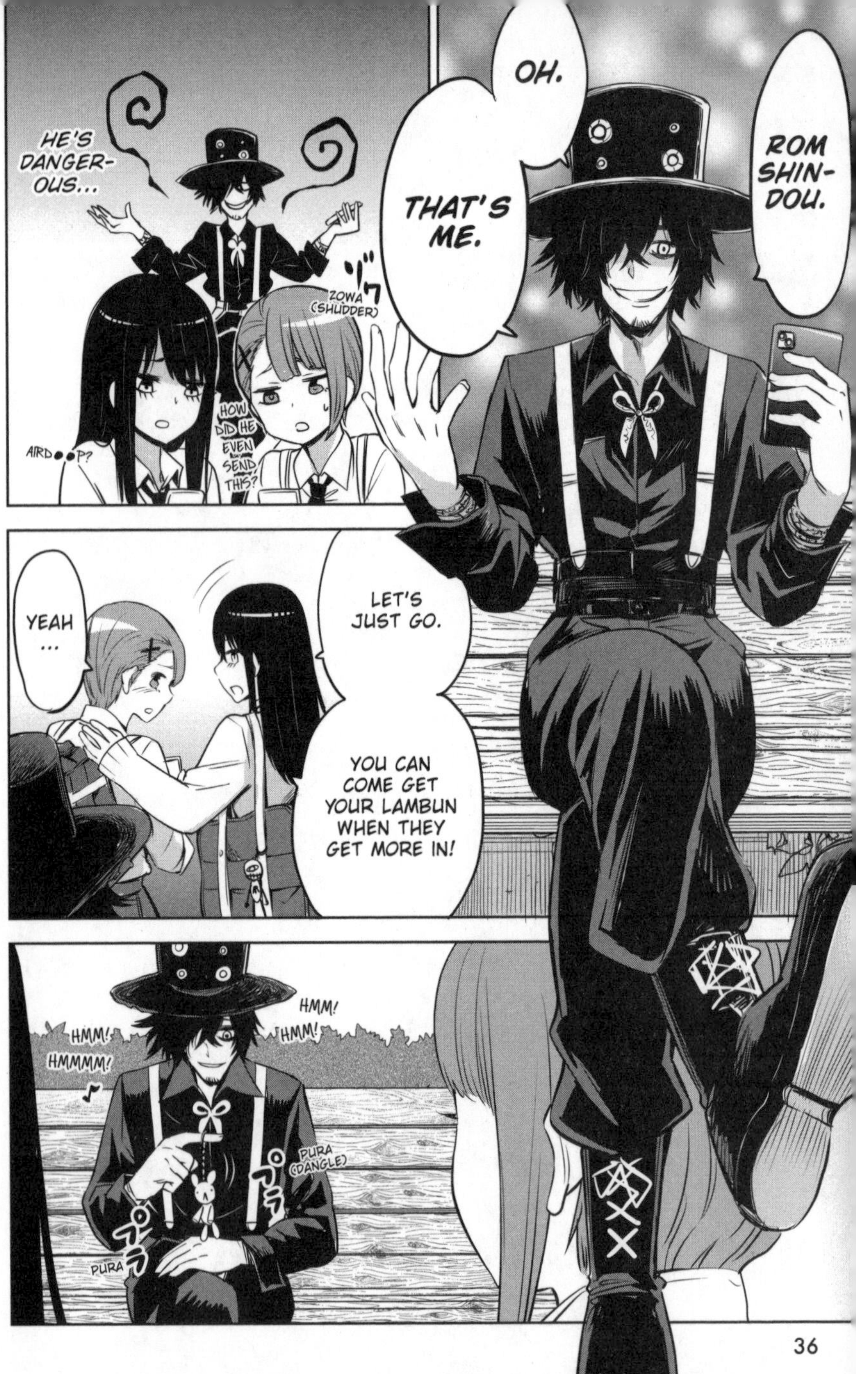
ROM SHIN-DOU.
OH.
THAT'S ME.
HE'S DANGER-OUS...
ZOWA (SHUDDER)
HOW DID HE EVEN SEND THIS?
AIRD●●P?
LET'S JUST GO.
YOU CAN COME GET YOUR LAMBUN WHEN THEY GET MORE IN!
YEAH ...
HMM!
HMM!
HMM!
HMMMM!
PURA (DANGLE)
PURA

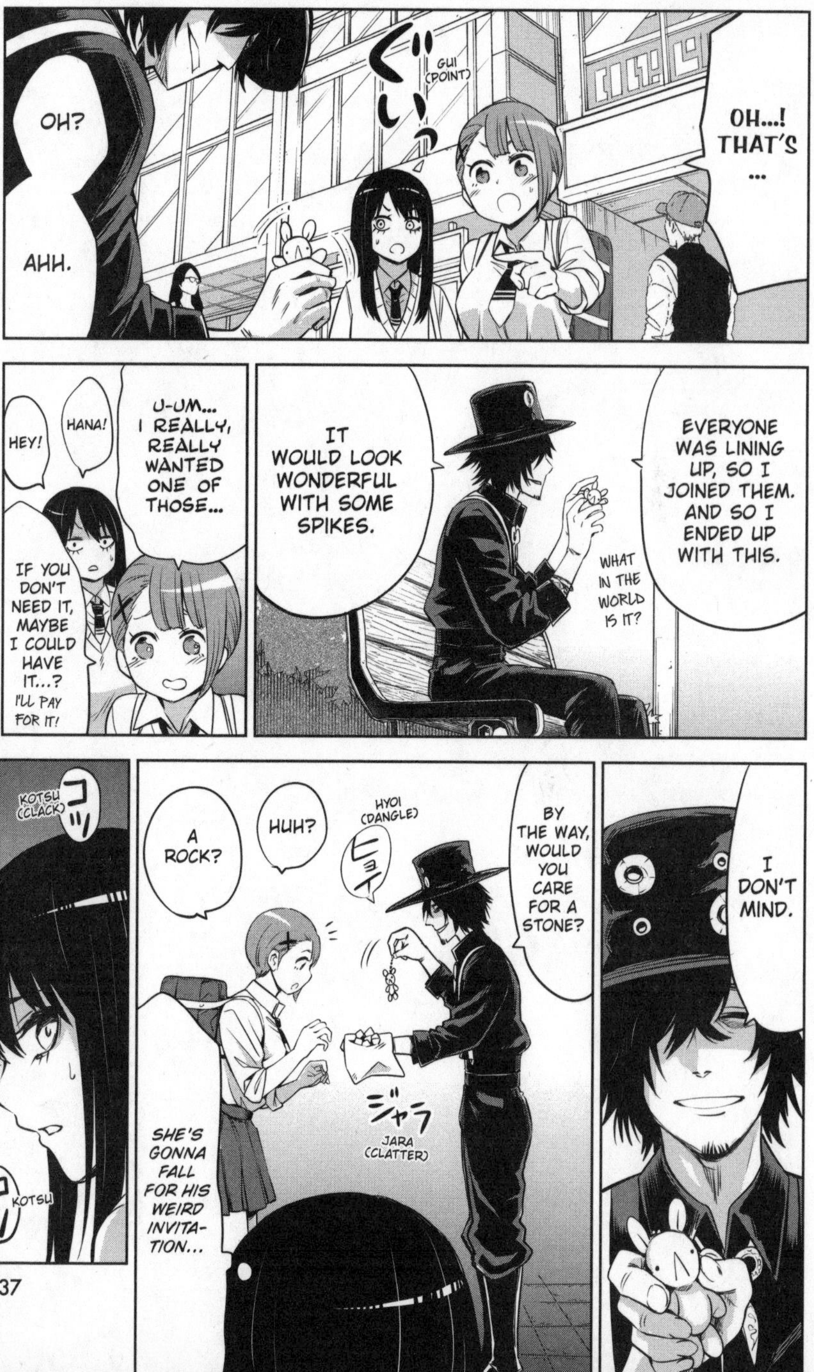
OH...! THAT'S ...
ぐいっ
GUI (POINT)
OH?
AHH.
EVERYONE WAS LINING UP, SO I JOINED THEM. AND SO I ENDED UP WITH THIS.
WHAT IN THE WORLD IS IT?
IT WOULD LOOK WONDERFUL WITH SOME SPIKES.
U-UM... I REALLY, REALLY WANTED ONE OF THOSE...
HANA!
HEY!
IF YOU DON'T NEED IT, MAYBE I COULD HAVE IT...?
I'LL PAY FOR IT!
I DON'T MIND.
BY THE WAY, WOULD YOU CARE FOR A STONE?
ヒョイ
HYOI (DANGLE)
HUH?
A ROCK?
ジャラ
JARA (CLATTER)
SHE'S GONNA FALL FOR HIS WEIRD INVITATION...
コッ
KOTSU (CLACK)
コッ
KOTSU

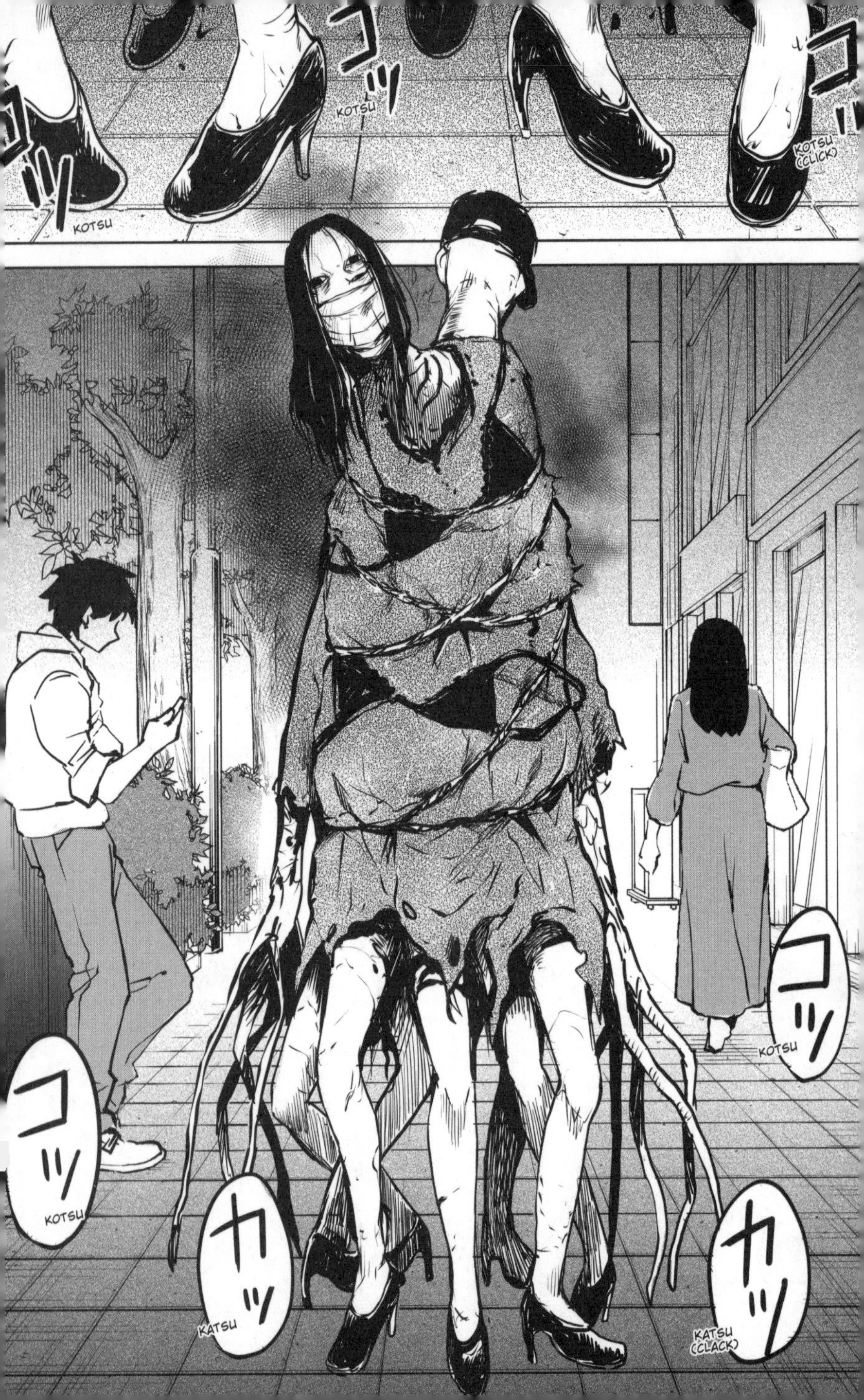
コッ
KOTSU (CLICK)
ゴッ
KOTSU
コッ
KOTSU
コッ
KOTSU
カッ
KATSU (CLACK)
コッ
KOTSU
カッ
KATSU

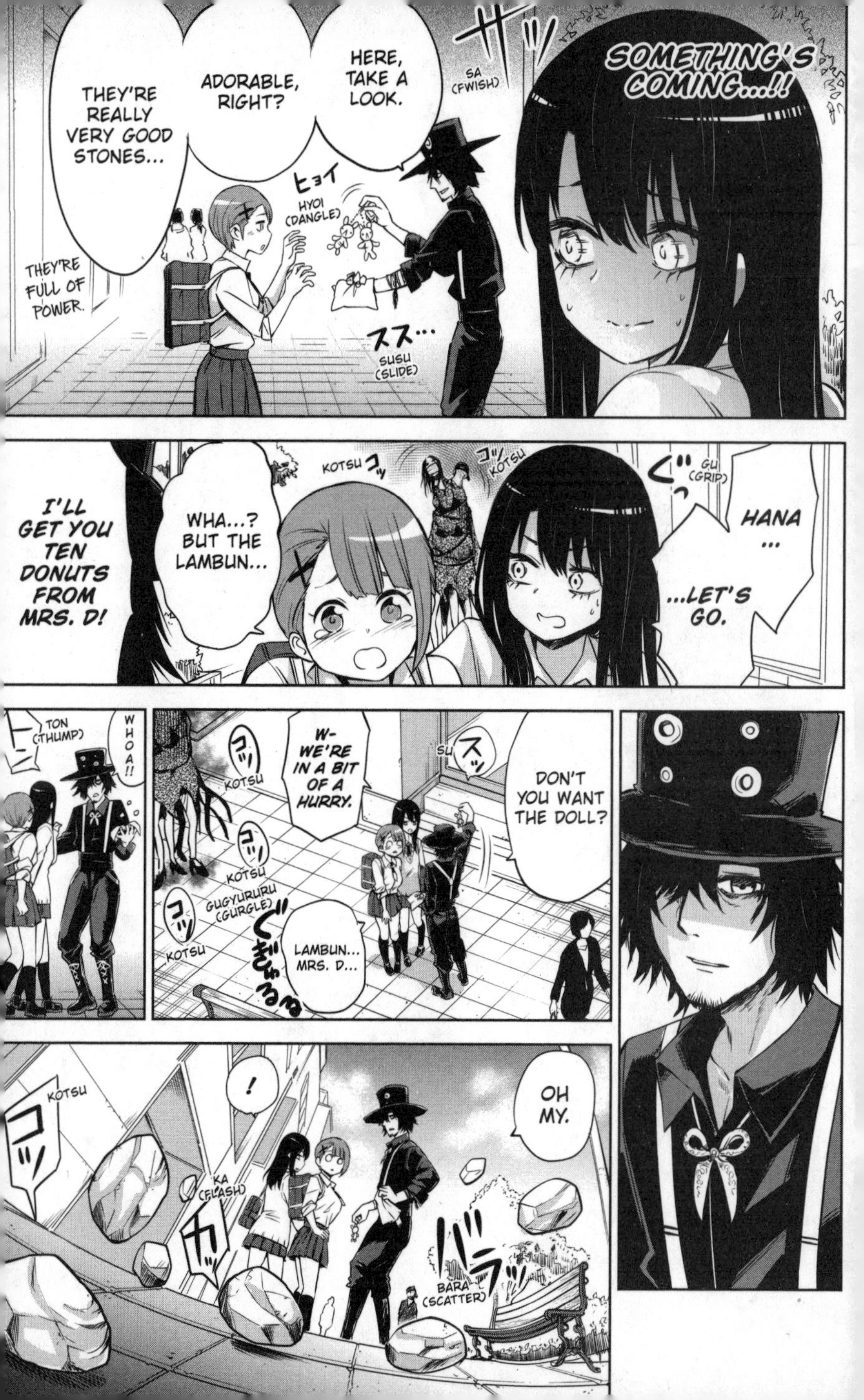
SOMETHING'S COMING...!!
SA (FWISH)
HERE, TAKE A LOOK.
ADORABLE, RIGHT?
THEY'RE REALLY VERY GOOD STONES...
HYOI (DANGLE)
THEY'RE FULL OF POWER.
SUSU (SLIDE)
GU (GRIP)
HANA ...
...LET'S GO.
KOTSU
KOTSU
WHA...? BUT THE LAMBUN...
I'LL GET YOU TEN DONUTS FROM MRS. D!
DON'T YOU WANT THE DOLL?
SU
W-WE'RE IN A BIT OF A HURRY.
KOTSU
KOTSU
KOTSU
GUGYURURU (GURGLE)
LAMBUN... MRS. D...
WHOA!!
TON (THUMP)
OH MY.
!
BARA (SCATTER)
KA (FLASH)
KOTSU

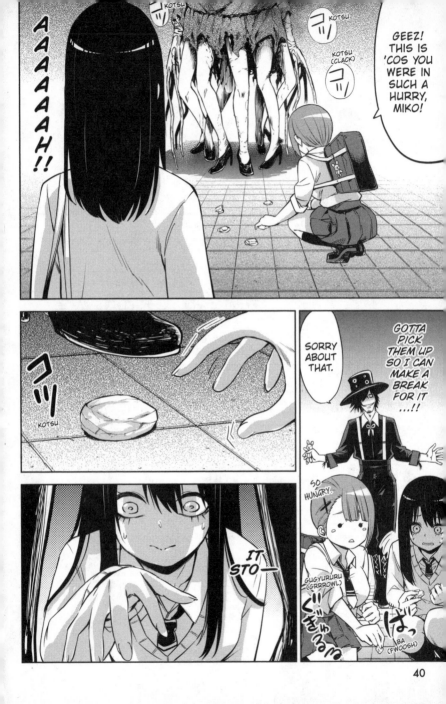

GEEZ! THIS IS 'COS YOU WERE IN SUCH A HURRY, MIKO!
KOTSU
KOTSU (CLACK)
KOTSU
KOTSU
AAAAAAH!!
GOTTA PICK THEM UP SO I CAN MAKE A BREAK FOR IT ...!!
SORRY ABOUT THAT.
SO HUNGRY.
GUGYURURU (GRRROWL)
BA (FWOOSH)
KOTSU
IT STO—

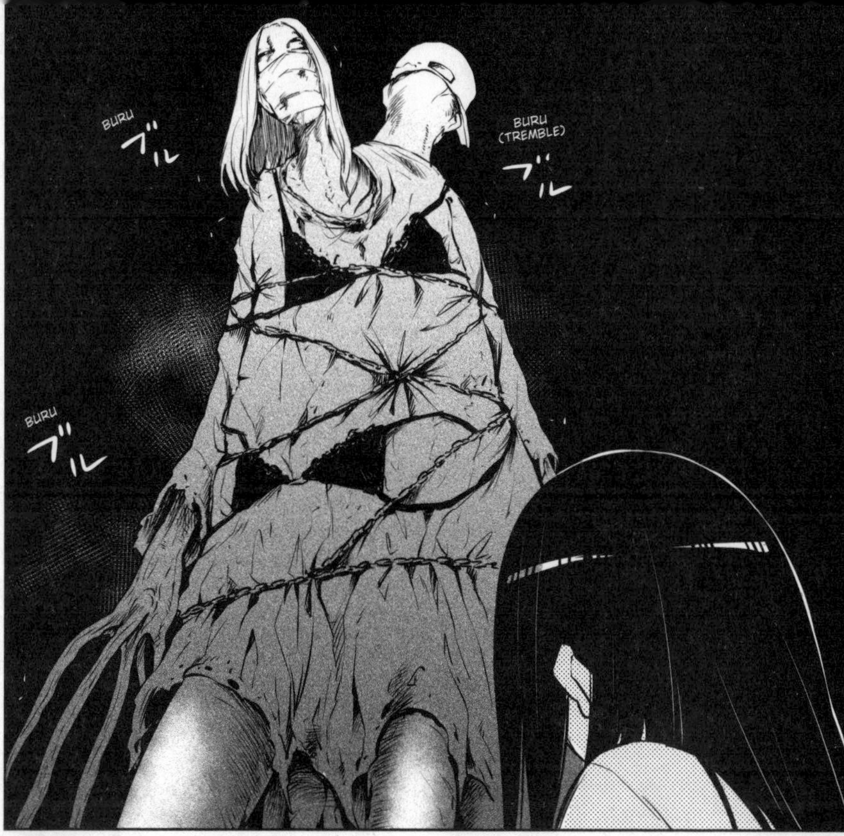
BURU (TREMBLE)
ブル
BURU
ブル
BURU
ブル
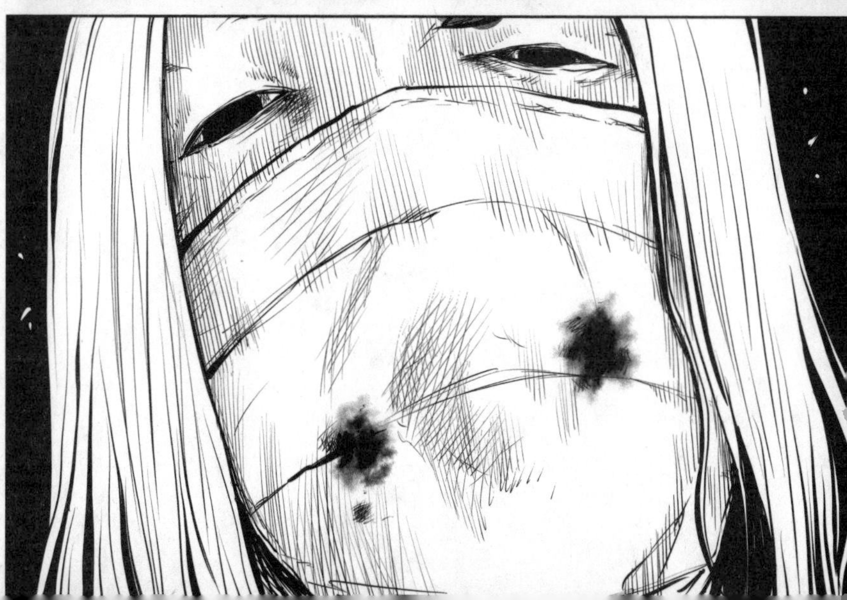

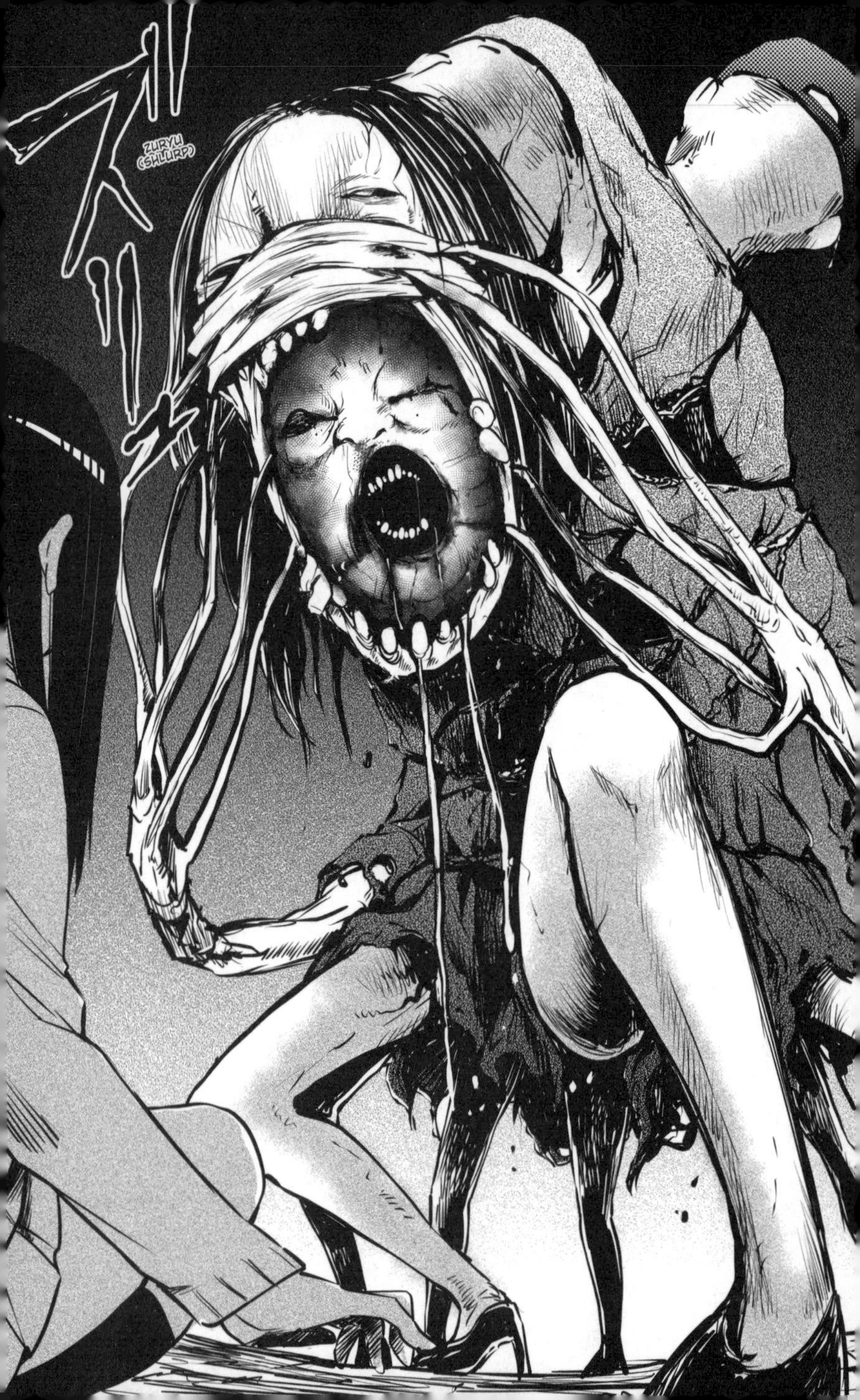
ZURYU
(SHLURP)

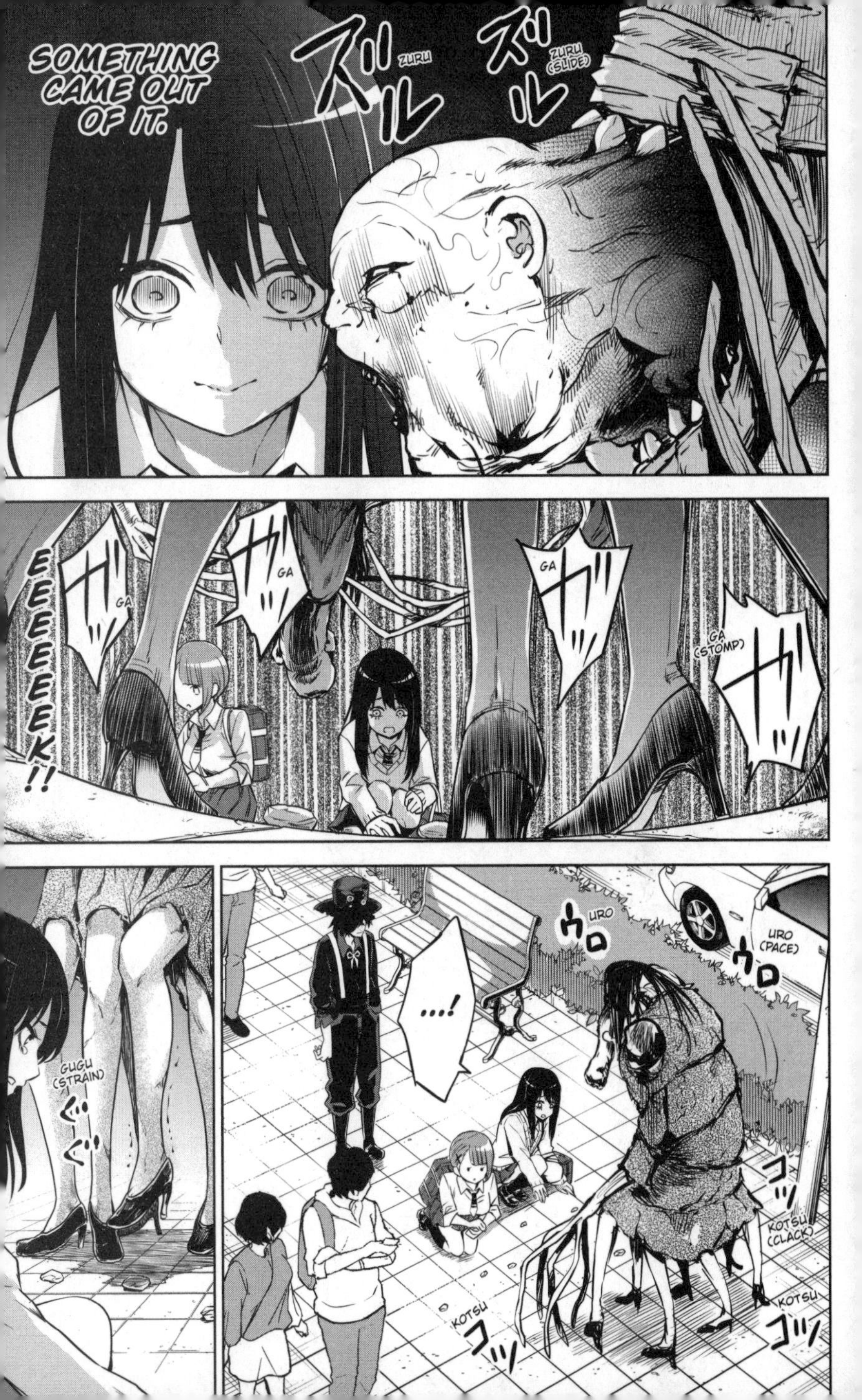
ZURU (SLIDE)
ZURU
SOMETHING CAME OUT OF IT.
GA (STOMP)
GA
GA
GA
EEEEEEEEK!!
URO (PACE)
URO
...!
KOTSU (CLACK)
KOTSU
KOTSU
GUGU (STRAIN)

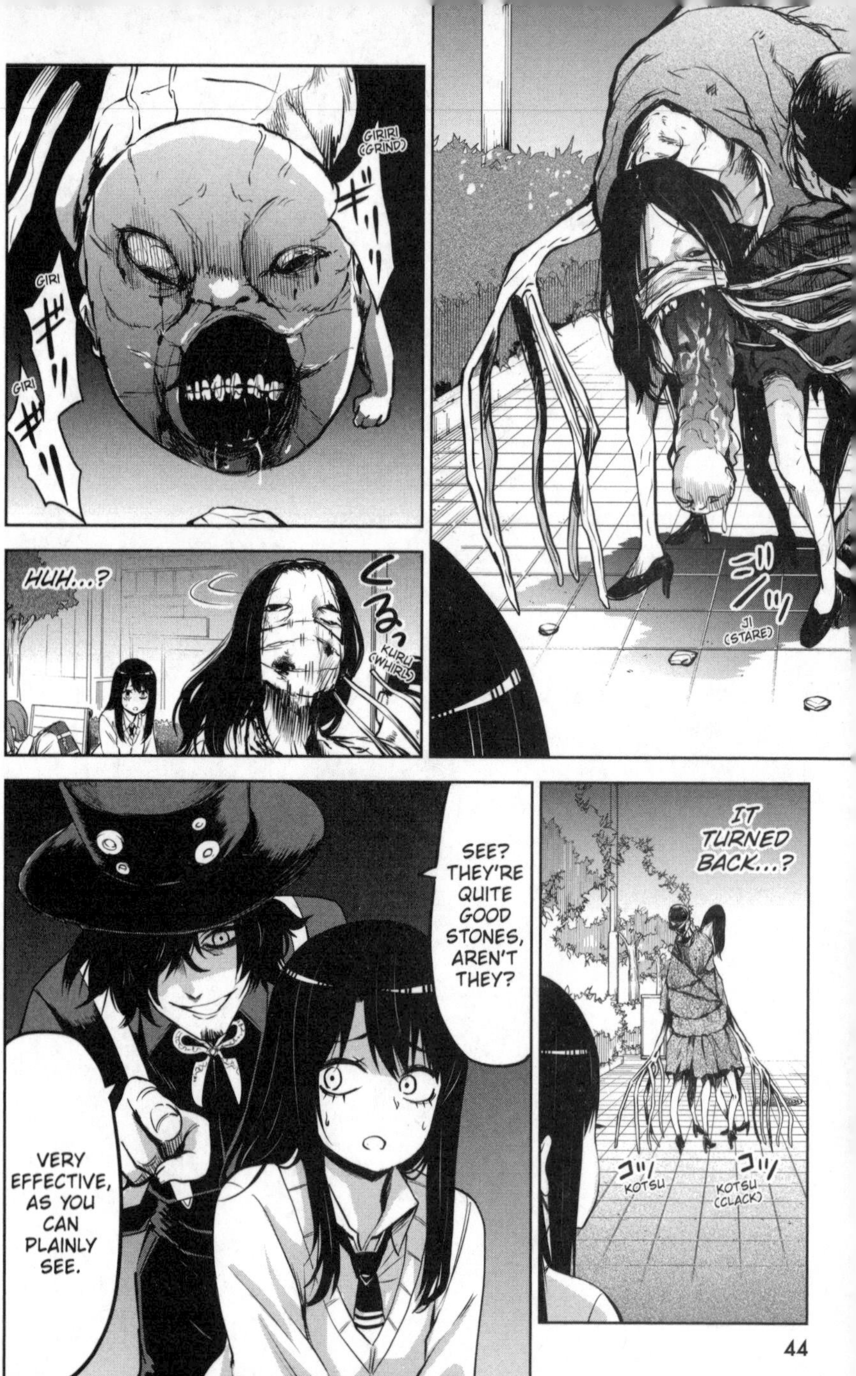
JI (STARE)
GIRIRI (GRIND)
GIRI
GIRI
HUH...?
KURU (WHIRL)
IT TURNED BACK...?
KOTSU
KOTSU (CLACK)
SEE? THEY'RE QUITE GOOD STONES, AREN'T THEY?
VERY EFFECTIVE, AS YOU CAN PLAINLY SEE.

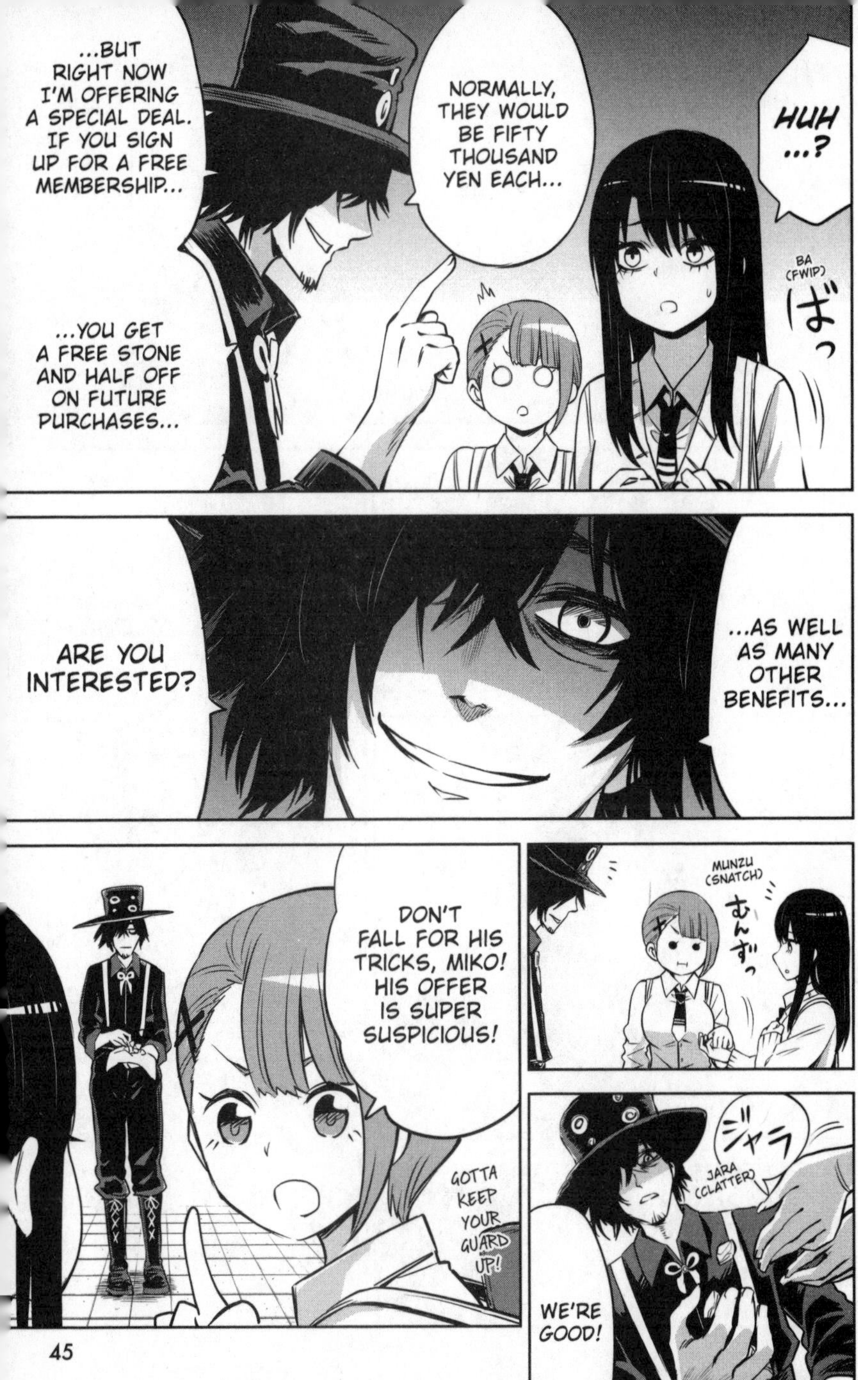
HUH ...?
BA (FWIP)
ばっ
NORMALLY, THEY WOULD BE FIFTY THOUSAND YEN EACH...
...BUT RIGHT NOW I'M OFFERING A SPECIAL DEAL. IF YOU SIGN UP FOR A FREE MEMBERSHIP...
...YOU GET A FREE STONE AND HALF OFF ON FUTURE PURCHASES...
...AS WELL AS MANY OTHER BENEFITS...
ARE YOU INTERESTED?
MUNZU (SNATCH)
むんずっ
ジャラ
JARA (CLATTER)
WE'RE GOOD!
DON'T FALL FOR HIS TRICKS, MIKO! HIS OFFER IS SUPER SUSPICIOUS!
GOTTA KEEP YOUR GUARD UP!

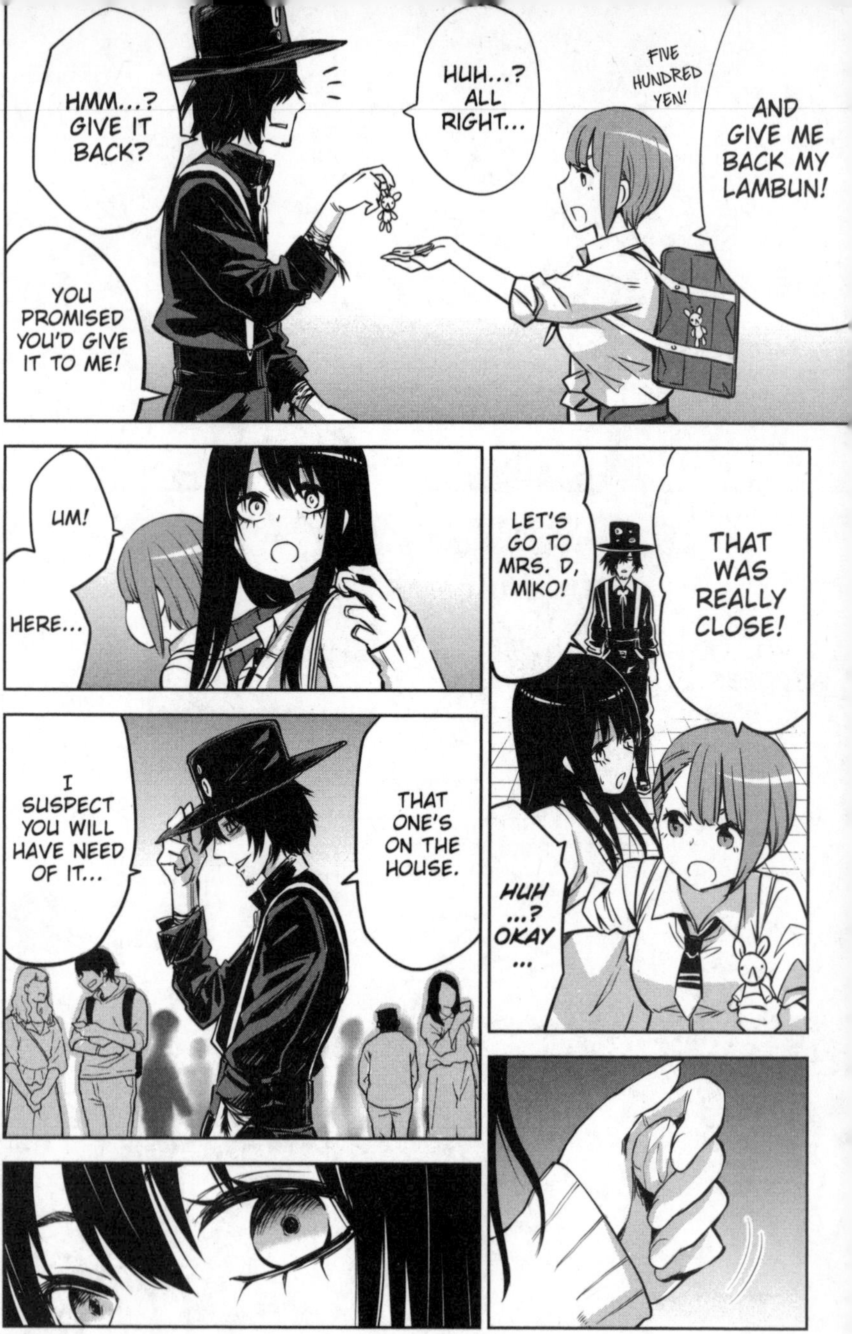
FIVE HUNDRED YEN!
AND GIVE ME BACK MY LAMBUN!
HUH...? ALL RIGHT...
HMM...? GIVE IT BACK?
YOU PROMISED YOU'D GIVE IT TO ME!
THAT WAS REALLY CLOSE!
LET'S GO TO MRS. D, MIKO!
HUH ...? OKAY ...
UM!
HERE...
THAT ONE'S ON THE HOUSE.
I SUSPECT YOU WILL HAVE NEED OF IT...

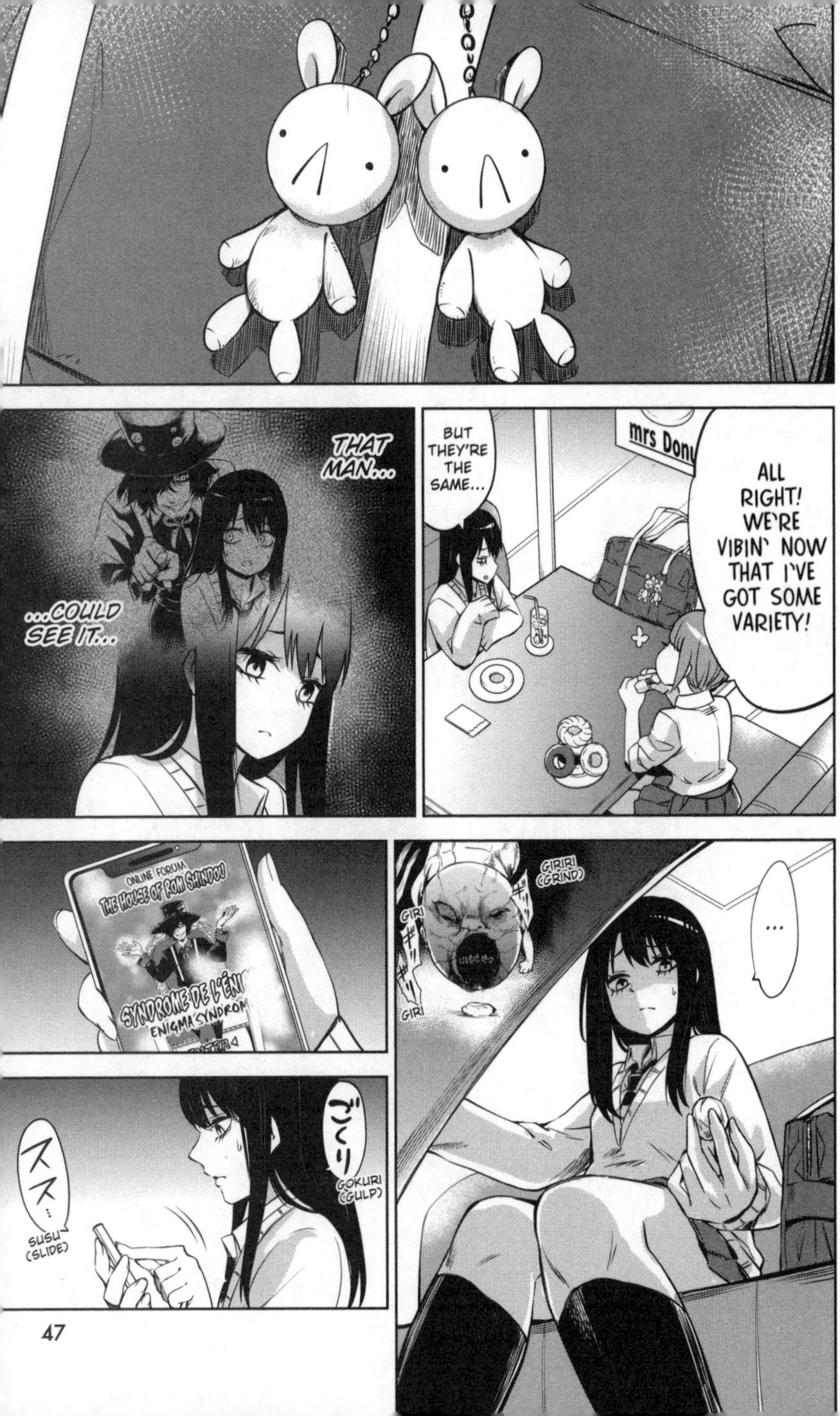
mrs Donu
ALL RIGHT! WE'RE VIBIN' NOW THAT I'VE GOT SOME VARIETY!
BUT THEY'RE THE SAME...
THAT MAN...
...COULD SEE IT...
...
GIRIRI (GRIND)
GIRI
GIRI
ONLINE FORUM
THE HOUSE OF ROM SHINDOU
ごくり
GOKURI (GULP)
スス…
SUSU (SLIDE)

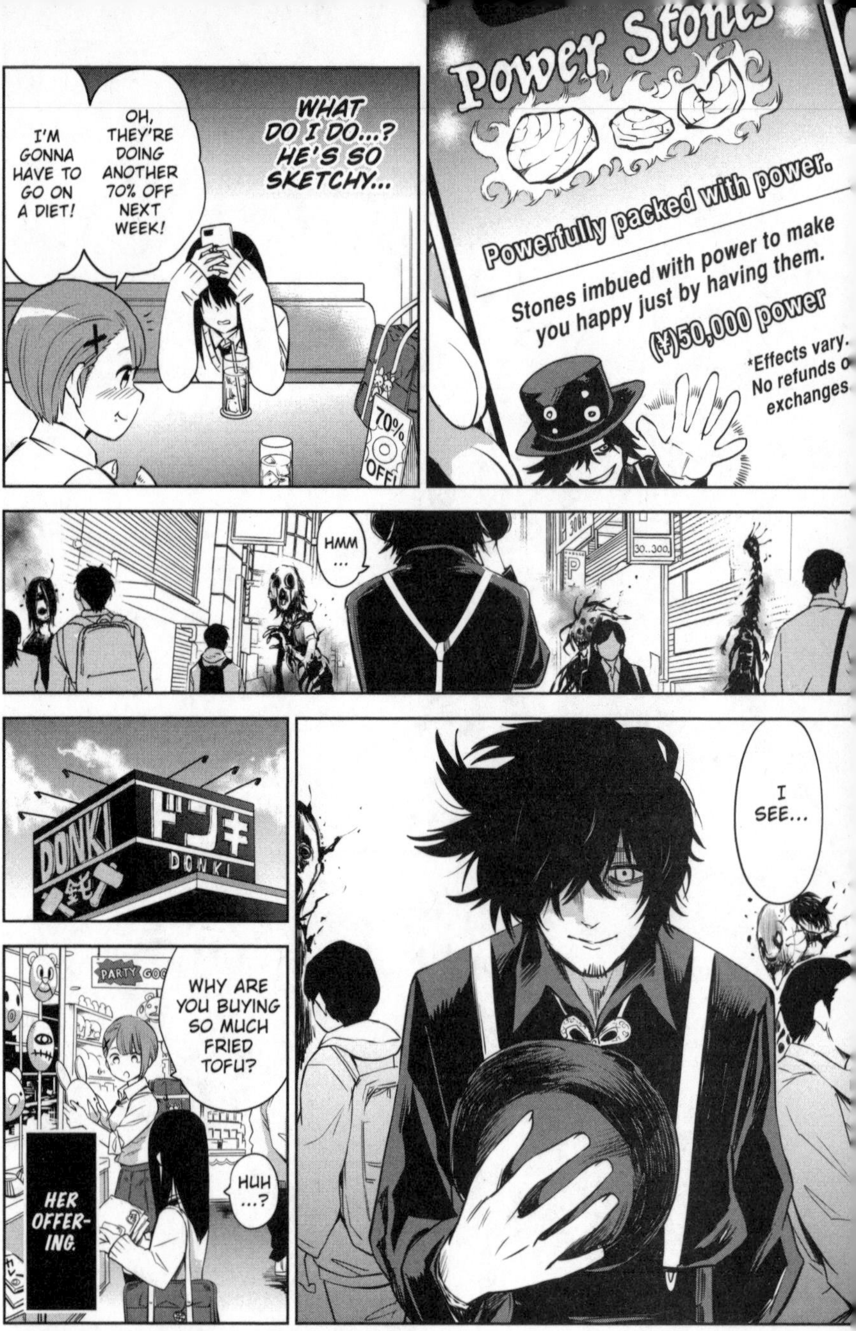
Power Stones
Powerfully packed with power.
Stones imbued with power to make you happy just by having them.
(¥)50,000 power
*Effects vary. No refunds o exchanges.
WHAT DO I DO...? HE'S SO SKETCHY...
OH, THEY'RE DOING ANOTHER 70% OFF NEXT WEEK!
I'M GONNA HAVE TO GO ON A DIET!
70% OFF
HMM ...
I SEE...
DONKI
ドンキ
DONKI
WHY ARE YOU BUYING SO MUCH FRIED TOFU?
HUH ...?
HER OFFERING.

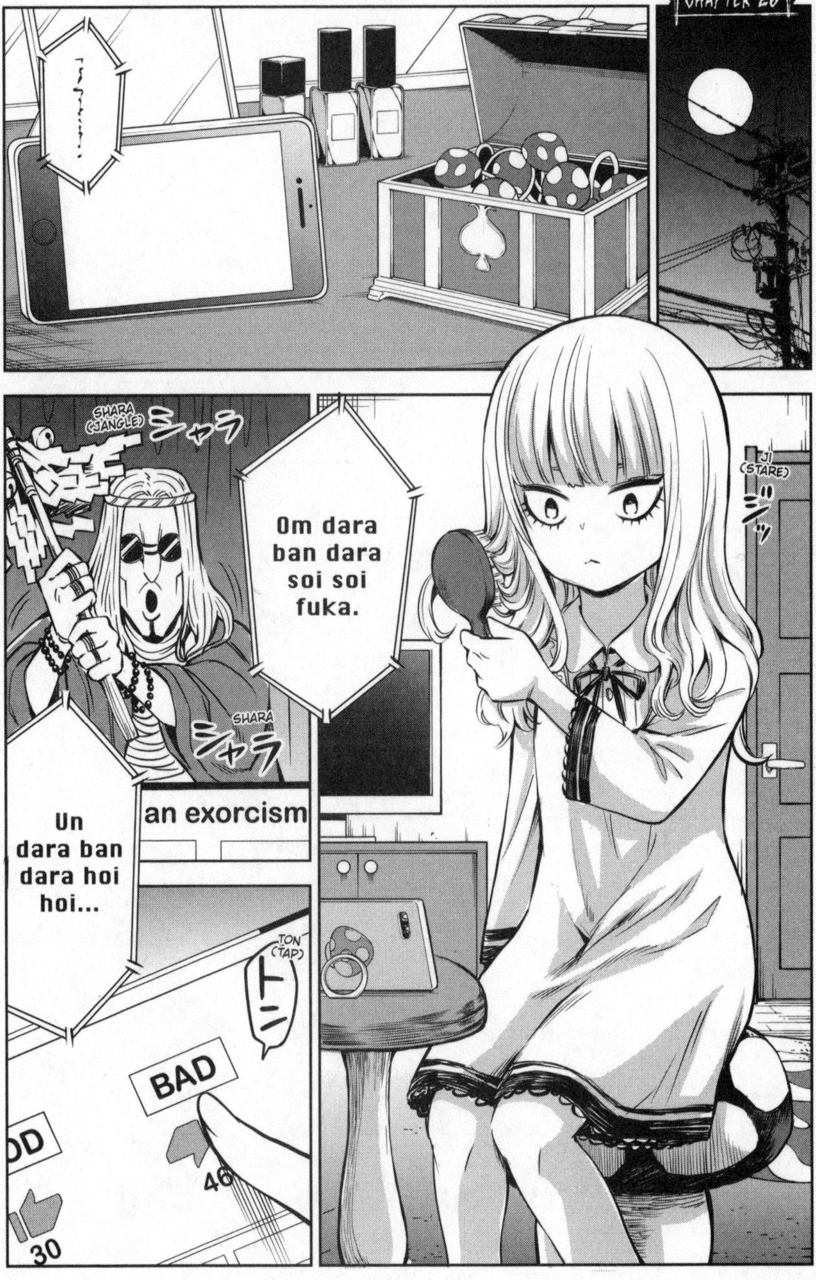
JI (STARE) ジッ
SHARA (JANGLE) シャラ
Om dara ban dara soi soi fuka.
SHARA シャラ
Un dara ban dara hoi hoi...
an exorcism
TON (TAP) トン
BAD
OD
46
30

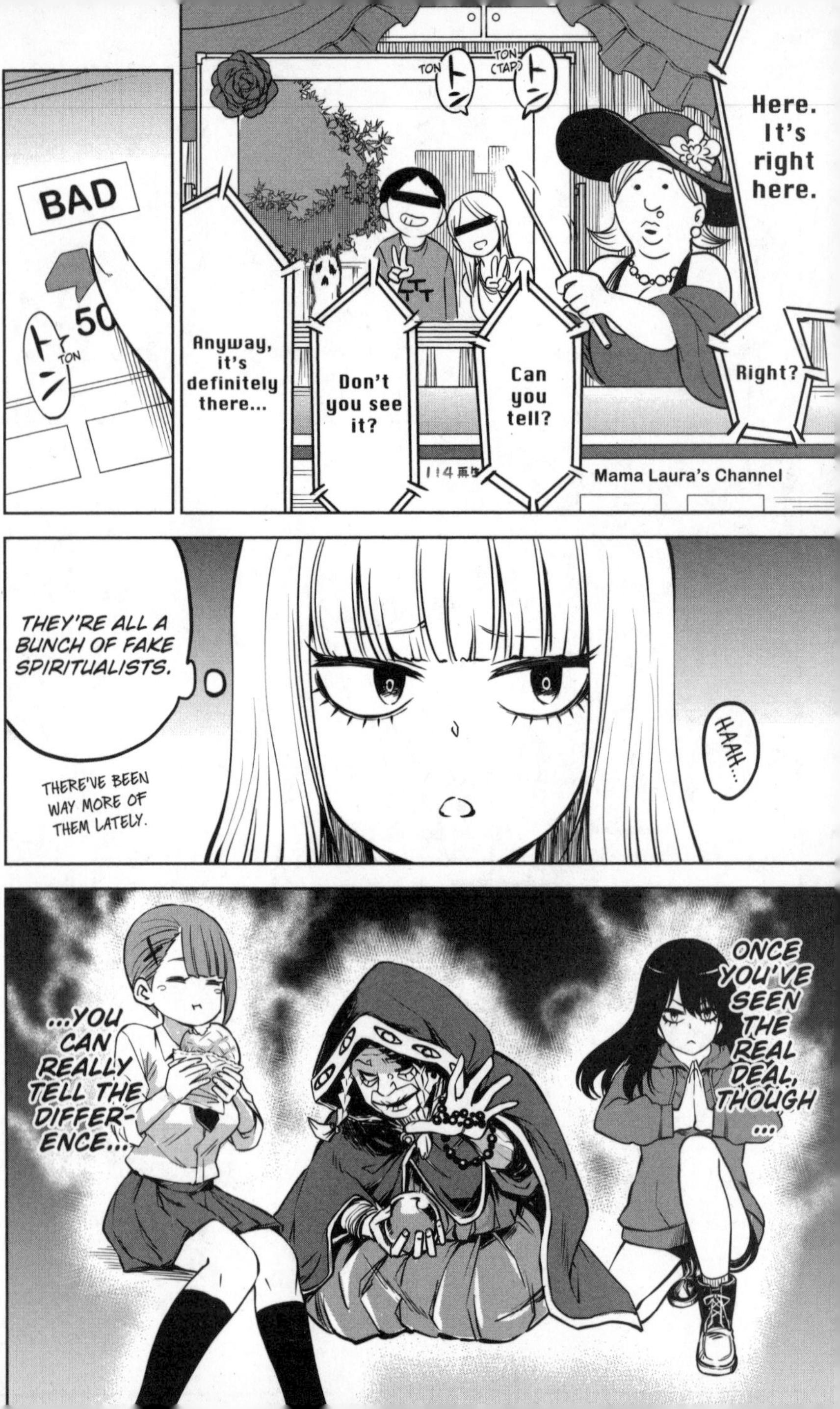

Here. It's right here.
TON (TAP)
TON
Right?
Can you tell?
Don't you see it?
Anyway, it's definitely there...
Mama Laura's Channel
BAD
50
TON
HAAH...
THEY'RE ALL A BUNCH OF FAKE SPIRITUALISTS.
THERE'VE BEEN WAY MORE OF THEM LATELY.
ONCE YOU'VE SEEN THE REAL DEAL, THOUGH...
...YOU CAN REALLY TELL THE DIFFER-ENCE...

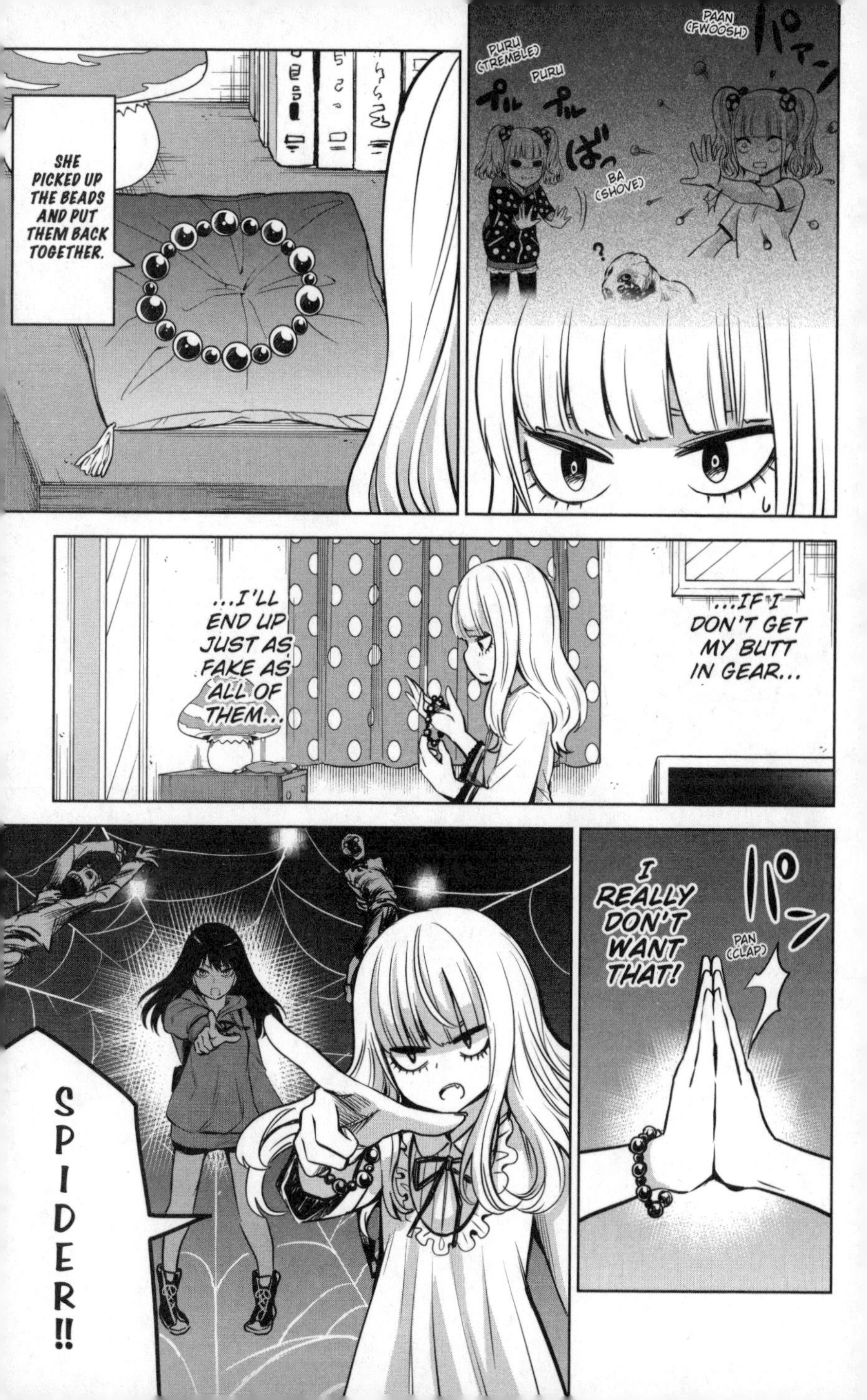

PAAN (FWOOSH)
パァン
PURU (TREMBLE)
PURU
プル プル
ばっ
BA (SHOVE)
?
SHE PICKED UP THE BEADS AND PUT THEM BACK TOGETHER.
...IF I DON'T GET MY BUTT IN GEAR...
...I'LL END UP JUST AS FAKE AS ALL OF THEM...
パン
PAN (CLAP)
I REALLY DON'T WANT THAT!
SPIDER!!

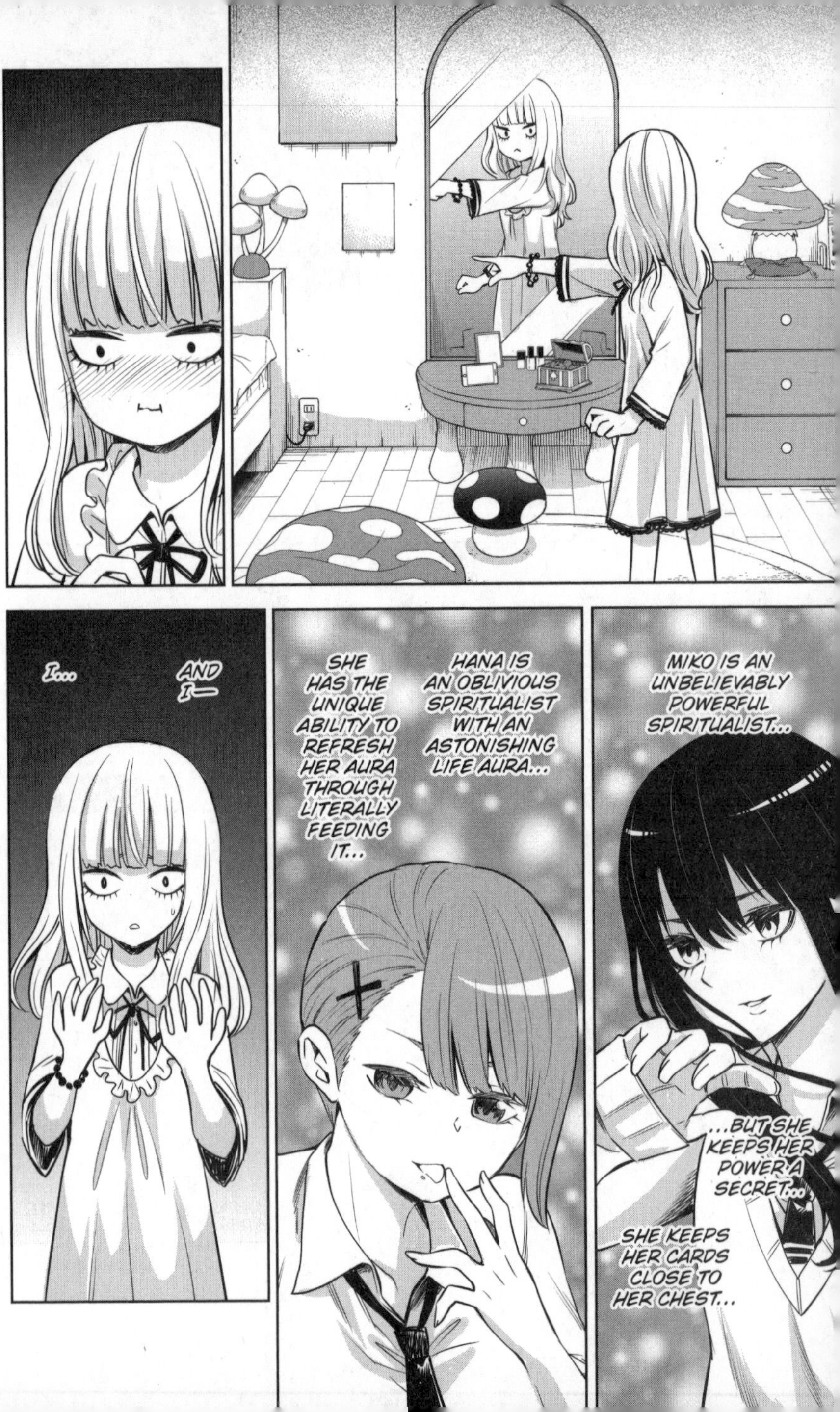
MIKO IS AN UNBELIEVABLY POWERFUL SPIRITUALIST...
...BUT SHE KEEPS HER POWER A SECRET...
SHE KEEPS HER CARDS CLOSE TO HER CHEST...
HANA IS AN OBLIVIOUS SPIRITUALIST WITH AN ASTONISHING LIFE AURA...
SHE HAS THE UNIQUE ABILITY TO REFRESH HER AURA THROUGH LITERALLY FEEDING IT...
AND I—
I...

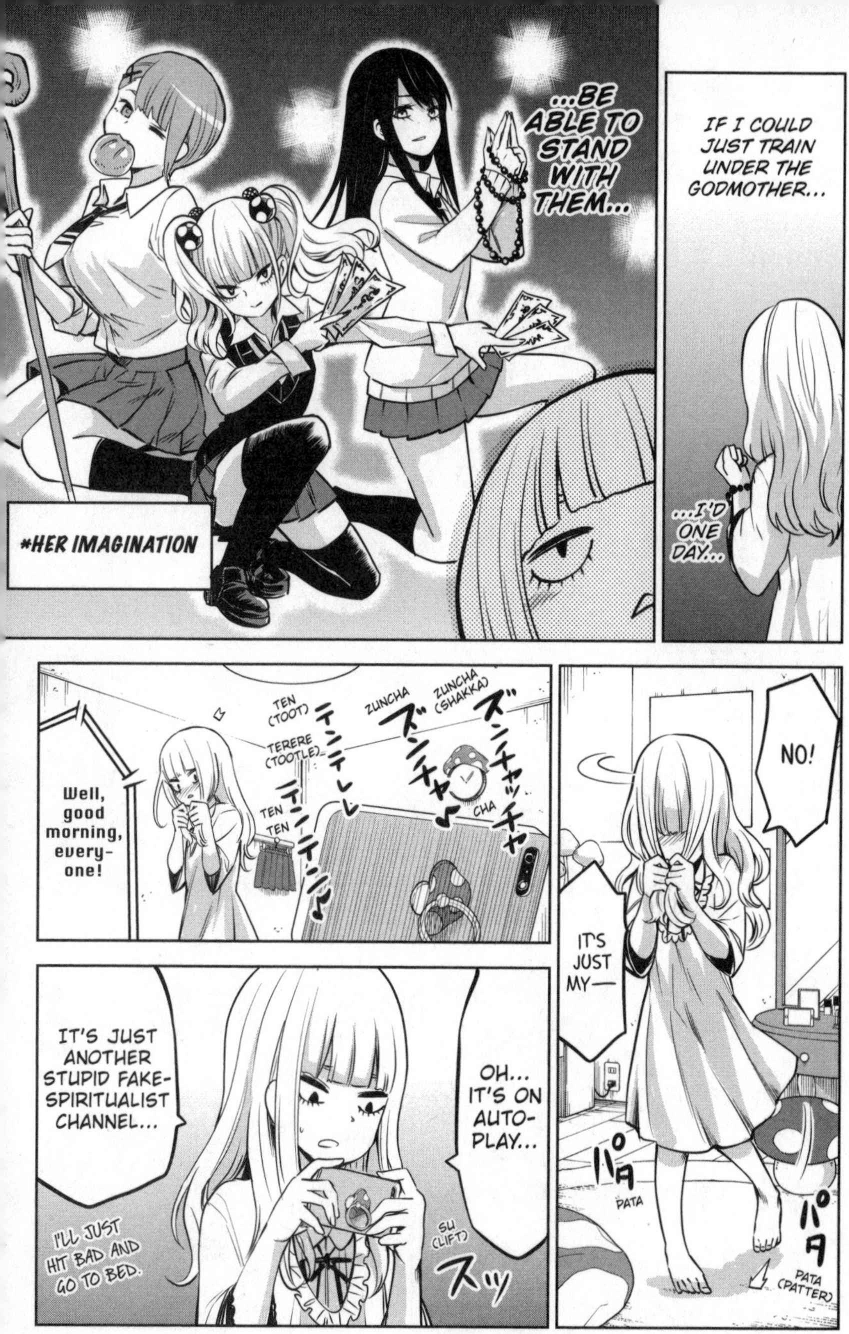
IF I COULD JUST TRAIN UNDER THE GODMOTHER...
...I'D ONE DAY...
...BE ABLE TO STAND WITH THEM...
#HER IMAGINATION
NO!
IT'S JUST MY—
パタ PATA
パタ PATA (PATTER)
ズンチャッチャ ZUNCHA (SHAKKA)
ズンチャ ZUNCHA
テンテレレ TEN (TOOT) TERERE (TOOTLE)
テンテン TEN TEN
CHA
Well, good morning, every-one!
OH... IT'S ON AUTO-PLAY...
IT'S JUST ANOTHER STUPID FAKE-SPIRITUALIST CHANNEL...
スッ SU (LIFT)
I'LL JUST HIT BAD AND GO TO BED.

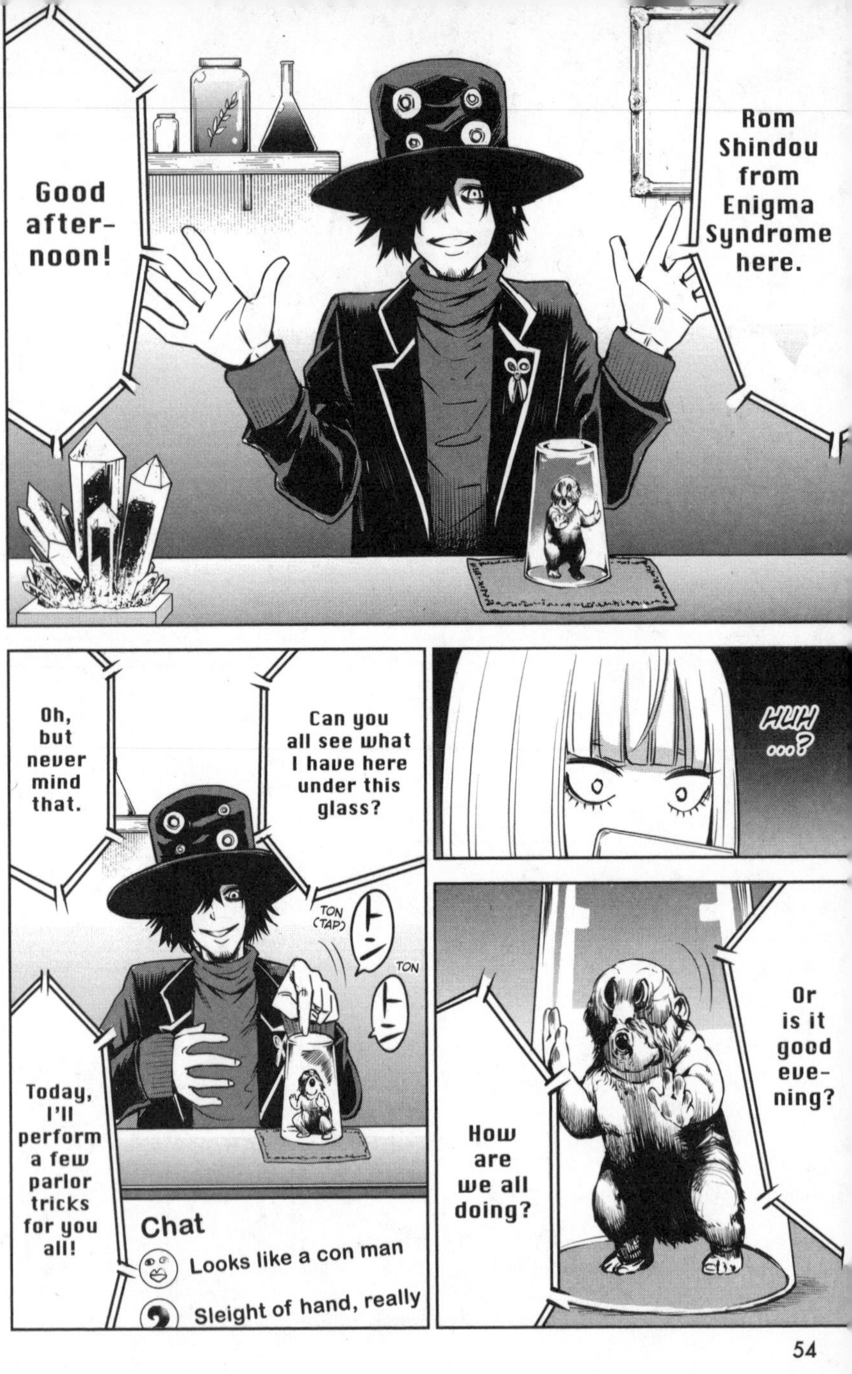
Rom Shindou from Enigma Syndrome here.
Good afternoon!
HUH...?
Or is it good evening?
How are we all doing?
Can you all see what I have here under this glass?
Oh, but never mind that.
TON (TAP)
TON
Today, I'll perform a few parlor tricks for you all!
Chat
Looks like a con man
Sleight of hand, really

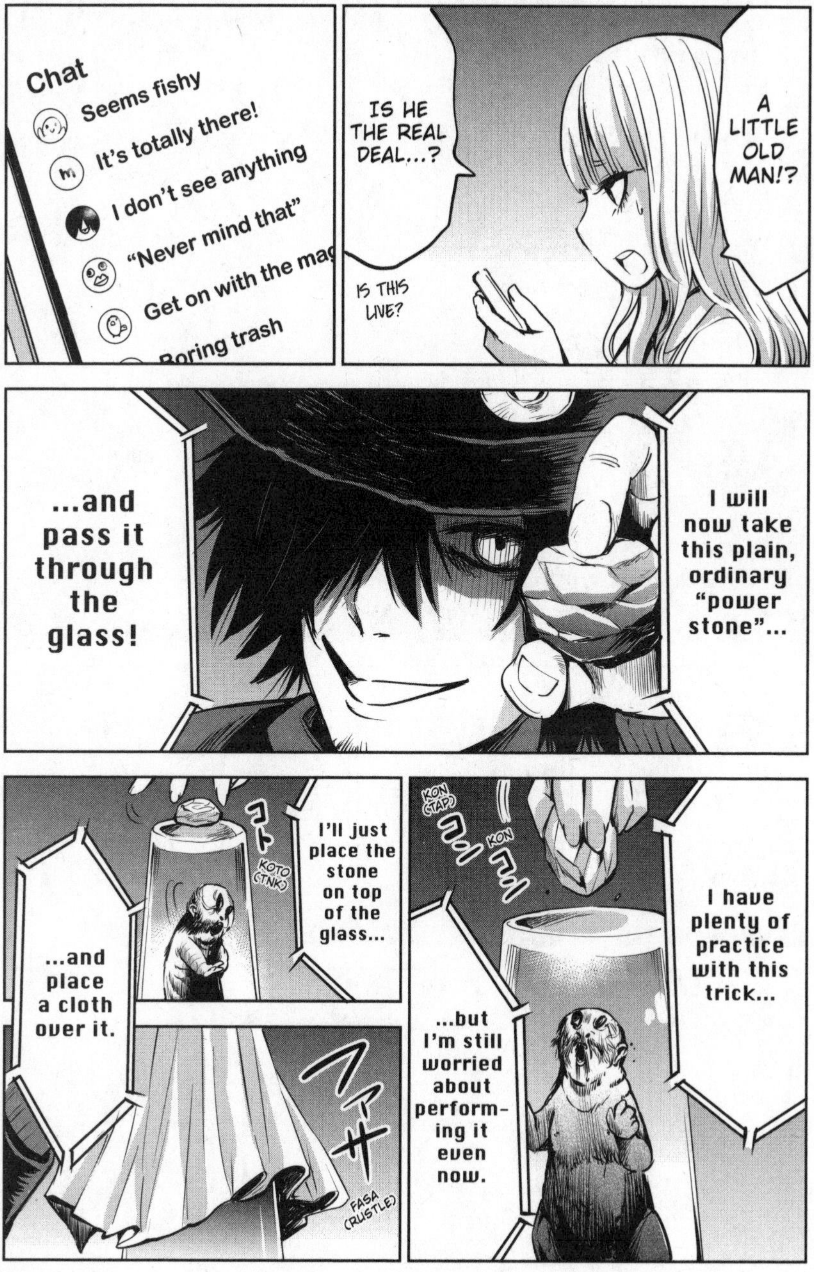
A LITTLE OLD MAN!?
IS HE THE REAL DEAL...?
IS THIS LIVE?
Chat
Seems fishy
It's totally there!
I don't see anything
"Never mind that"
Get on with the mag
Boring trash
I will now take this plain, ordinary "power stone"...
...and pass it through the glass!
コン
KON (TAP)
コン
KON
I have plenty of practice with this trick...
...but I'm still worried about performing it even now.
コト
KOTO (TNK)
I'll just place the stone on top of the glass...
...and place a cloth over it.
ファサ
FASA (RUSTLE)

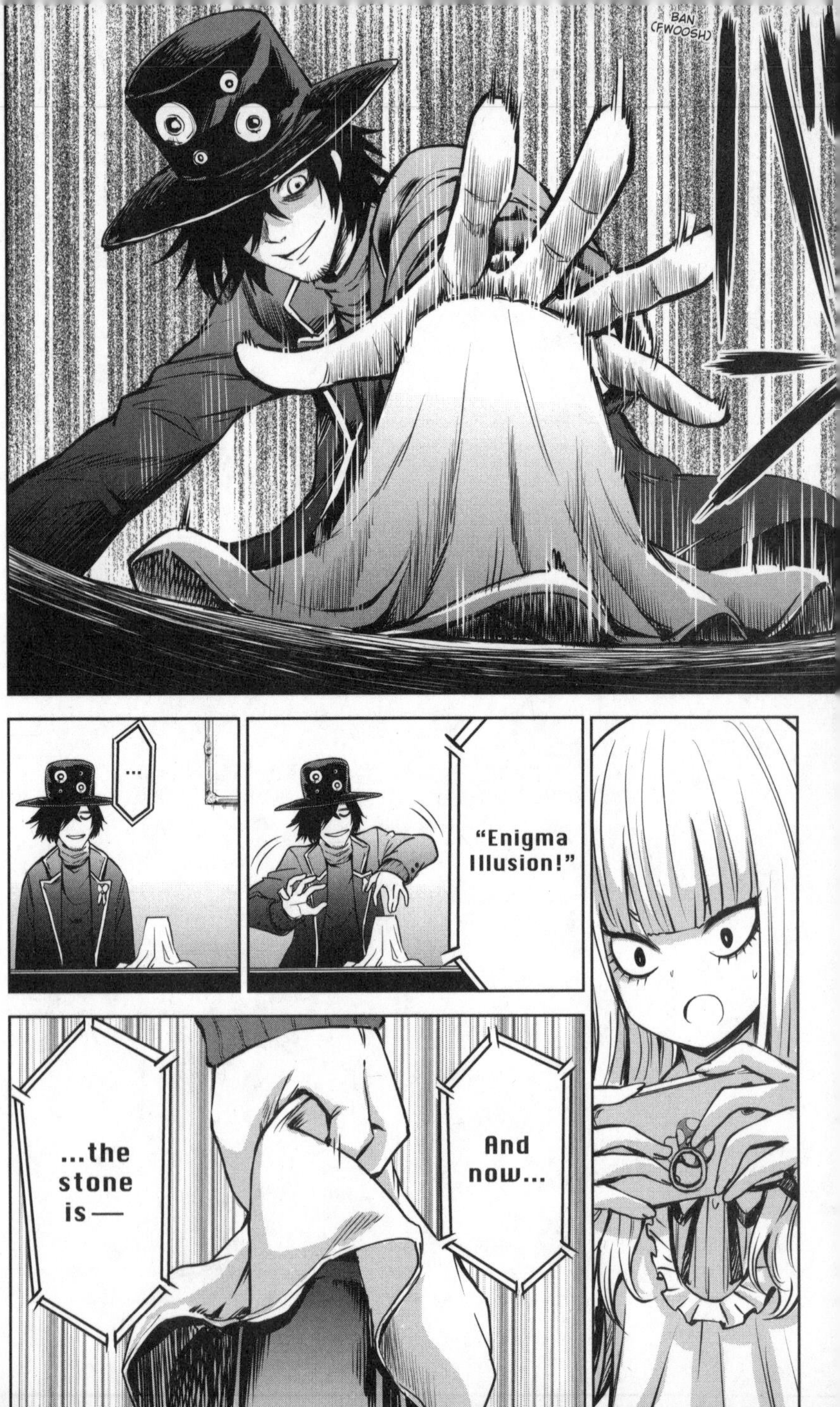
BAN (FWOOSH)
"Enigma Illusion!"
...
And now...
...the stone is—

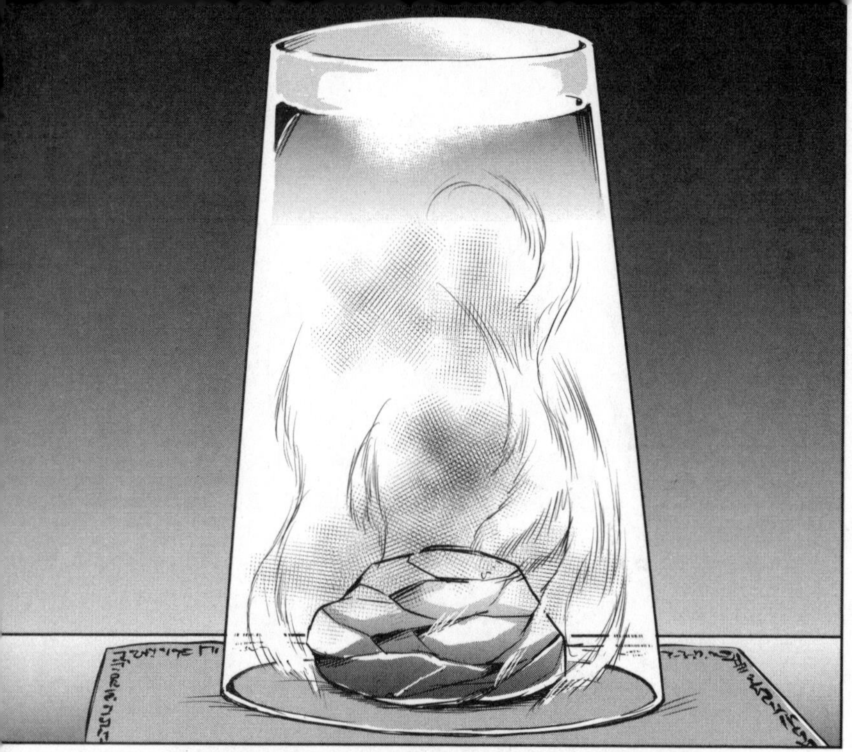

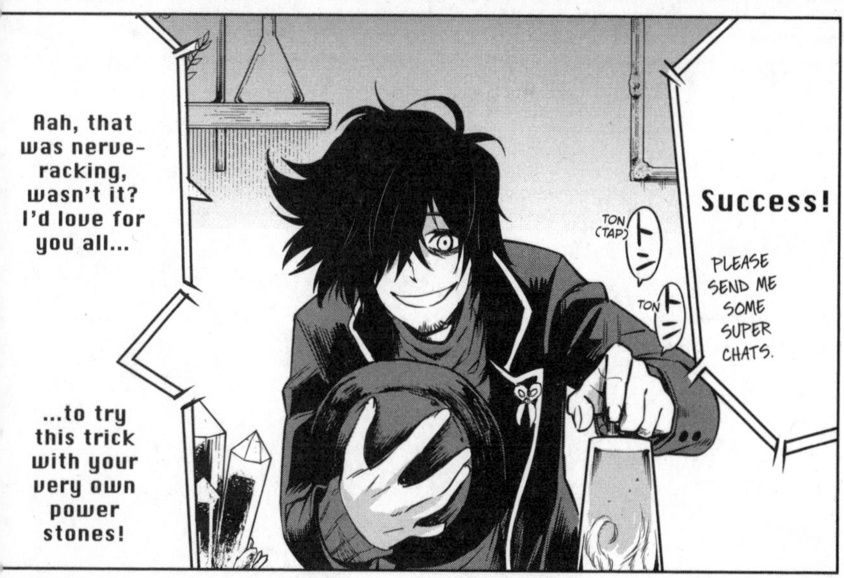
Success!
PLEASE SEND ME SOME SUPER CHATS.
TON (TAP)
TON
Aah, that was nerve-racking, wasn't it? I'd love for you all...
...to try this trick with your very own power stones!

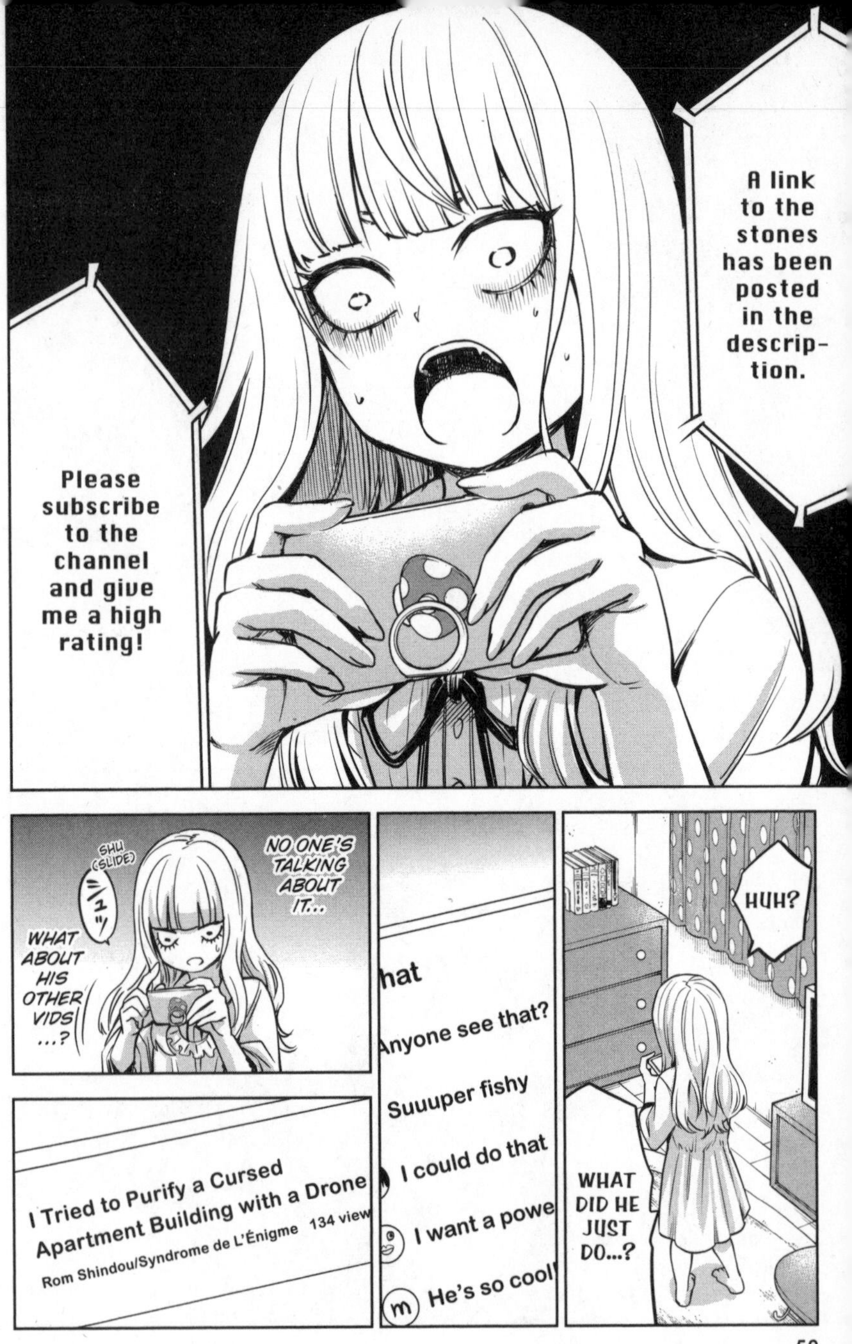
A link to the stones has been posted in the description.
Please subscribe to the channel and give me a high rating!
HUH?
WHAT DID HE JUST DO...?
hat
Anyone see that?
Suuuper fishy
I could do that
I want a powe
He's so cool
NO ONE'S TALKING ABOUT IT...
SHU (SLIDE)
WHAT ABOUT HIS OTHER VIDS ...?
I Tried to Purify a Cursed Apartment Building with a Drone
Rom Shindou/Syndrome de L'Énigme
134 view

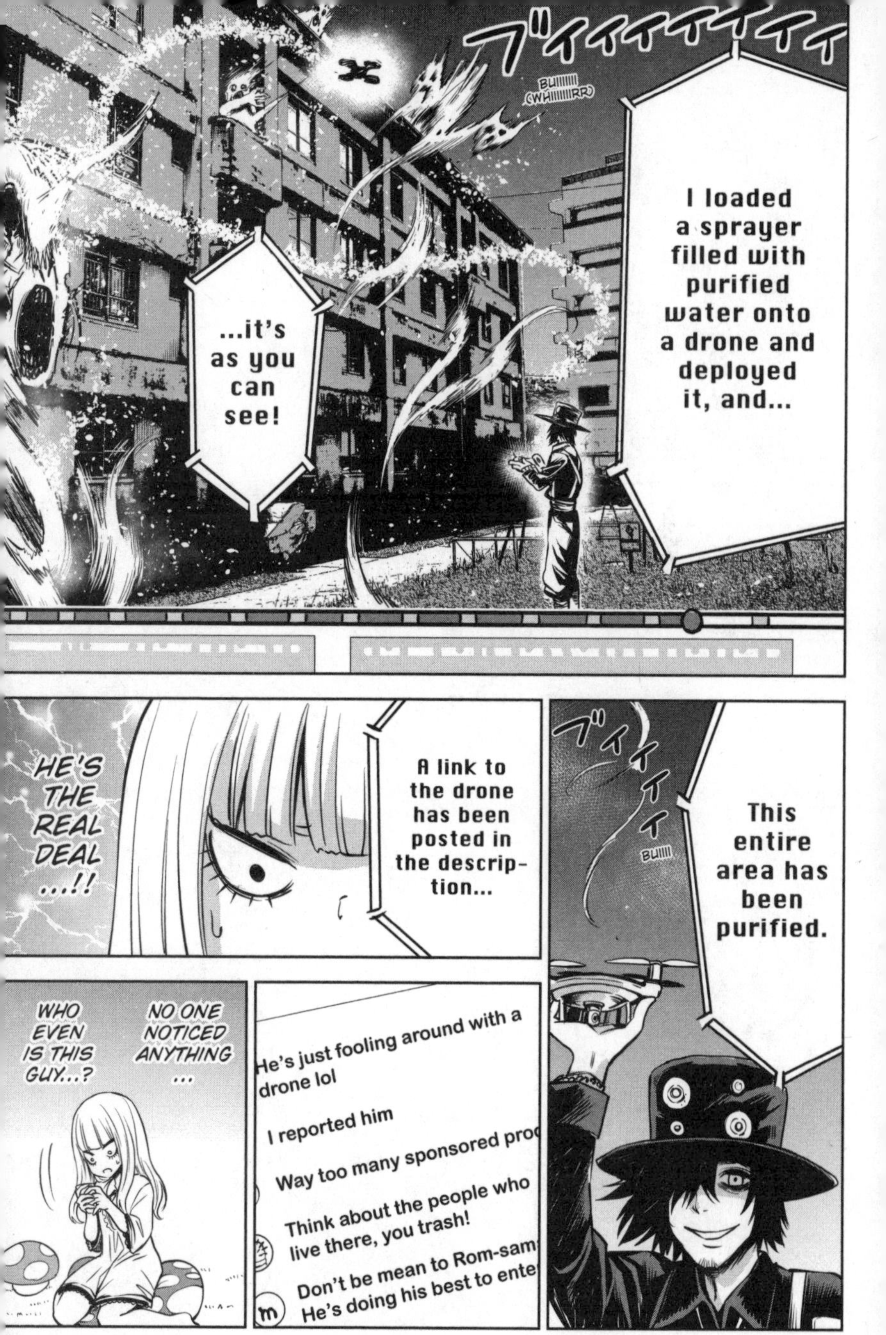
BUIIIIIII (WHIIIIIIRR)
I loaded a sprayer filled with purified water onto a drone and deployed it, and...
...it's as you can see!
BUIIII
This entire area has been purified.
A link to the drone has been posted in the descrip-tion...
HE'S THE REAL DEAL...!!
He's just fooling around with a drone lol
I reported him
Way too many sponsored pro
Think about the people who live there, you trash!
Don't be mean to Rom-sam
He's doing his best to ente
NO ONE NOTICED ANYTHING...
WHO EVEN IS THIS GUY...?

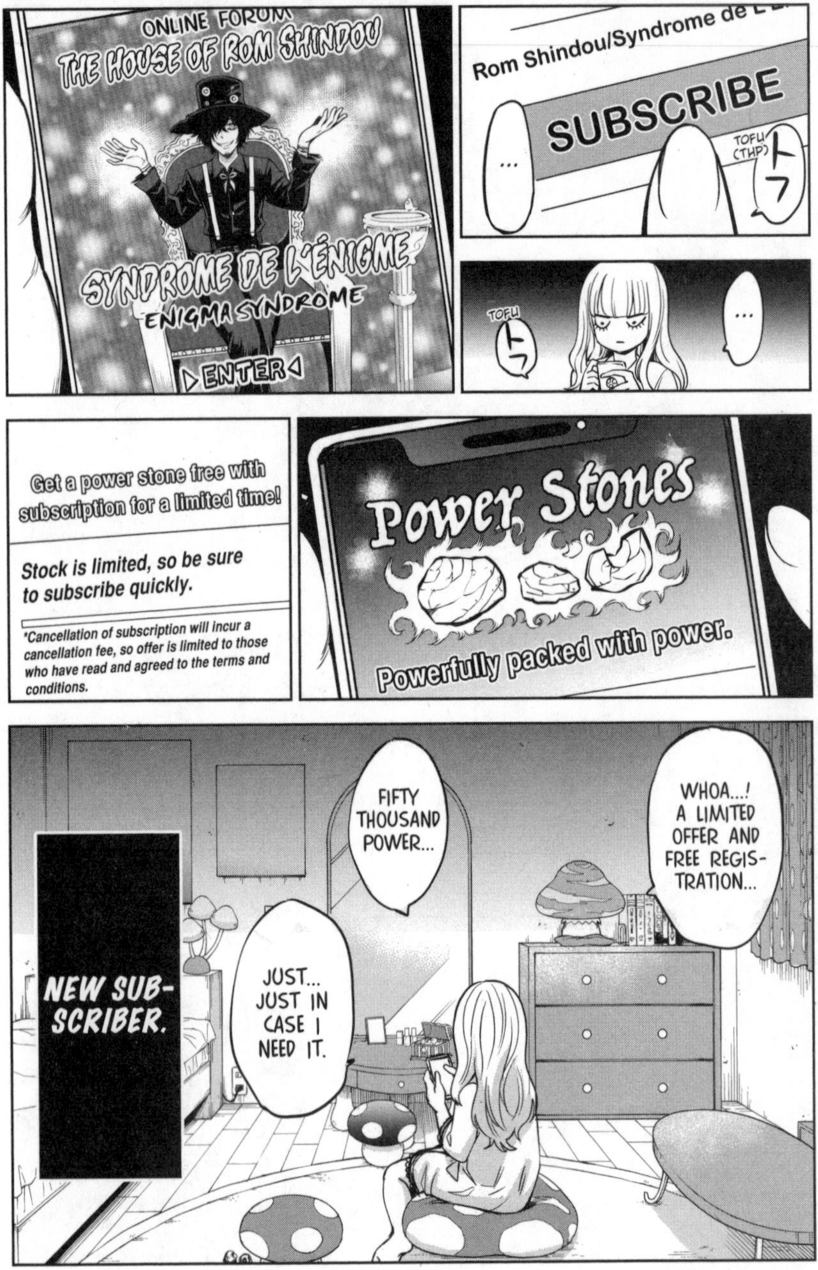
Rom Shindou/Syndrome de L
SUBSCRIBE
...
TOFU (THP) トフ
...
TOFU トフ
ONLINE FORUM
THE HOUSE OF ROM SHINDOU
SYNDROME DE L'ÉNIGME
ENIGMA SYNDROME
▷ENTER◁
Power Stones
Powerfully packed with power.
Get a power stone free with subscription for a limited time!
Stock is limited, so be sure to subscribe quickly.
*Cancellation of subscription will incur a cancellation fee, so offer is limited to those who have read and agreed to the terms and conditions.
WHOA...! A LIMITED OFFER AND FREE REGISTRATION...
FIFTY THOUSAND POWER...
JUST... JUST IN CASE I NEED IT.
NEW SUBSCRIBER.

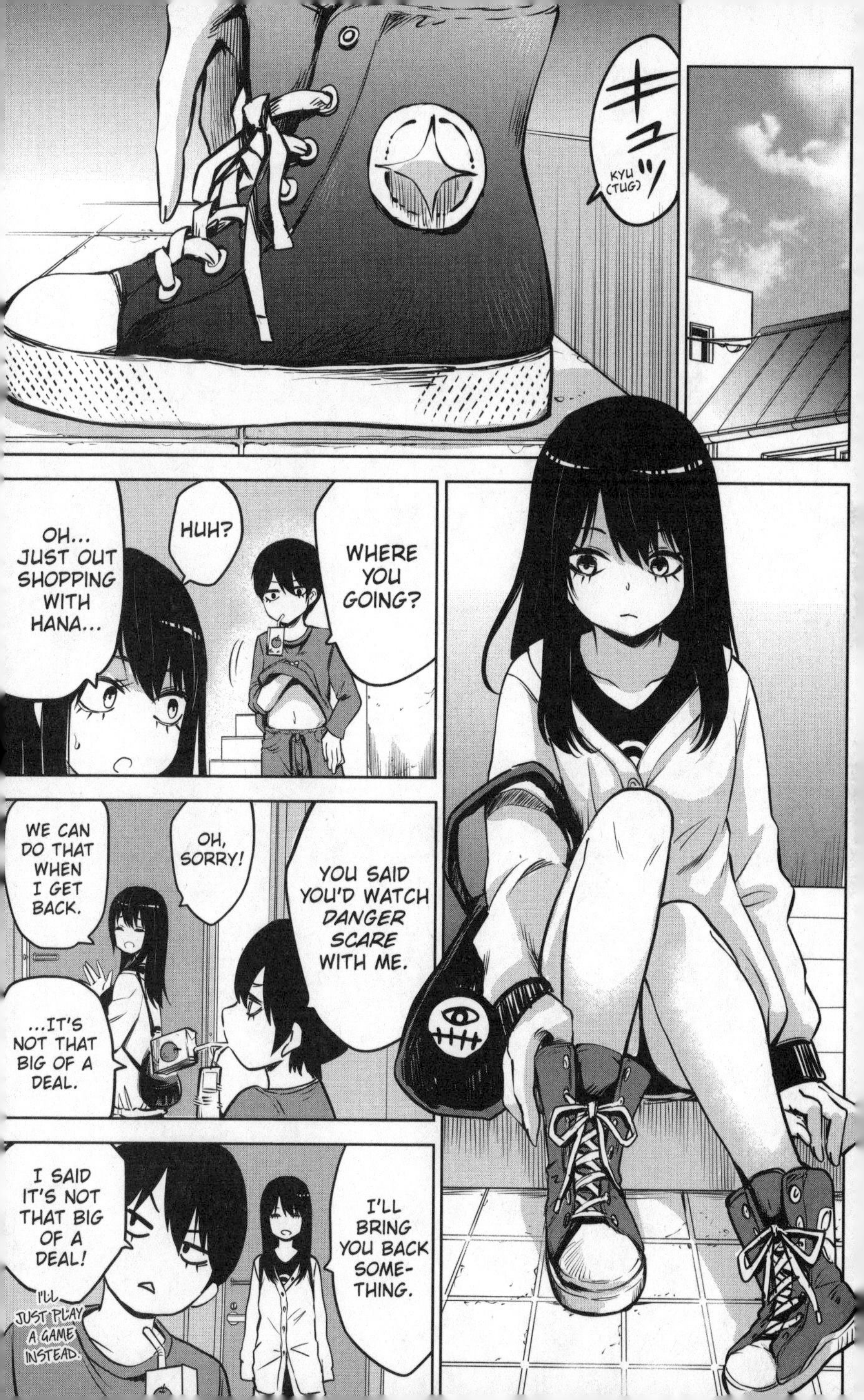
キュッ
KYU (TUG)
WHERE YOU GOING?
HUH?
OH... JUST OUT SHOPPING WITH HANA...
YOU SAID YOU'D WATCH *DANGER SCARE* WITH ME.
OH, SORRY!
WE CAN DO THAT WHEN I GET BACK.
...IT'S NOT THAT BIG OF A DEAL.
I'LL BRING YOU BACK SOME-THING.
I SAID IT'S NOT THAT BIG OF A DEAL!
I'LL JUST PLAY A GAME INSTEAD.

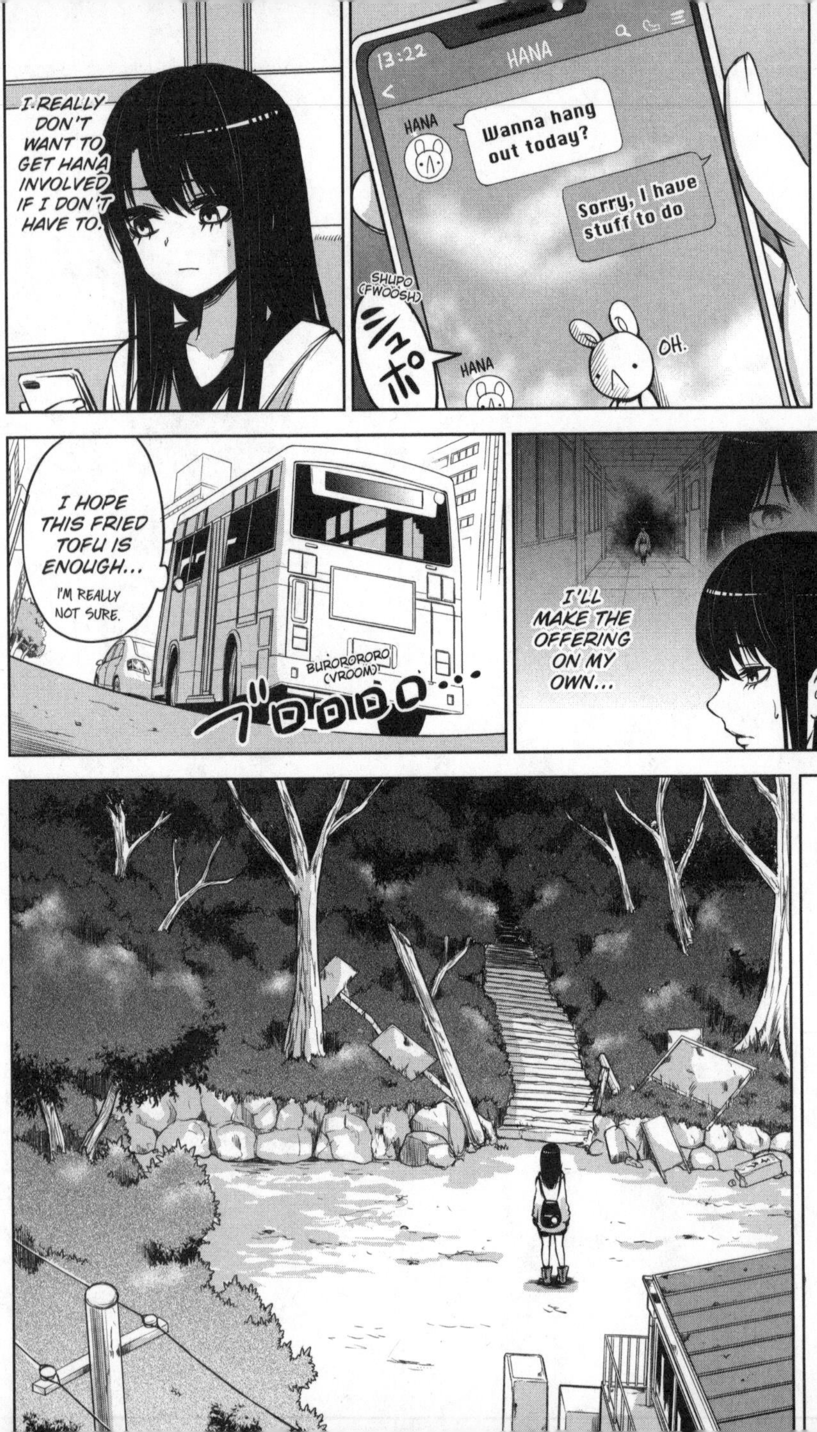
13:22
HANA
HANA
Wanna hang out today?
Sorry, I have stuff to do
SHUPO (FWOOSH)
シュポ
HANA
OH.
I REALLY DON'T WANT TO GET HANA INVOLVED IF I DON'T HAVE TO.
I'LL MAKE THE OFFERING ON MY OWN...
I HOPE THIS FRIED TOFU IS ENOUGH...
I'M REALLY NOT SURE.
BURORORORO (VROOM)
ブロロロロ…

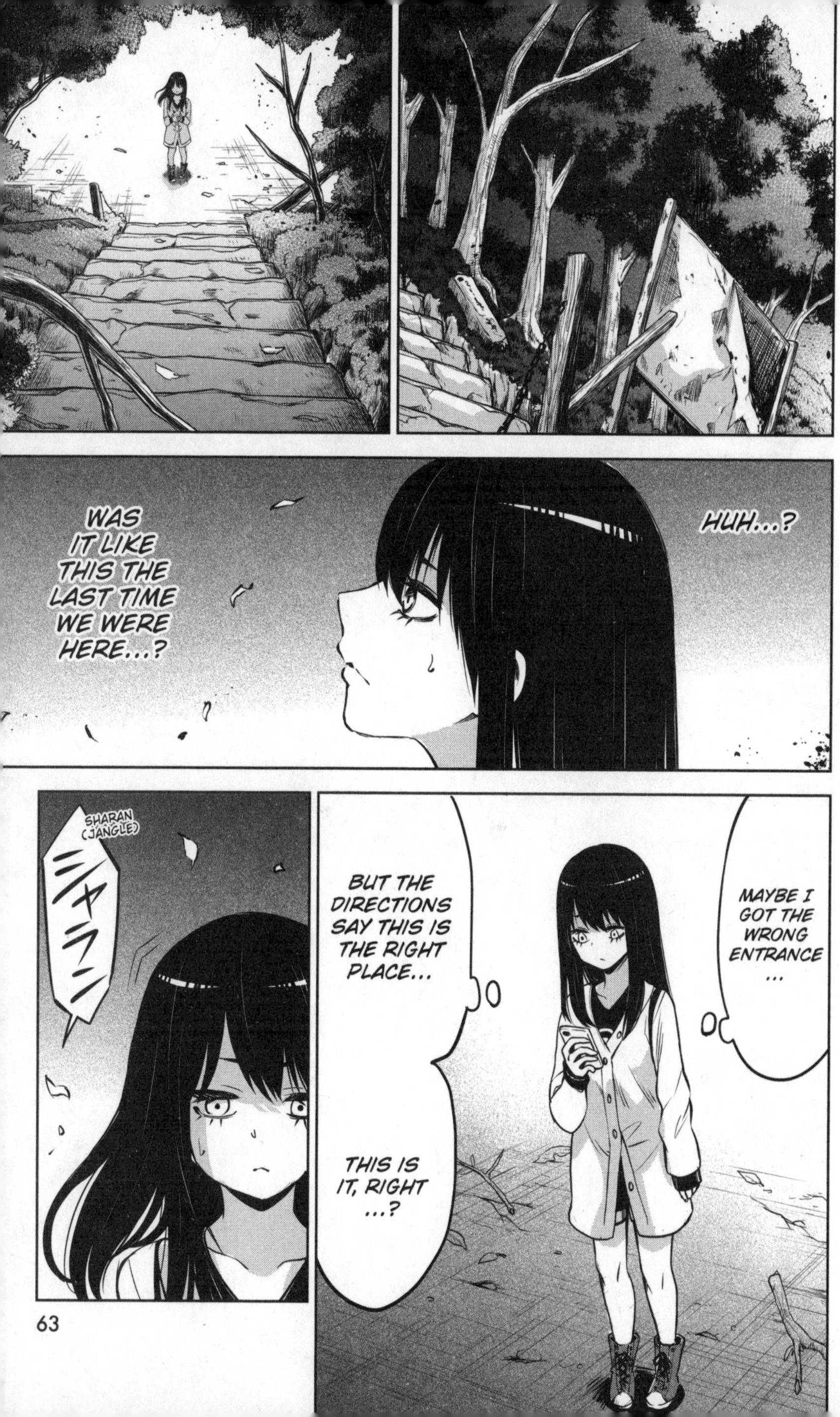
HUH...?
WAS IT LIKE THIS THE LAST TIME WE WERE HERE...?
MAYBE I GOT THE WRONG ENTRANCE...
BUT THE DIRECTIONS SAY THIS IS THE RIGHT PLACE...
THIS IS IT, RIGHT...?
シャラン
SHARAN (JANGLE)

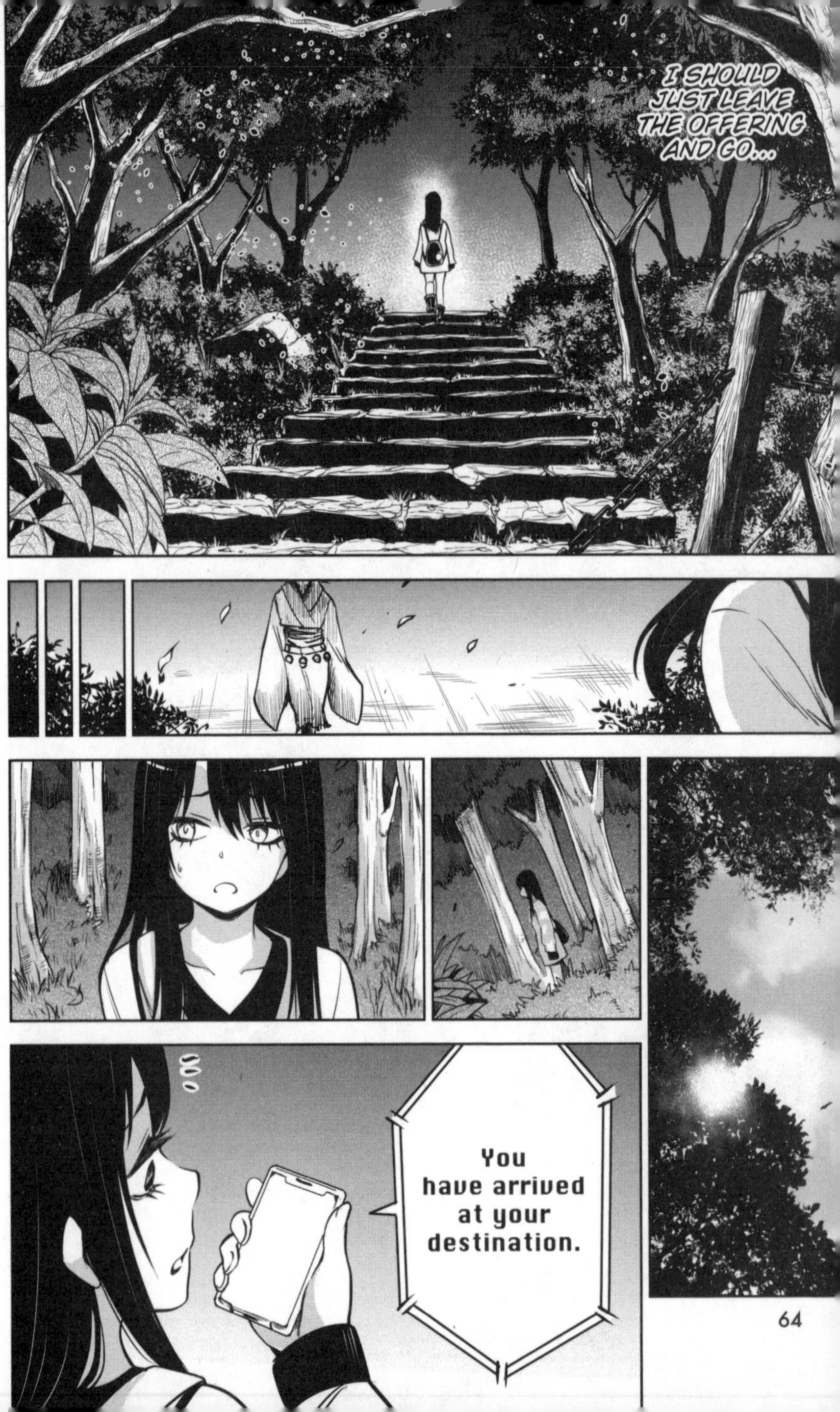
I SHOULD JUST LEAVE THE OFFERING AND GO...
You have arrived at your destination.

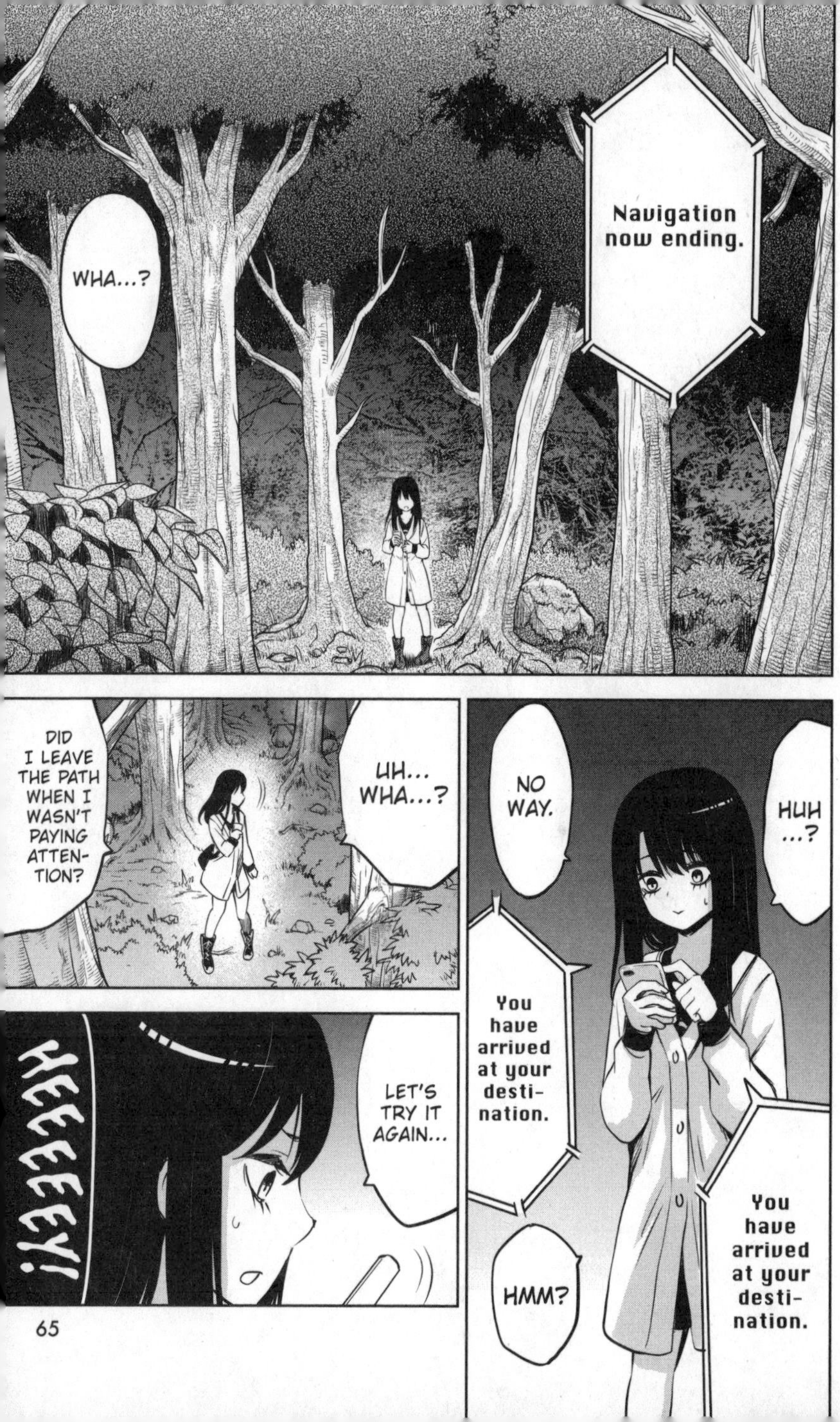

Navigation now ending.
WHA...?
HUH ...?
NO WAY.
You have arrived at your destination.
You have arrived at your destination.
HMM?
UH... WHA...?
DID I LEAVE THE PATH WHEN I WASN'T PAYING ATTENTION?
LET'S TRY IT AGAIN...
HEEEEEY!

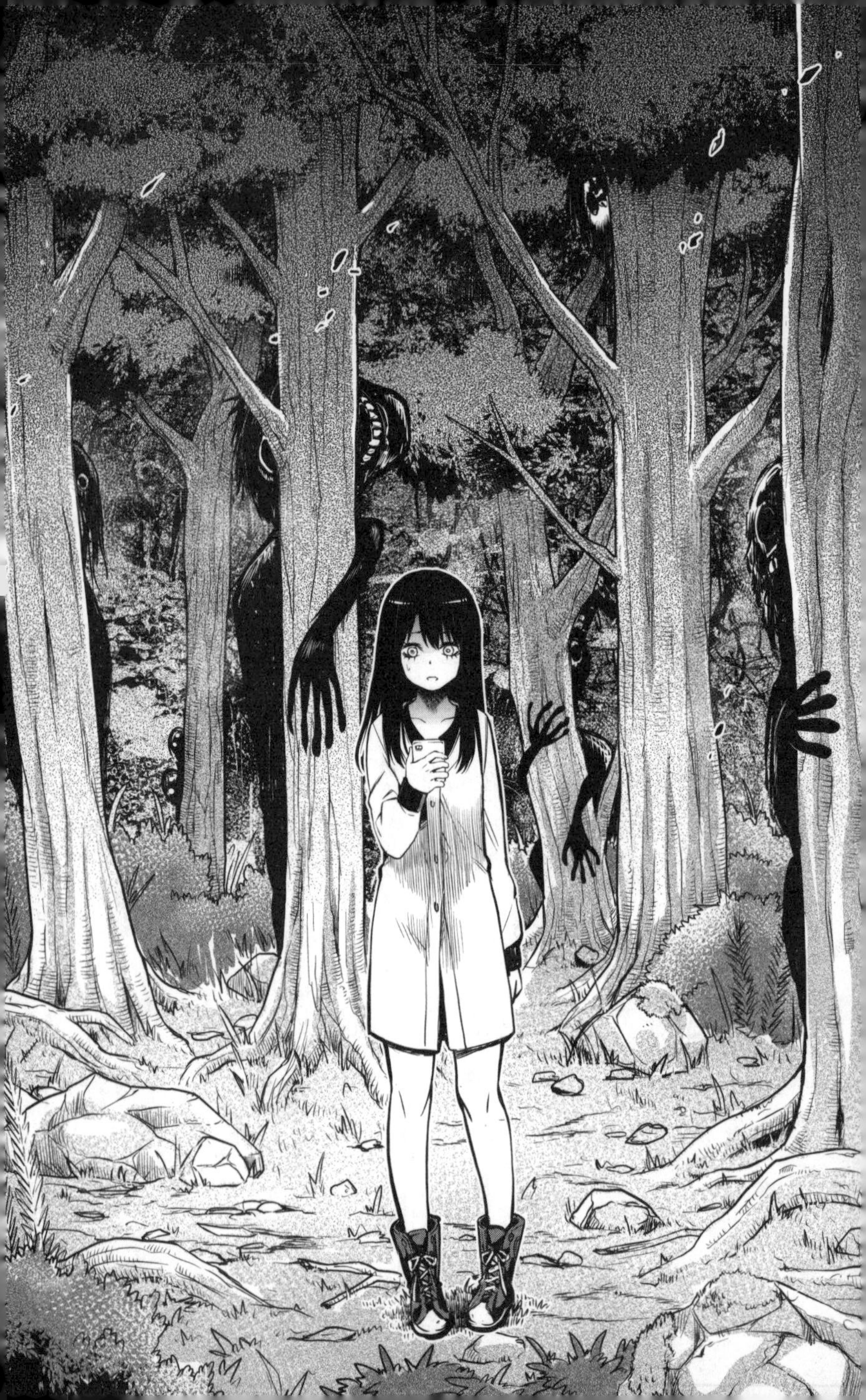

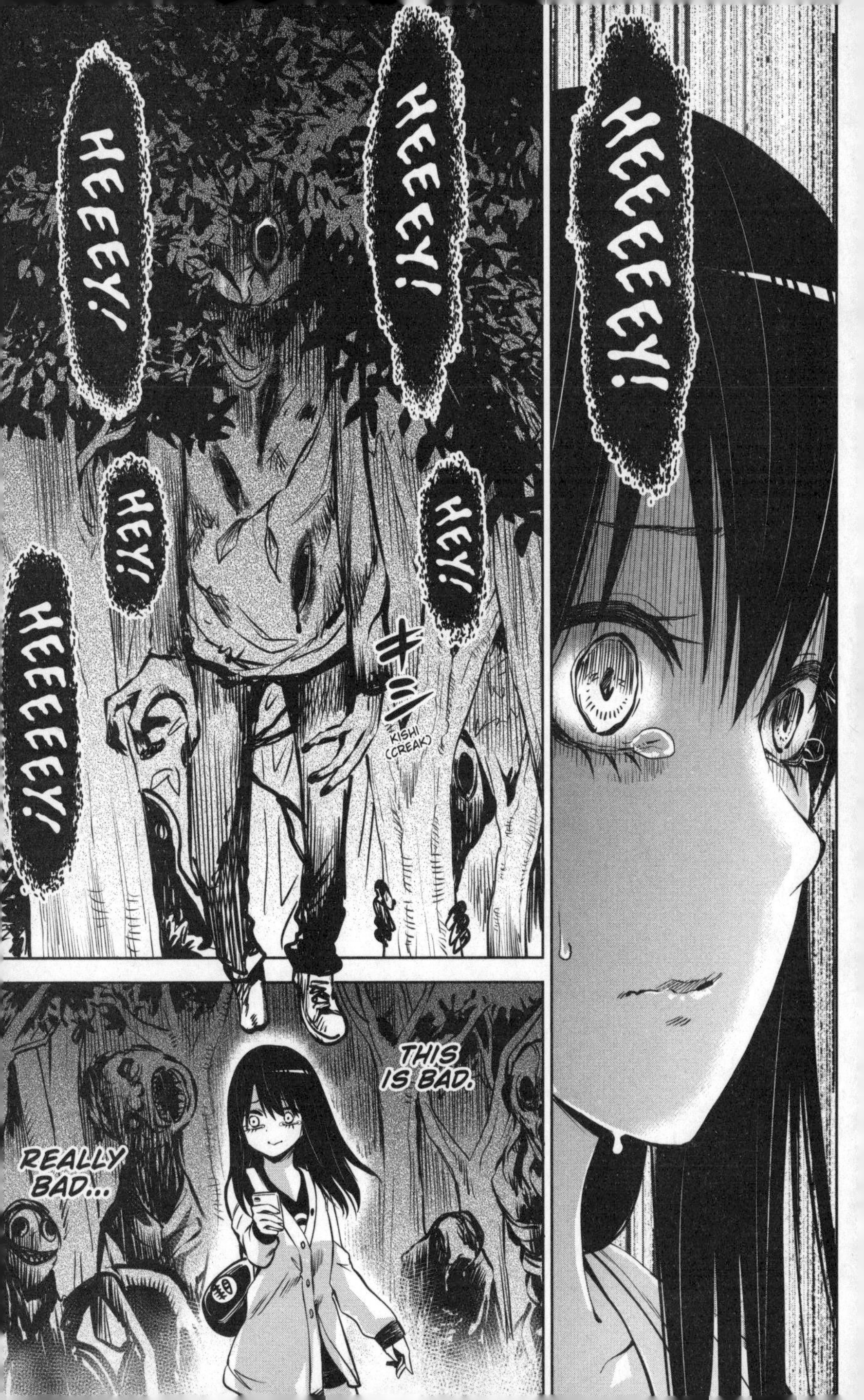
HEEEEEY!
HEEEY!
HEEEY!
HEY!
HEY!
HEEEEEEY!
KISHI (CREAK)
THIS IS BAD.
REALLY BAD...

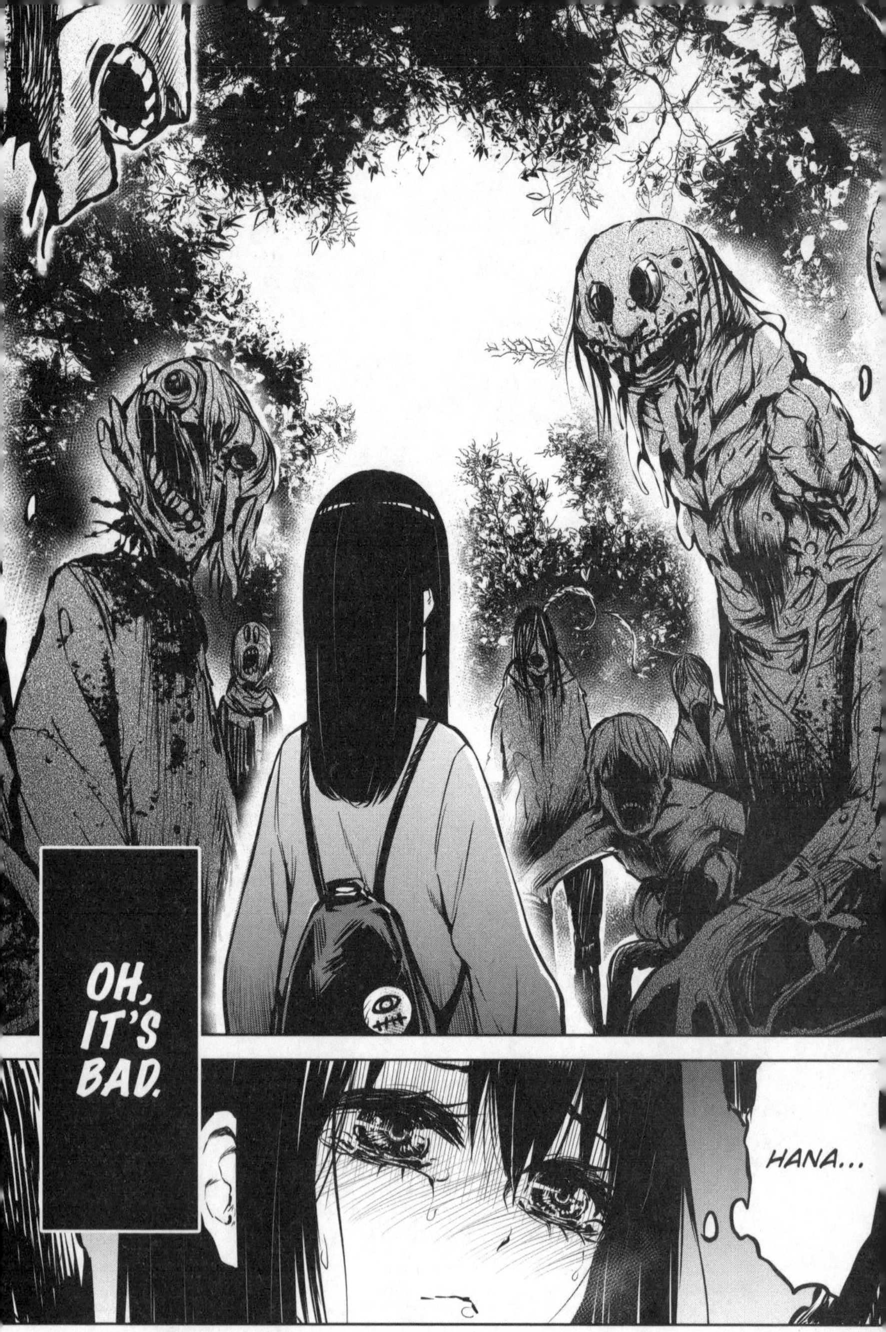
OH, IT'S BAD.
HANA...

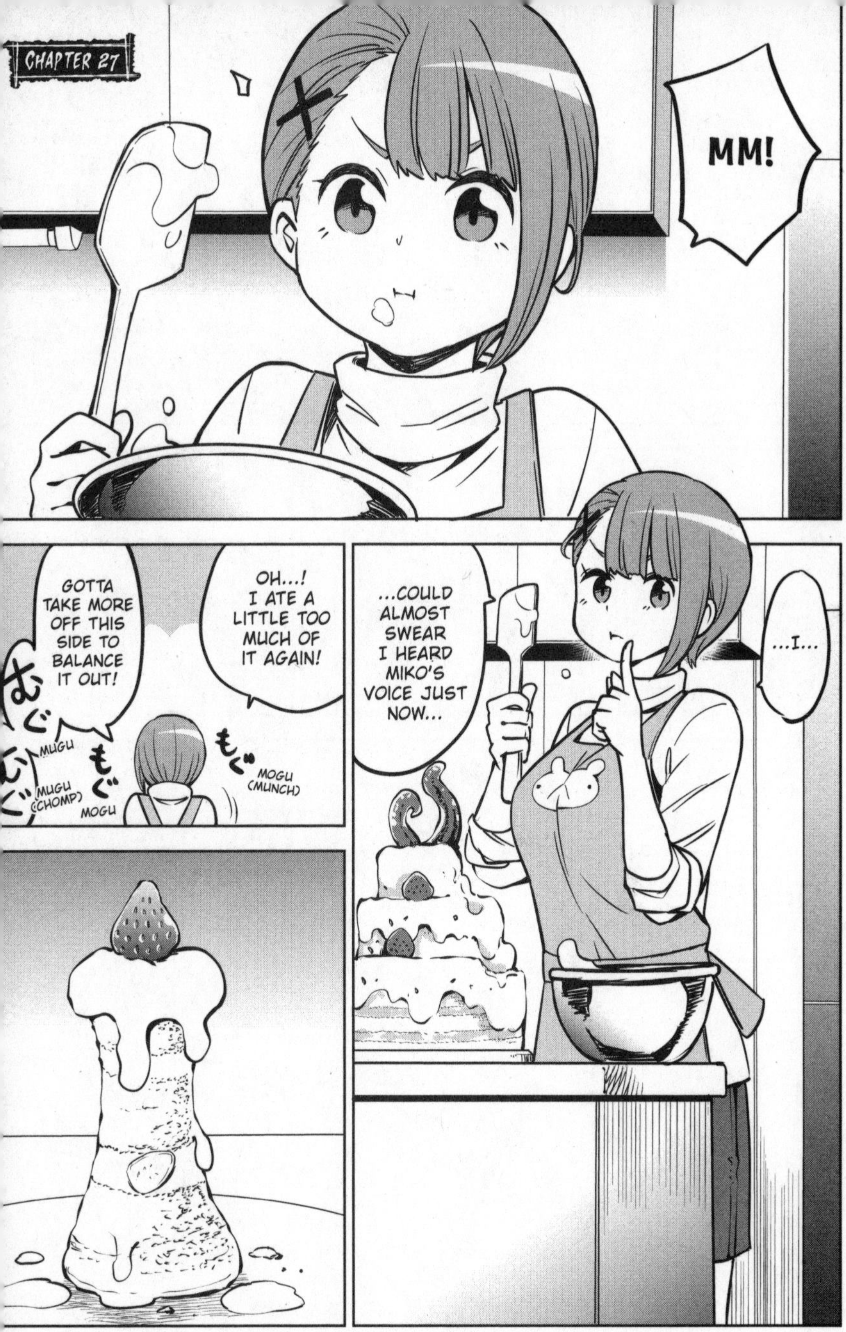
CHAPTER 27
MM!
...I...
...COULD ALMOST SWEAR I HEARD MIKO'S VOICE JUST NOW...
OH...! I ATE A LITTLE TOO MUCH OF IT AGAIN!
GOTTA TAKE MORE OFF THIS SIDE TO BALANCE IT OUT!
もぐ MOGU (MUNCH)
もぐ MOGU
むぐ MUGU
むぐ MUGU (CHOMP)

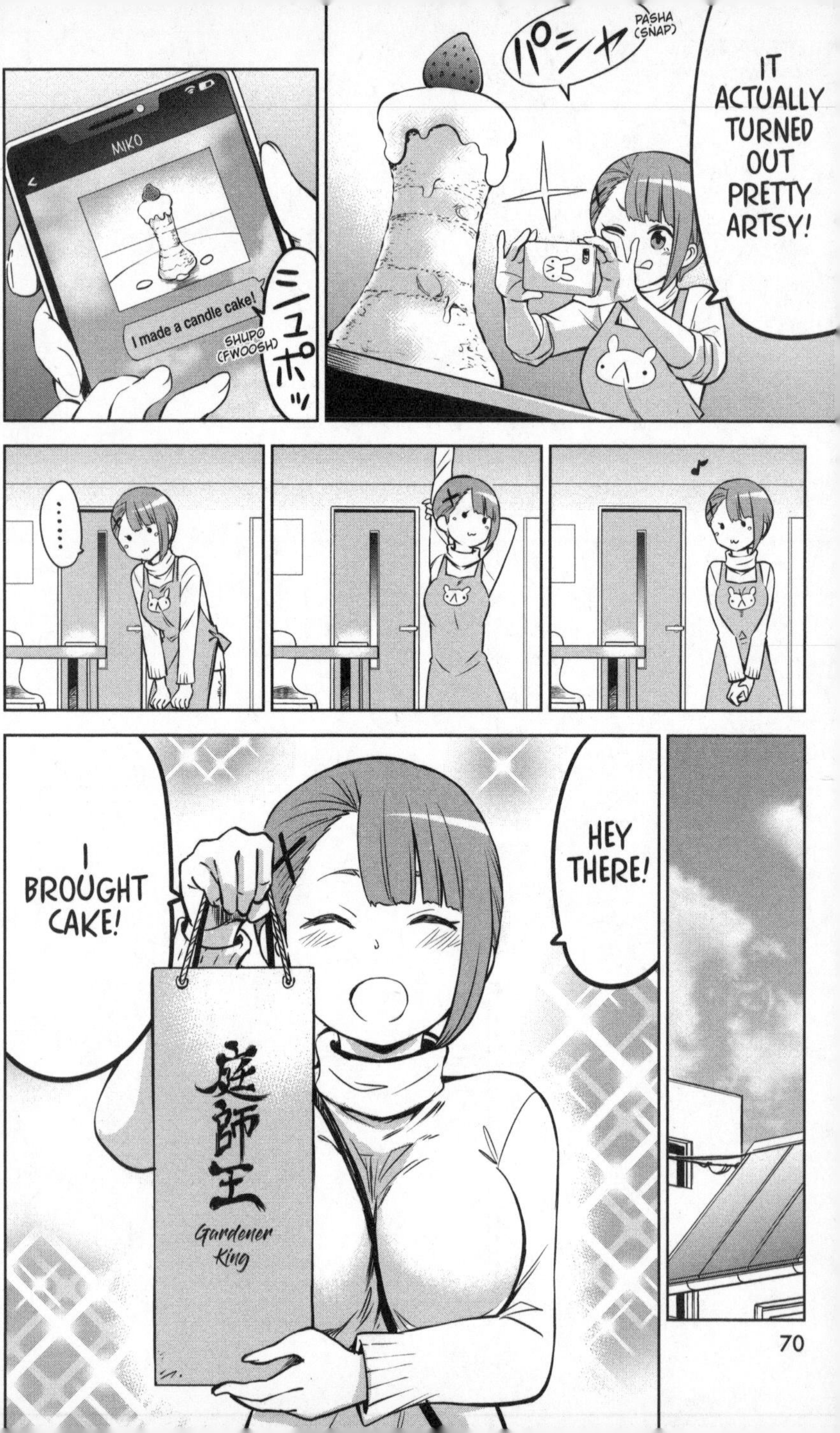
パシャ
PASHA (SNAP)
IT ACTUALLY TURNED OUT PRETTY ARTSY!
MIKO
I made a candle cake!
シュポッ
SHUPO (FWOOSH)
......
HEY THERE!
I BROUGHT CAKE!
庭師王
Gardener King

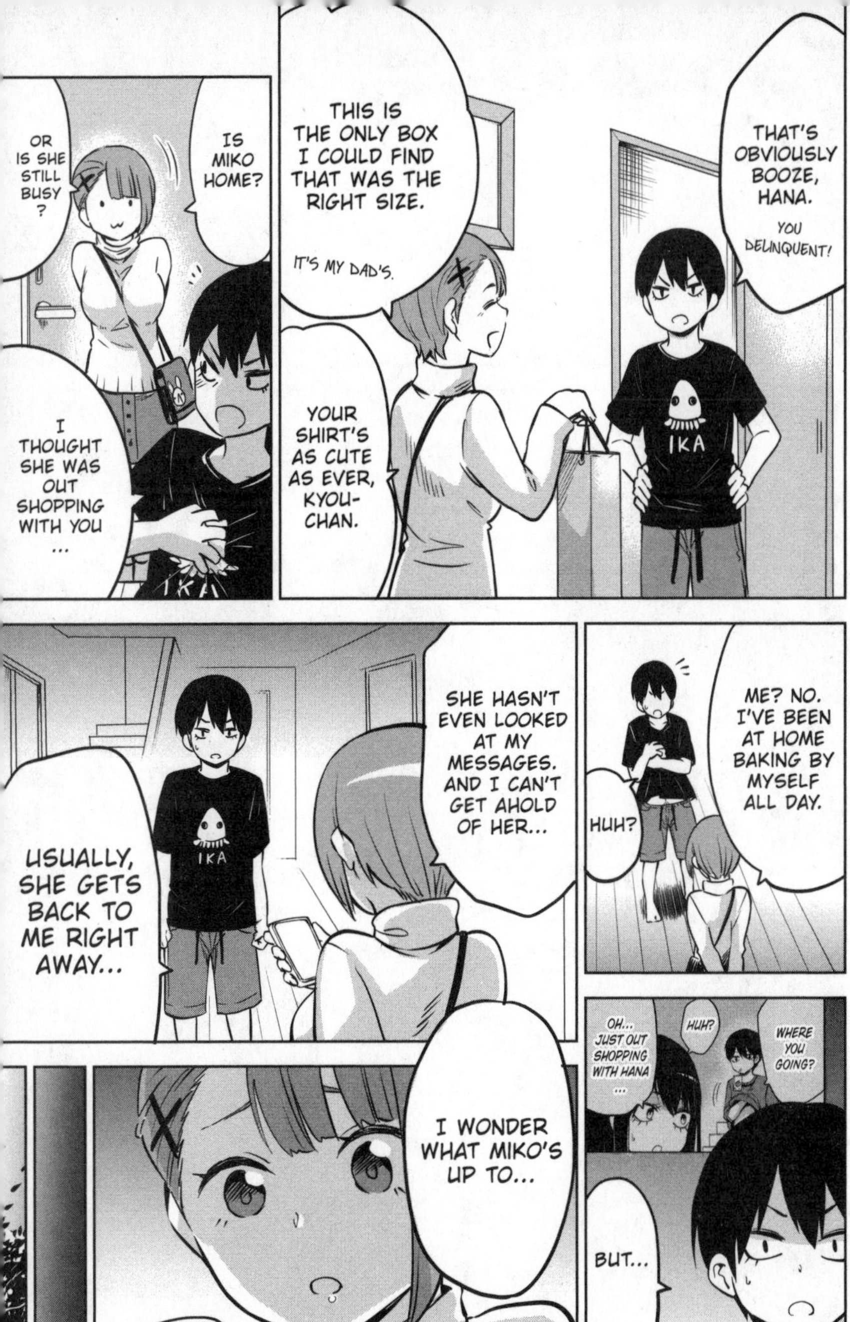
THAT'S OBVIOUSLY BOOZE, HANA.
YOU DELINQUENT!
THIS IS THE ONLY BOX I COULD FIND THAT WAS THE RIGHT SIZE.
IT'S MY DAD'S.
YOUR SHIRT'S AS CUTE AS EVER, KYOU-CHAN.
IS MIKO HOME?
OR IS SHE STILL BUSY?
I THOUGHT SHE WAS OUT SHOPPING WITH YOU...
ME? NO. I'VE BEEN AT HOME BAKING BY MYSELF ALL DAY.
HUH?
SHE HASN'T EVEN LOOKED AT MY MESSAGES. AND I CAN'T GET AHOLD OF HER...
USUALLY, SHE GETS BACK TO ME RIGHT AWAY...
WHERE YOU GOING?
HUH?
OH... JUST OUT SHOPPING WITH HANA...
BUT...
I WONDER WHAT MIKO'S UP TO...

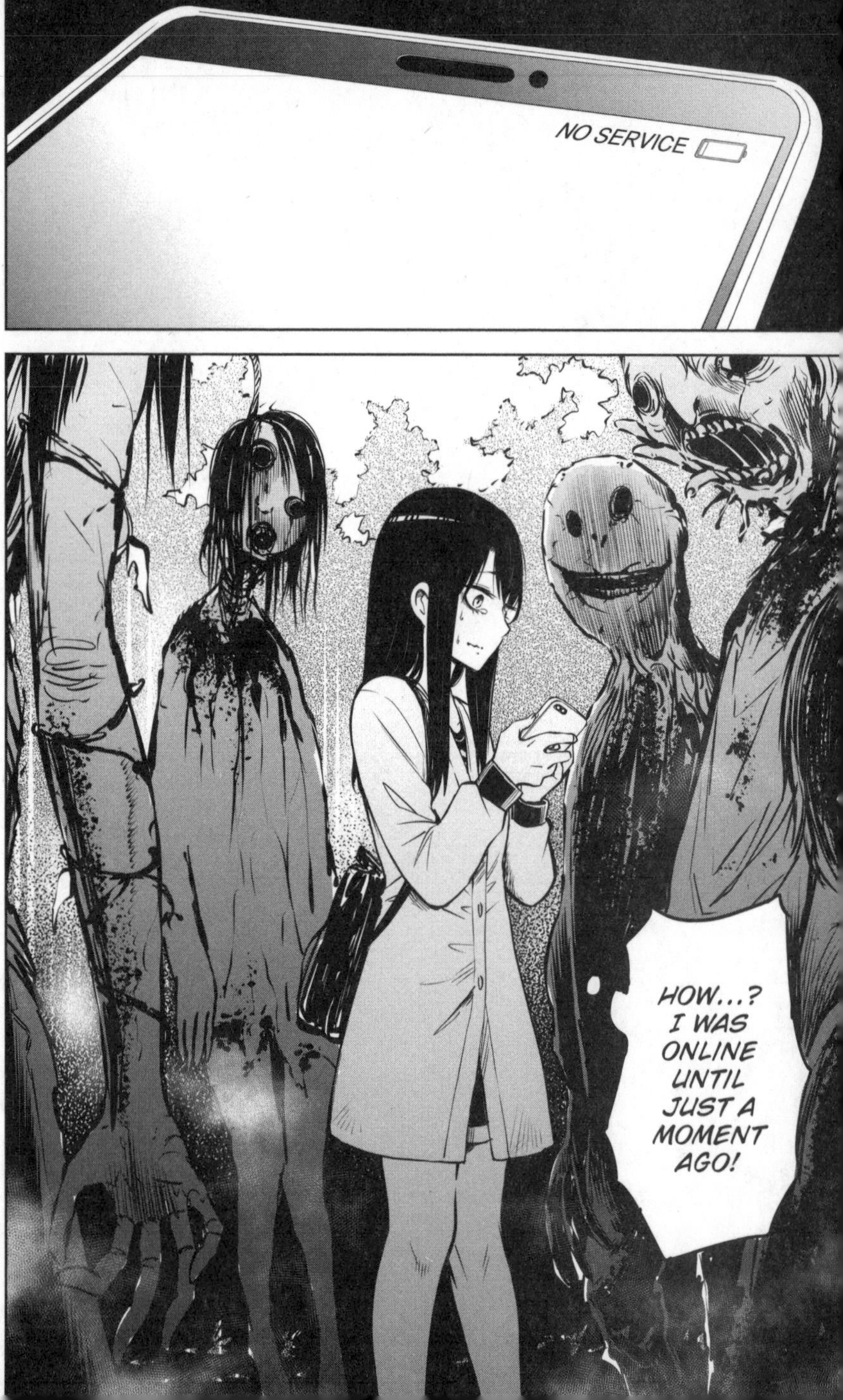
NO SERVICE
HOW...? I WAS ONLINE UNTIL JUST A MOMENT AGO!

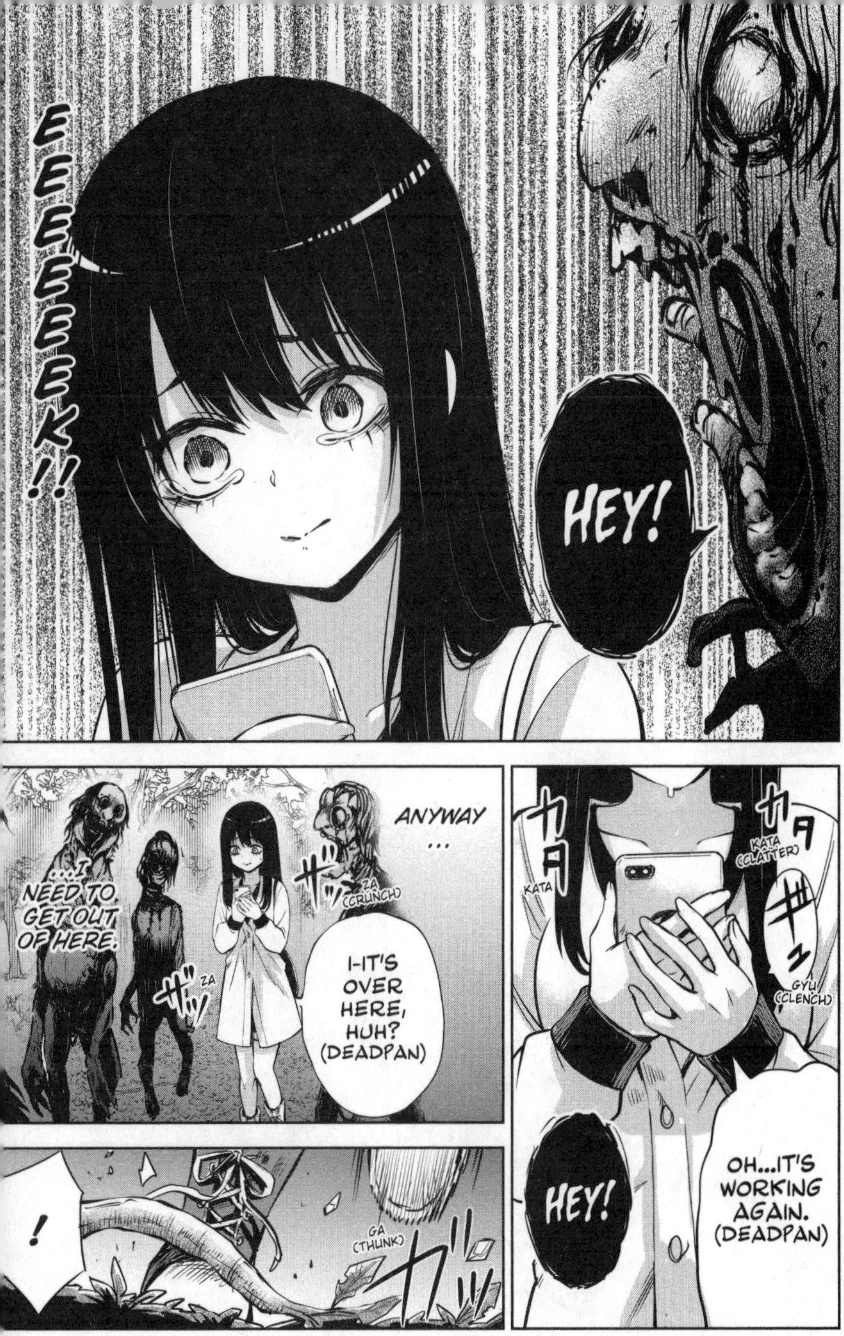
HEY!
EEEEEEEK!!
KATA (CLATTER)
KATA
GYU (CLENCH)
OH...IT'S WORKING AGAIN. (DEADPAN)
HEY!
ANYWAY ...
ZA (CRUNCH)
I-IT'S OVER HERE, HUH? (DEADPAN)
ZA
...I NEED TO GET OUT OF HERE.
GA (THUNK)
!

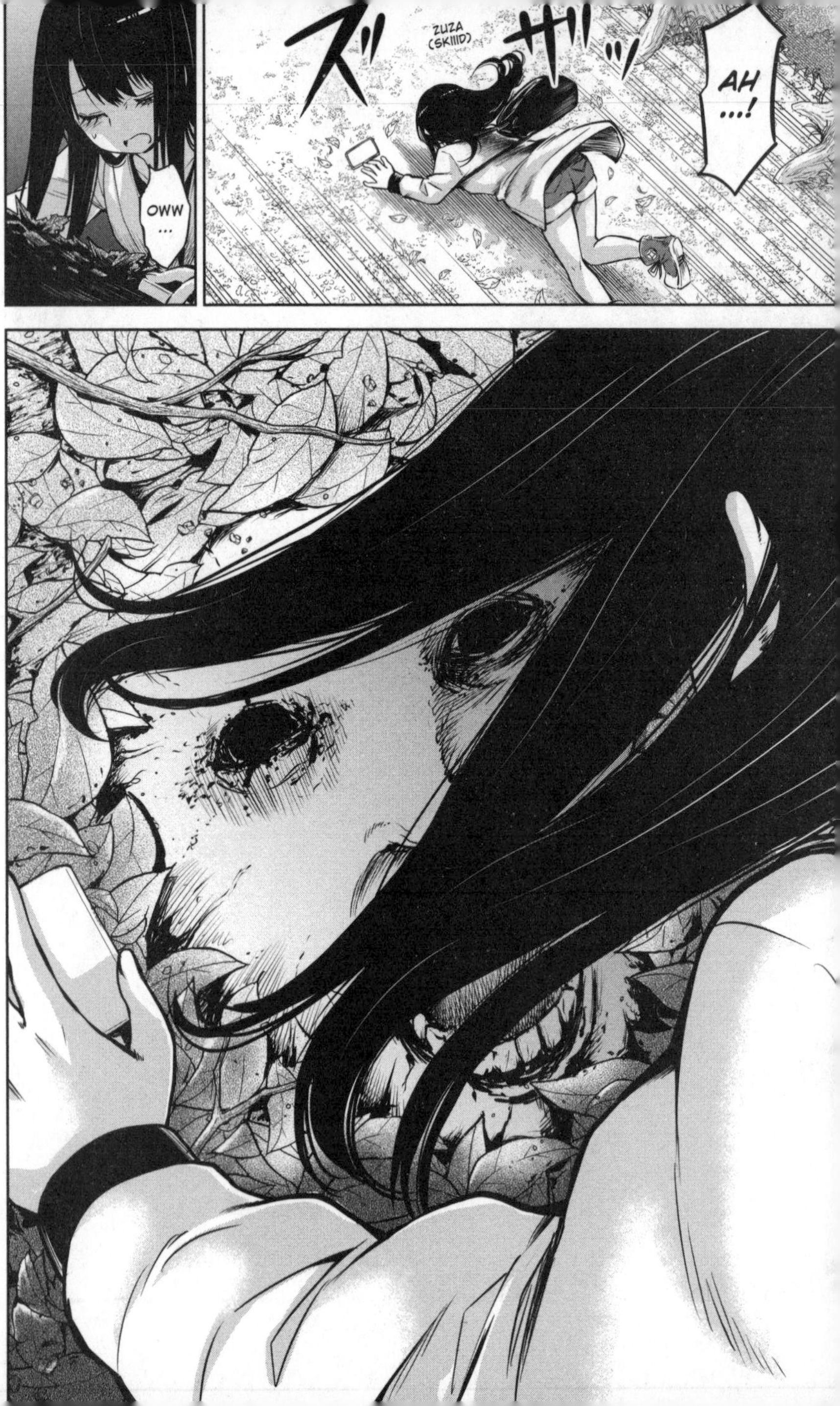
AH ...!
ズザッ
ZUZA (SKIIID)
OWW ...

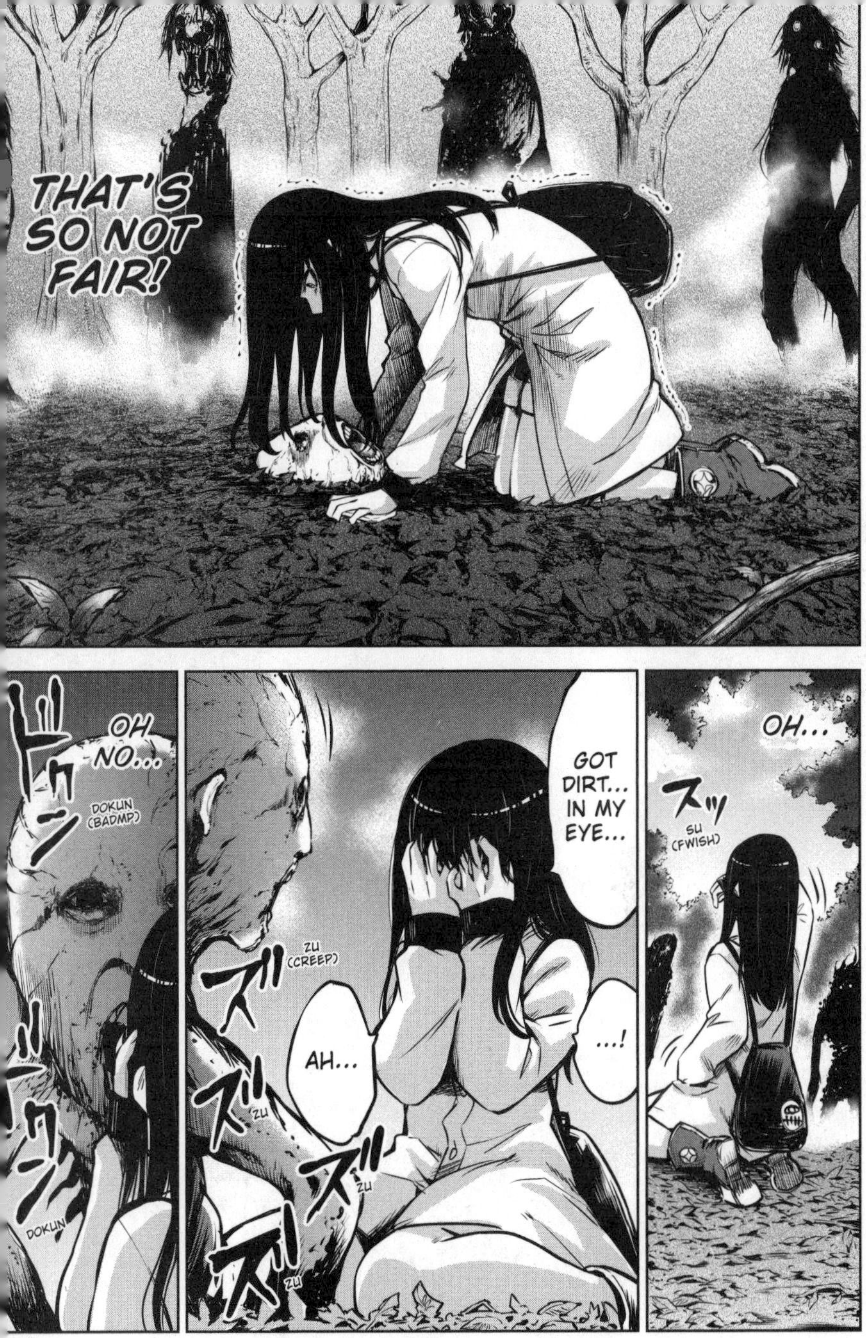

THAT'S SO NOT FAIR!
OH...
スッ
SU (FWISH)
GOT DIRT... IN MY EYE...
...!
AH...
ズ
ZU (CREEP)
ズ
ZU
ズ
ZU
ズ
ZU
OH NO...
ドクン
DOKUN (BADMP)
ドクン
DOKUN

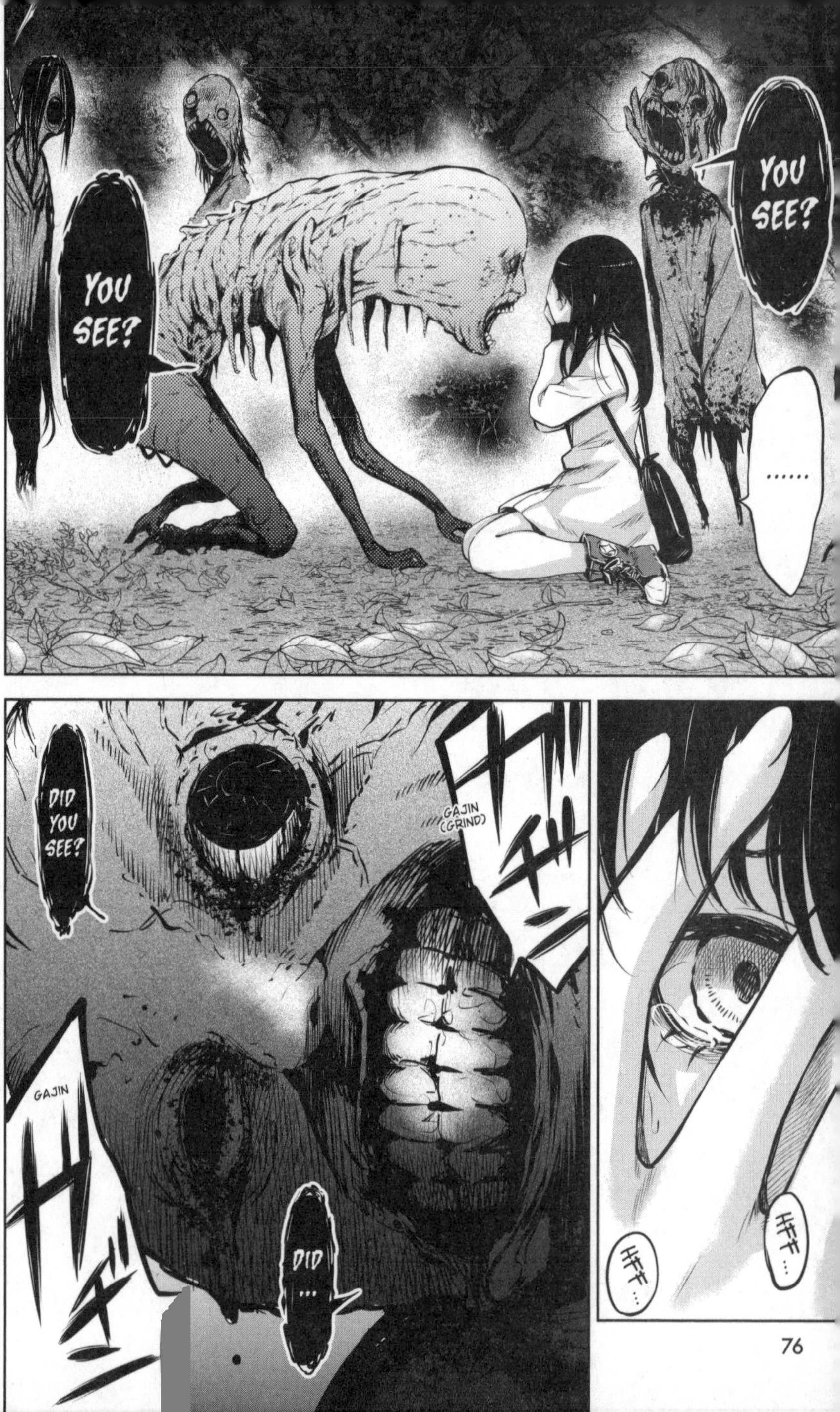
YOU SEE?
......
YOU SEE?
HFF...
HFF...
GAJIN (GRIND)
DID YOU SEE?
GAJIN
DID ...

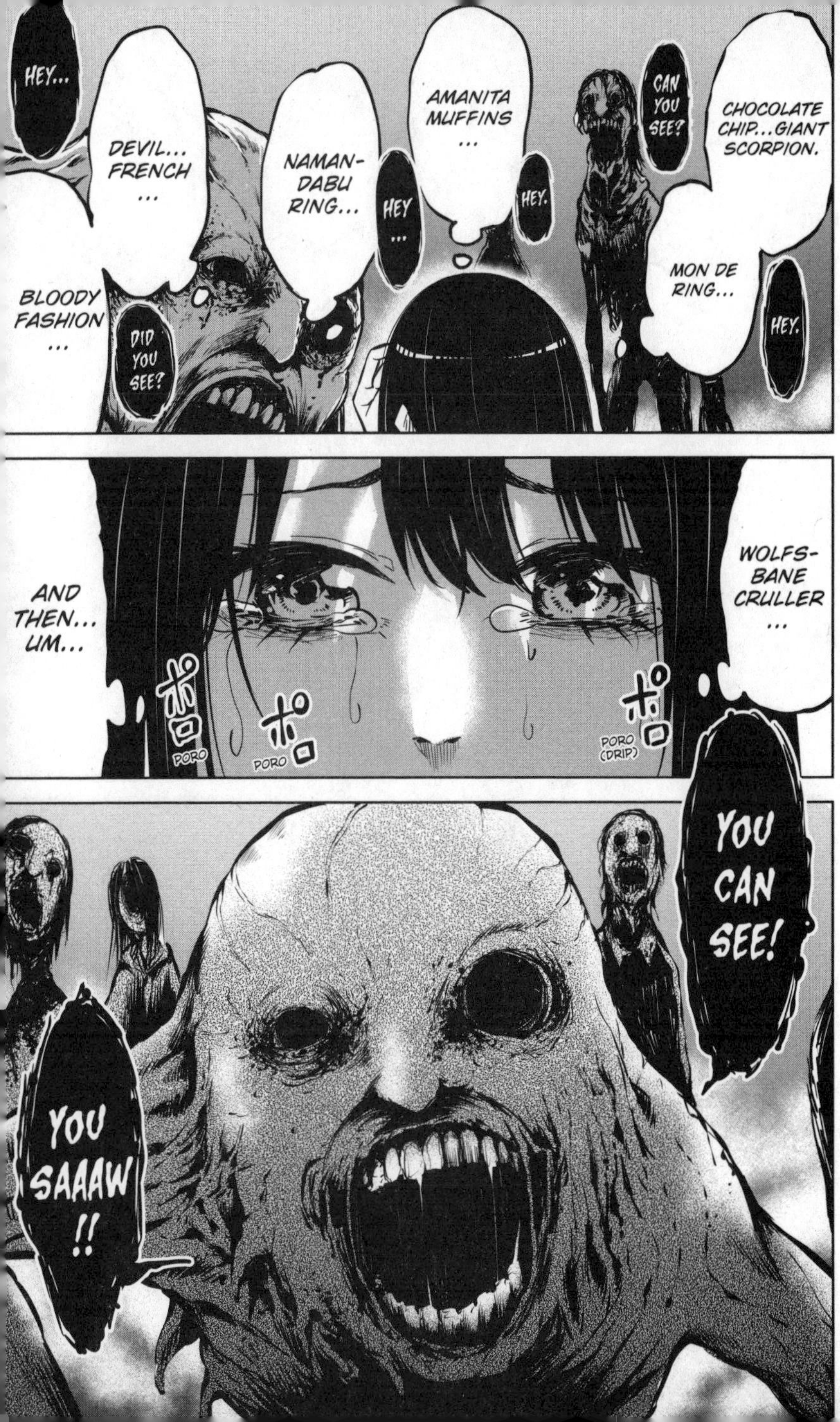
CHOCOLATE CHIP...GIANT SCORPION.
CAN YOU SEE?
AMANITA MUFFINS ...
HEY.
MON DE RING...
HEY.
HEY ...
NAMAN-DABU RING...
DEVIL... FRENCH ...
HEY...
BLOODY FASHION ...
DID YOU SEE?
WOLFS-BANE CRULLER ...
ポロ
PORO (DRIP)
ポロ
PORO
ポロ
PORO
AND THEN... UM...
YOU CAN SEE!
YOU SAAAW !!

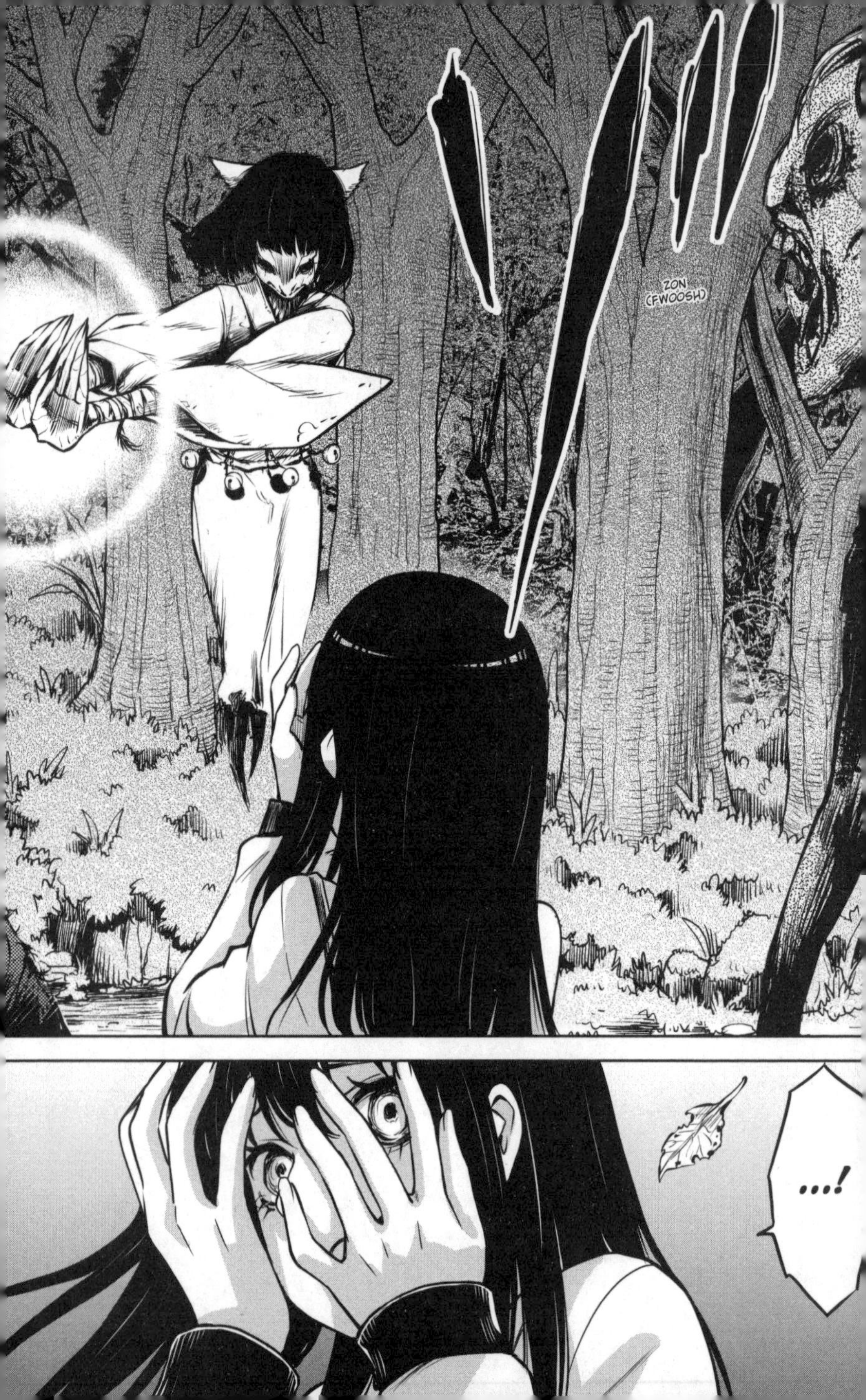
ZON
(FWOOSH)
...!

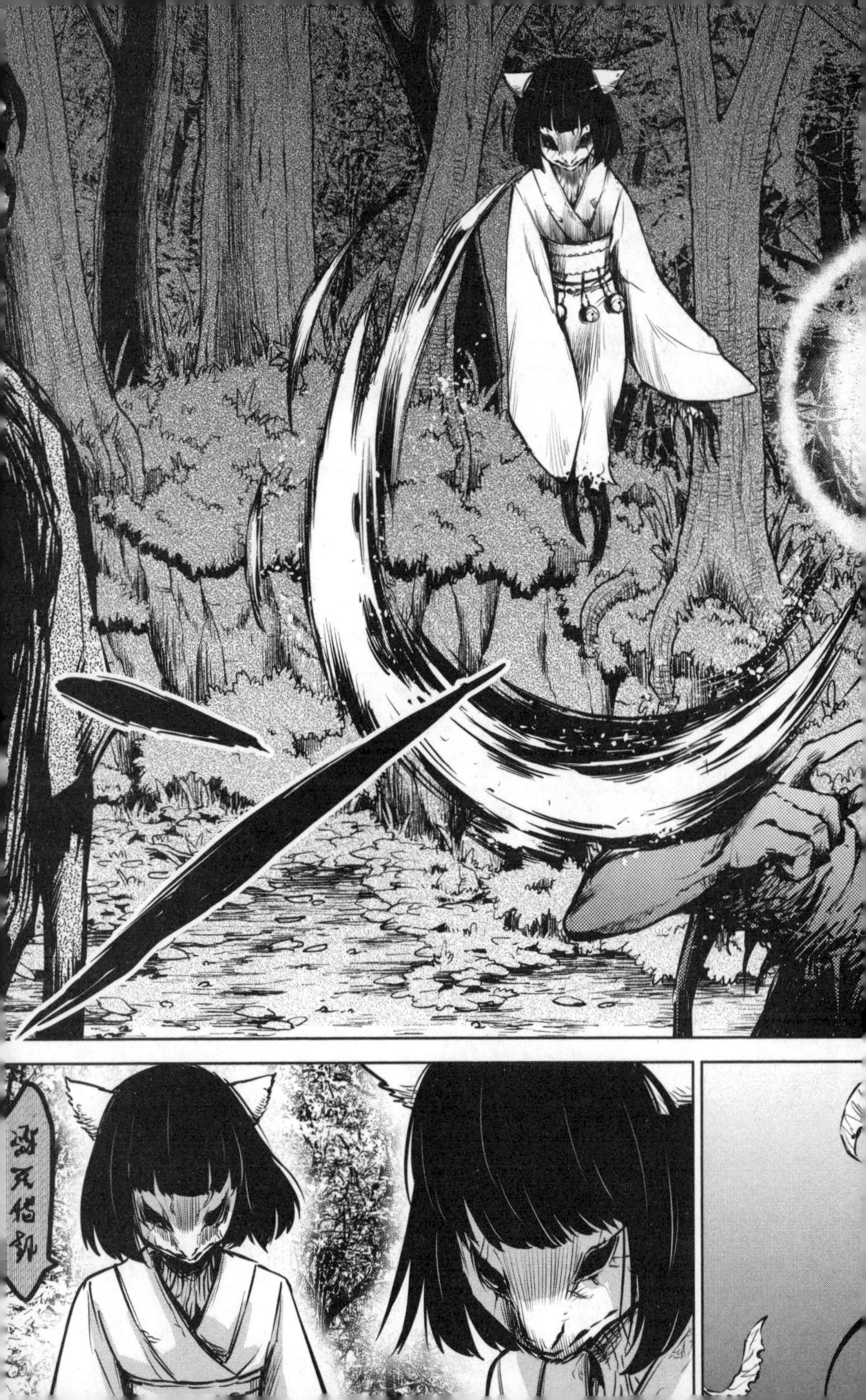

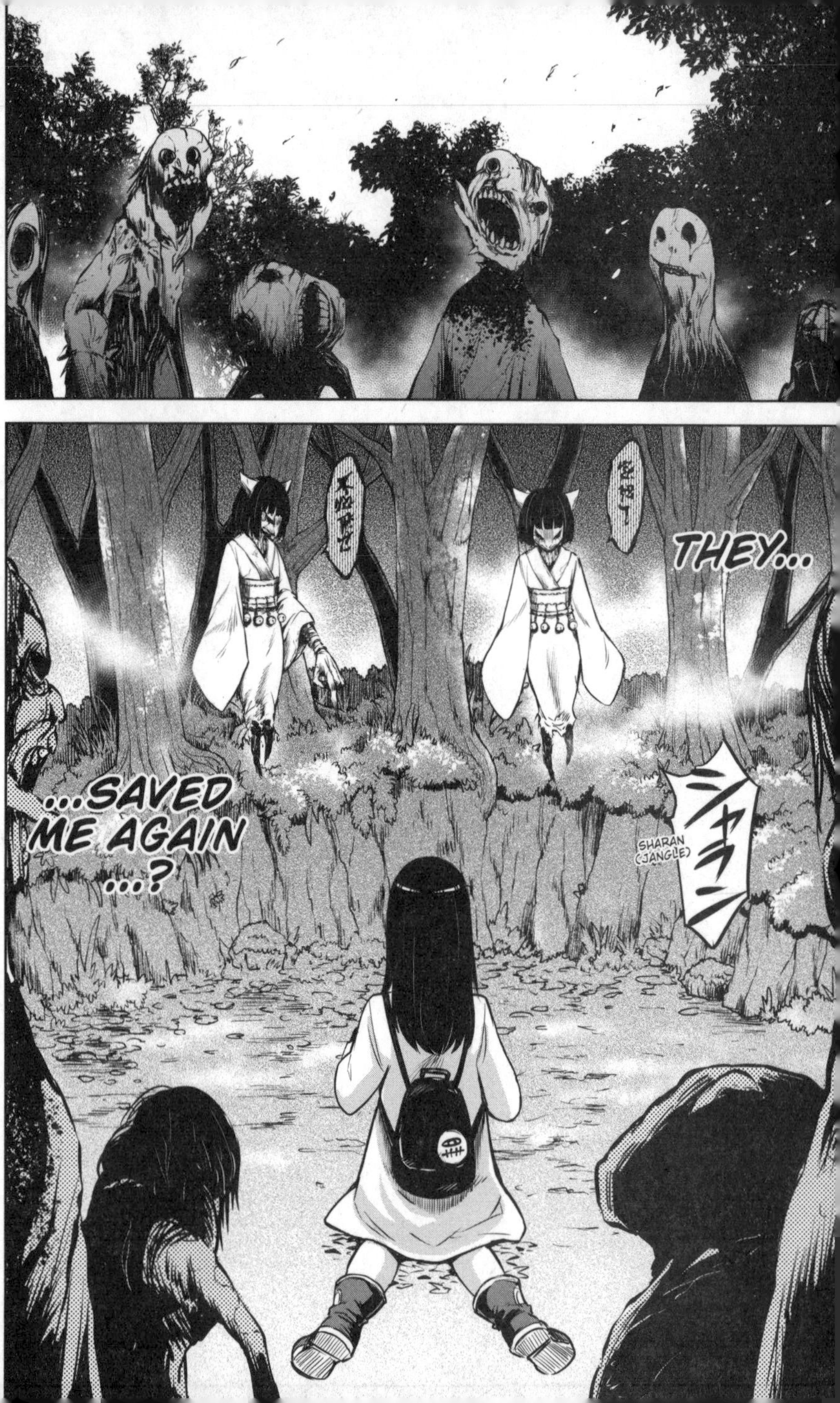
THEY...
シャラン
SHARAN (JANGLE)
...SAVED ME AGAIN ...?

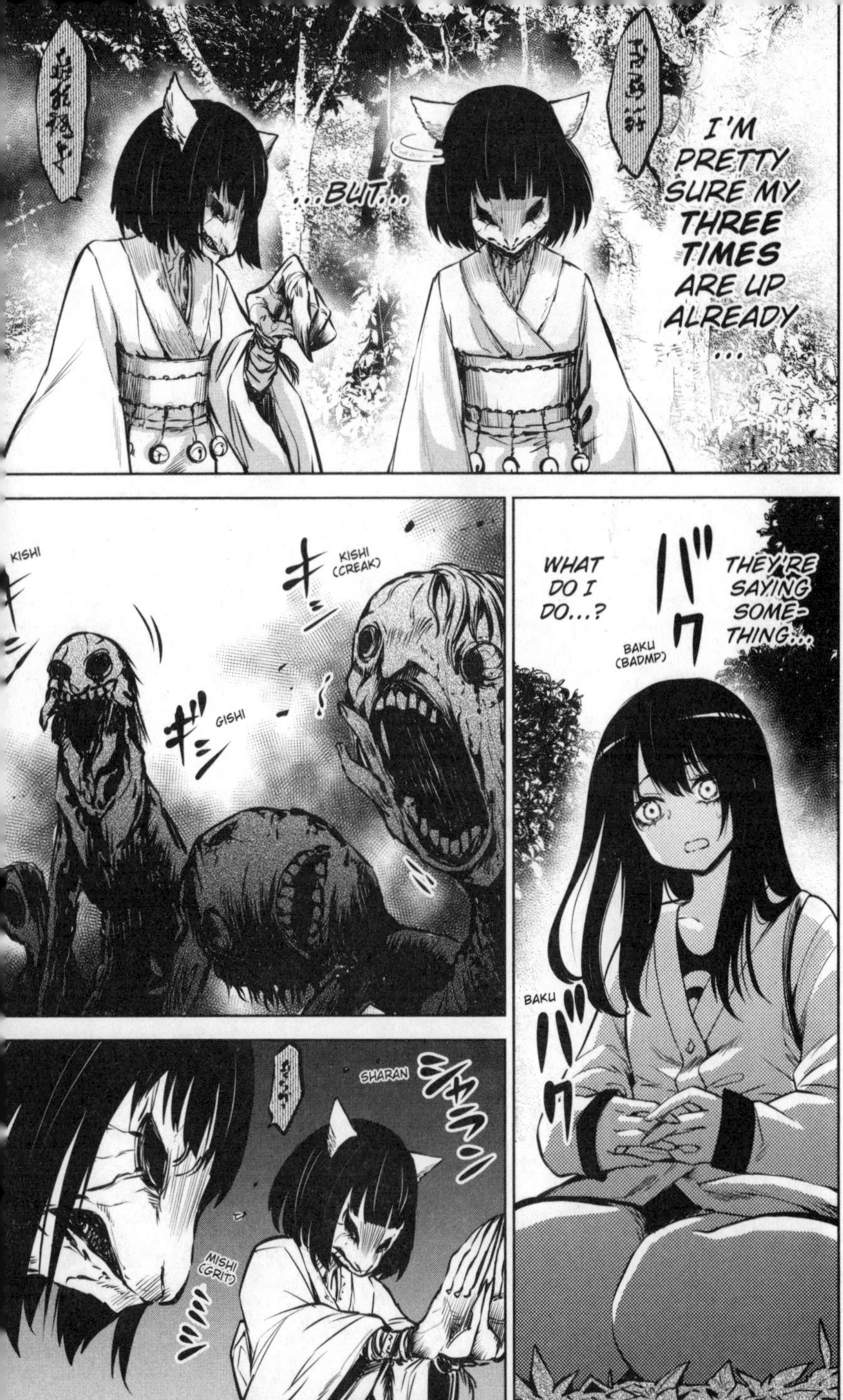
I'M PRETTY SURE MY THREE TIMES ARE UP ALREADY...
...BUT...
THEY'RE SAYING SOME-THING...
BAKU (BADMP)
WHAT DO I DO...?
BAKU
KISHI (CREAK)
GISHI
KISHI
SHARAN
MISHI (GRIT)

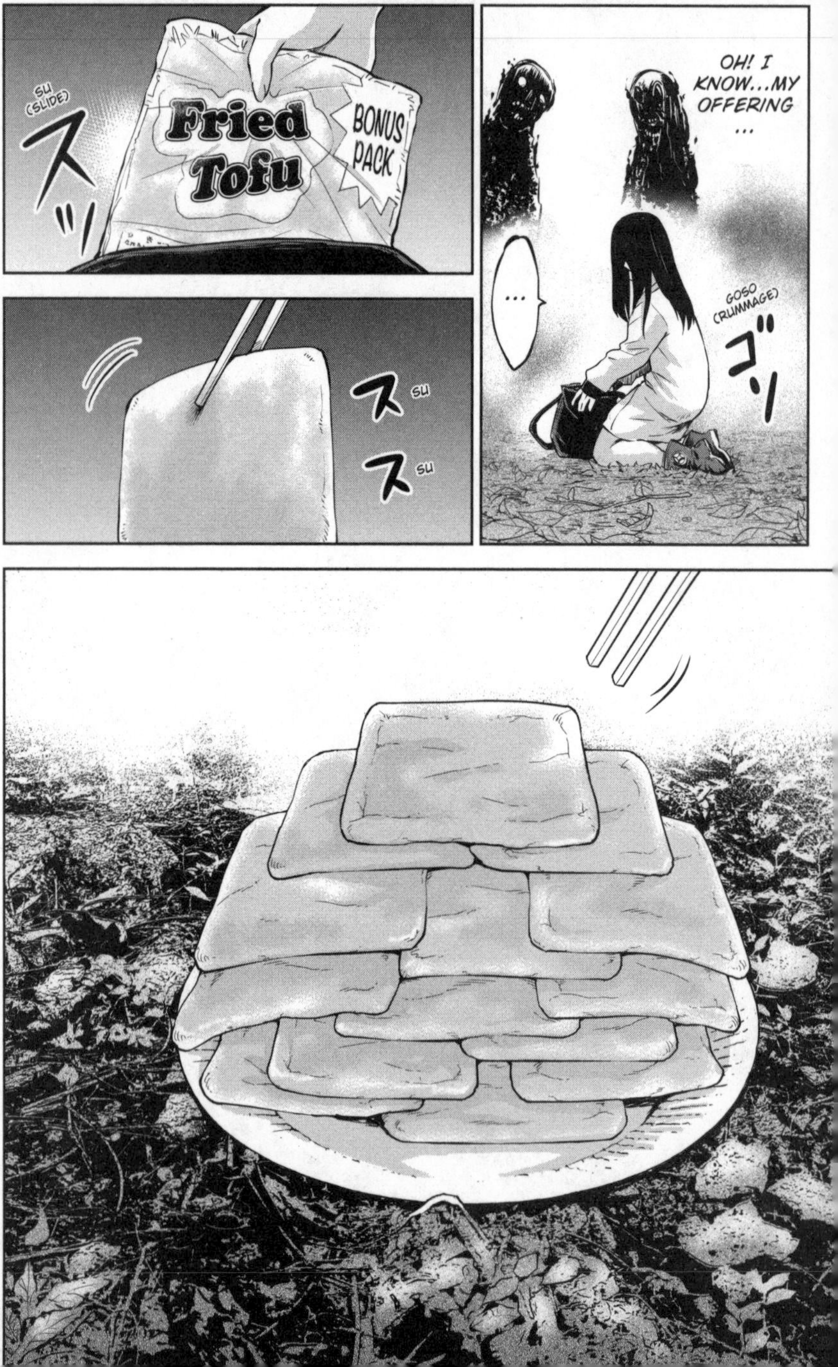
OH! I KNOW...MY OFFERING ...
...
GOSO (RUMMAGE)
SU (SLIDE)
Fried Tofu
BONUS PACK
SU
SU

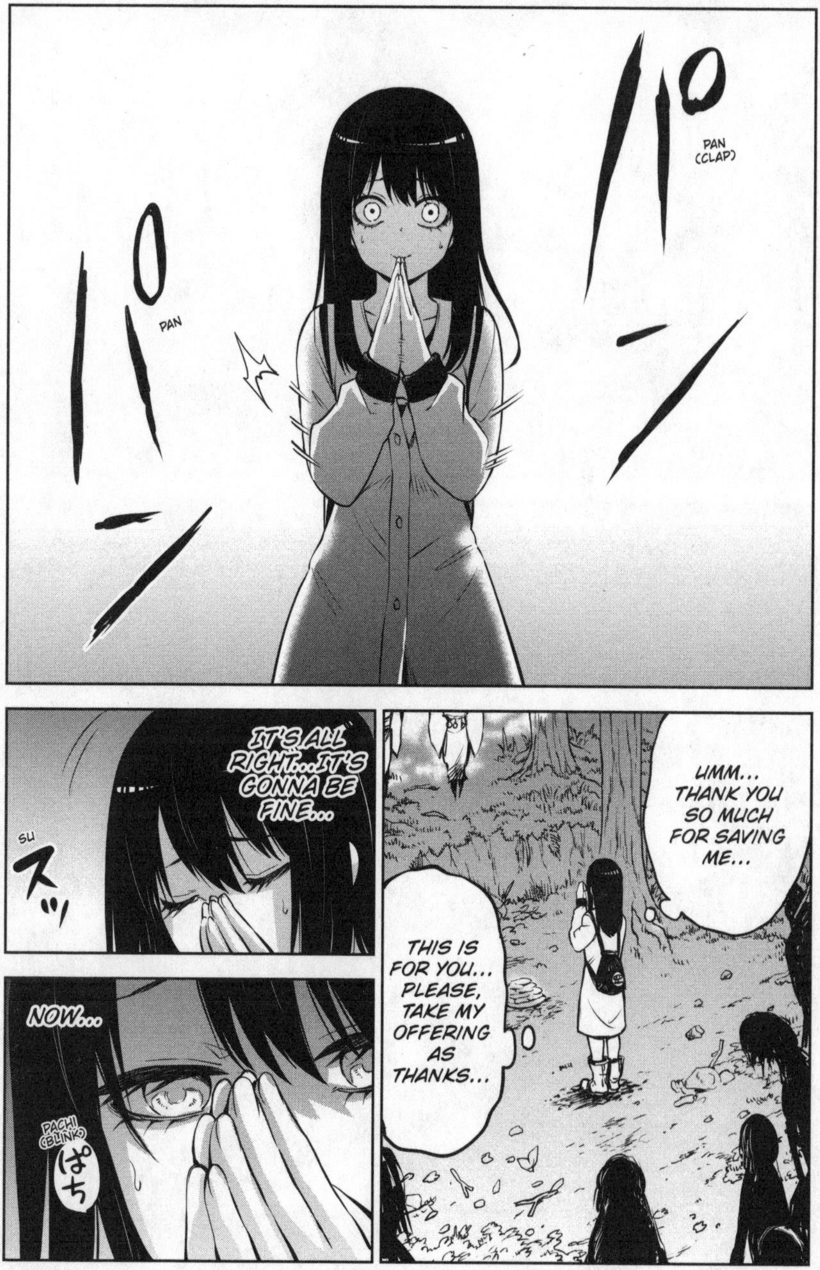
パーン
PAN (CLAP)
パーン
PAN
UMM... THANK YOU SO MUCH FOR SAVING ME...
THIS IS FOR YOU... PLEASE, TAKE MY OFFERING AS THANKS...
IT'S ALL RIGHT...IT'S GONNA BE FINE...
SU
スッ
NOW...
PACHI (BLINK)
ぱち

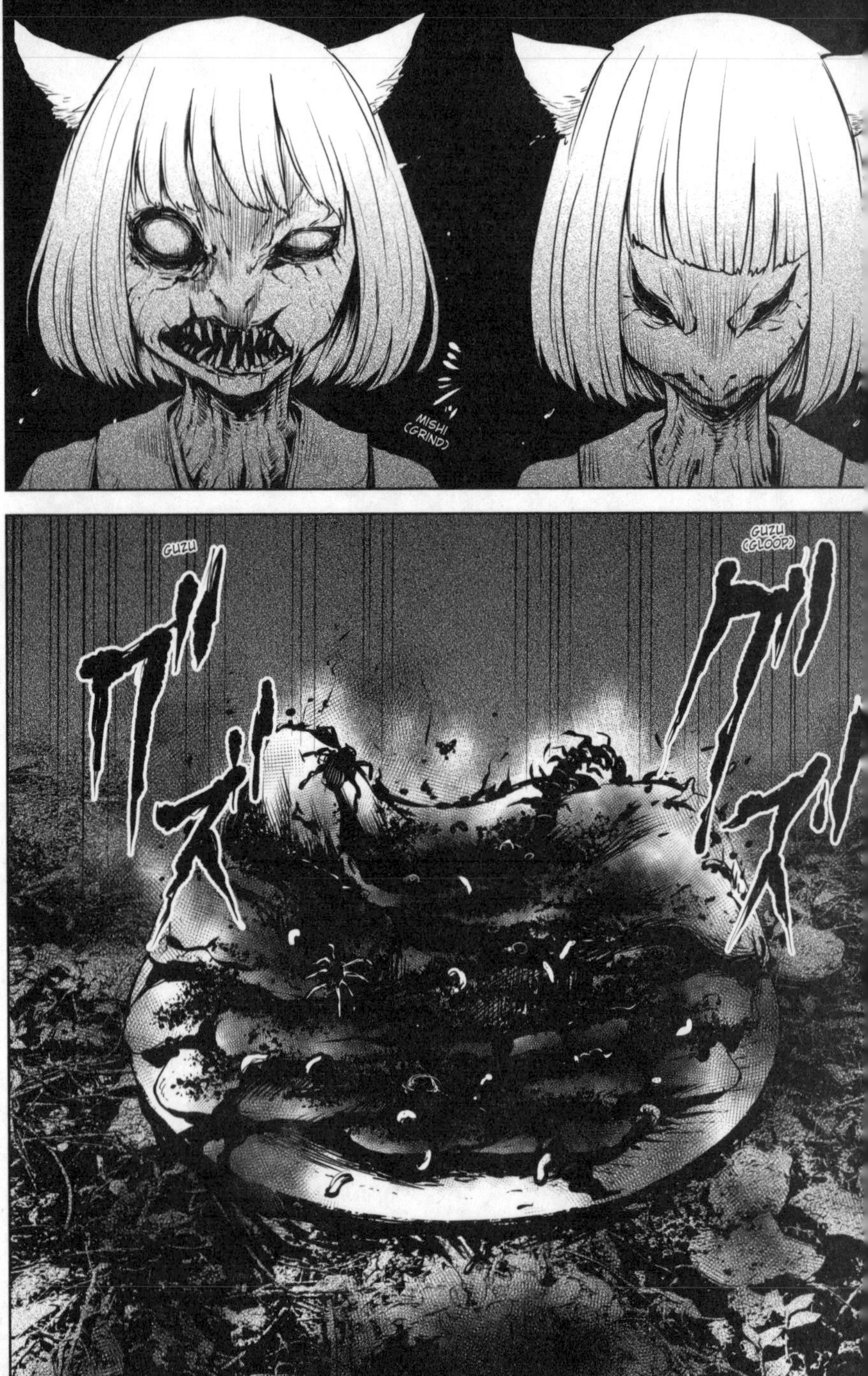
MISHI (GRIND)
GUZU (GLOOP)
グズ
GUZU
グズ

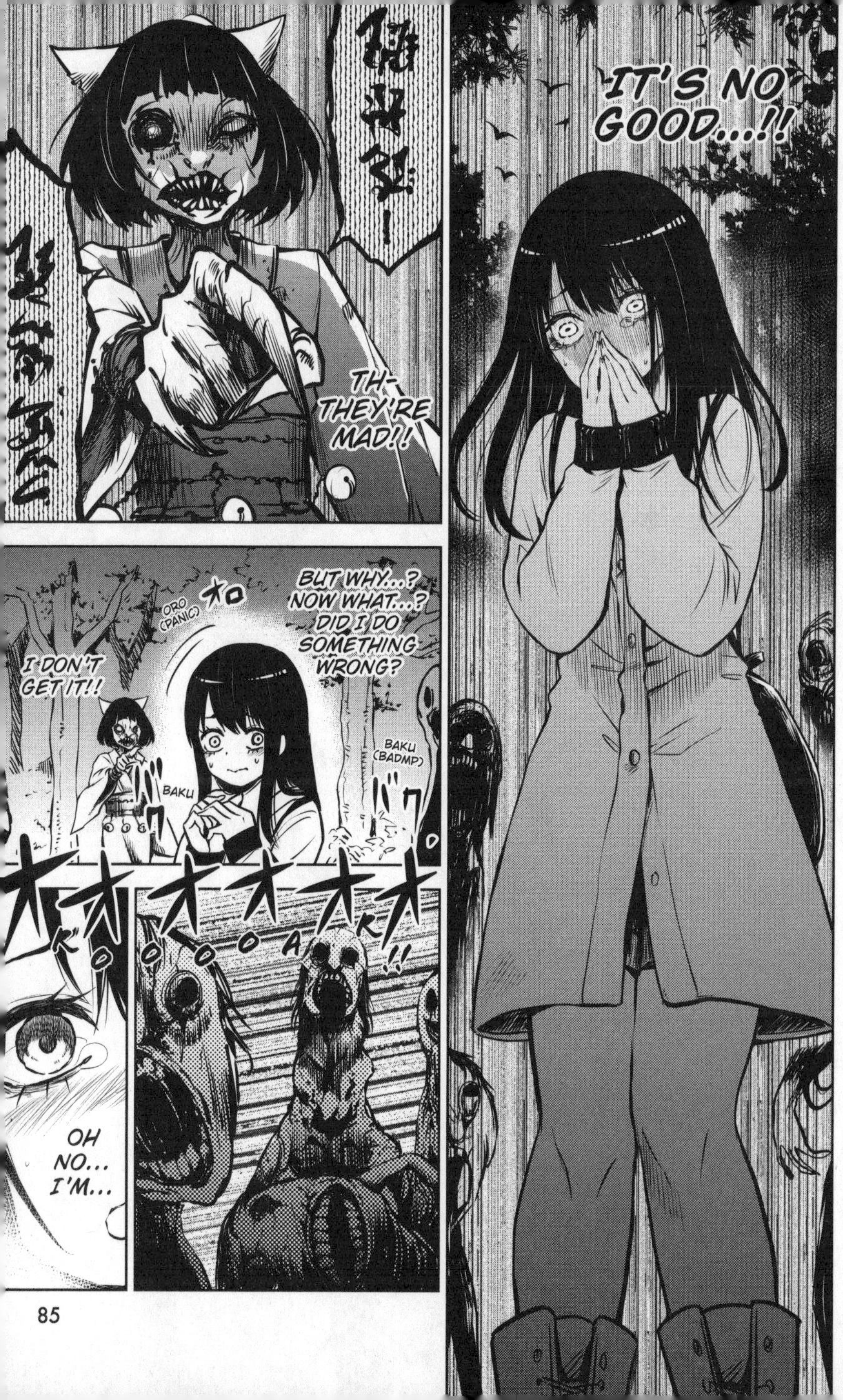
IT'S NO GOOD...!!
TH-THEY'RE MAD!!
BUT WHY...? NOW WHAT...? DID I DO SOMETHING WRONG?
ORO (PANIC) オロ
I DON'T GET IT!!
BAKU (BADMP) バク
BAKU
KOOOOAR!!
OH NO... I'M...

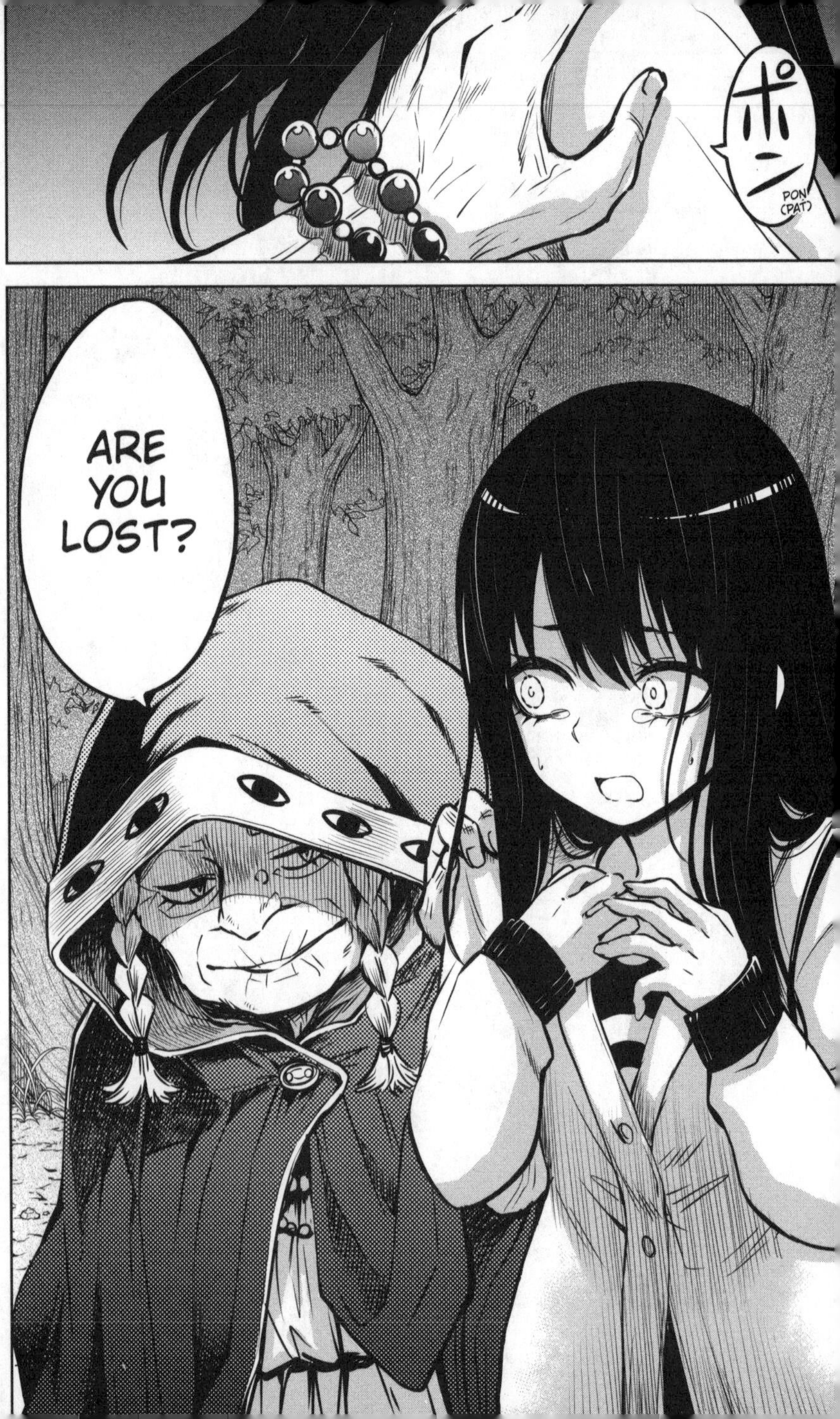
ポン
PON (PAT)
ARE YOU LOST?

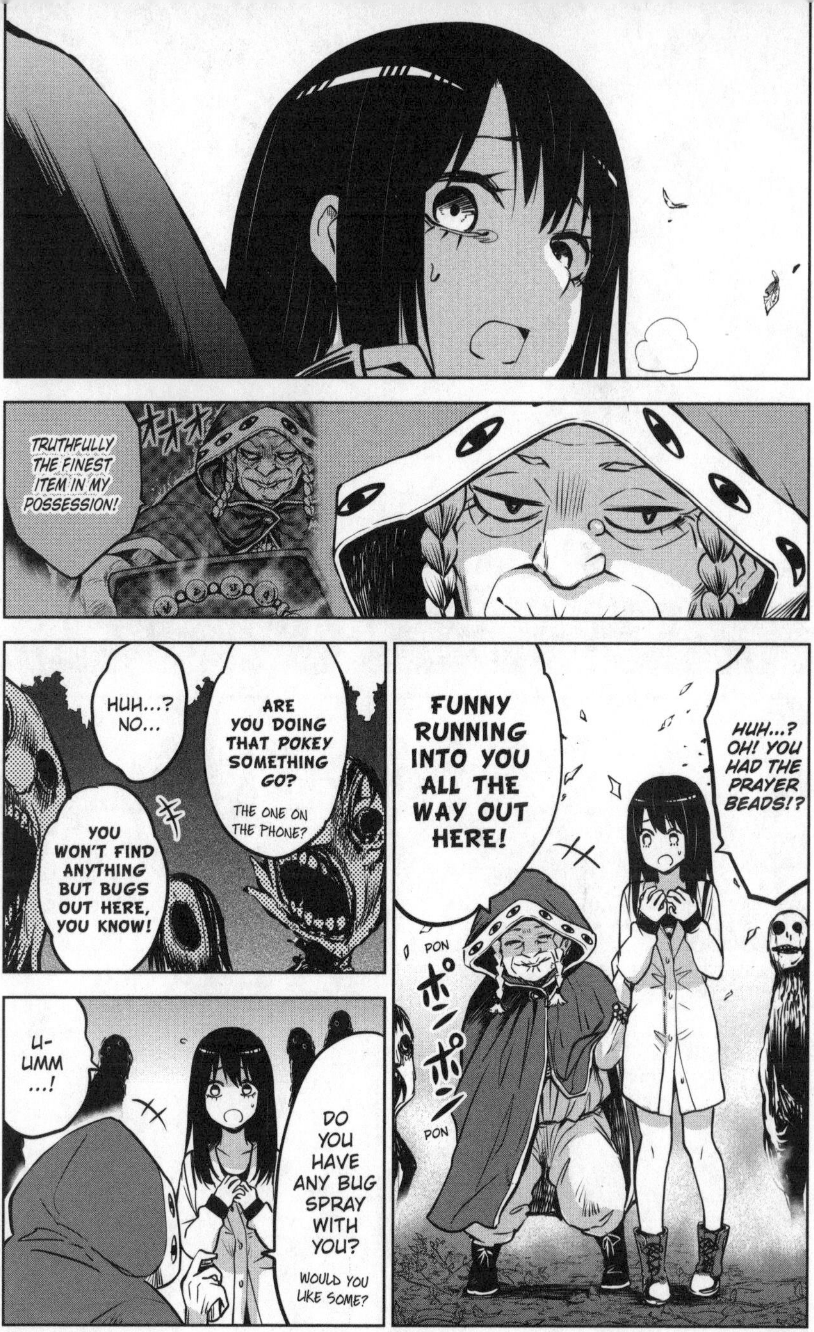
TRUTHFULLY THE FINEST ITEM IN MY POSSESSION!
HUH...? OH! YOU HAD THE PRAYER BEADS!?
FUNNY RUNNING INTO YOU ALL THE WAY OUT HERE!
PON
PON
ARE YOU DOING THAT POKEY SOMETHING GO?
THE ONE ON THE PHONE?
HUH...? NO...
YOU WON'T FIND ANYTHING BUT BUGS OUT HERE, YOU KNOW!
DO YOU HAVE ANY BUG SPRAY WITH YOU?
WOULD YOU LIKE SOME?
U-UMM...!

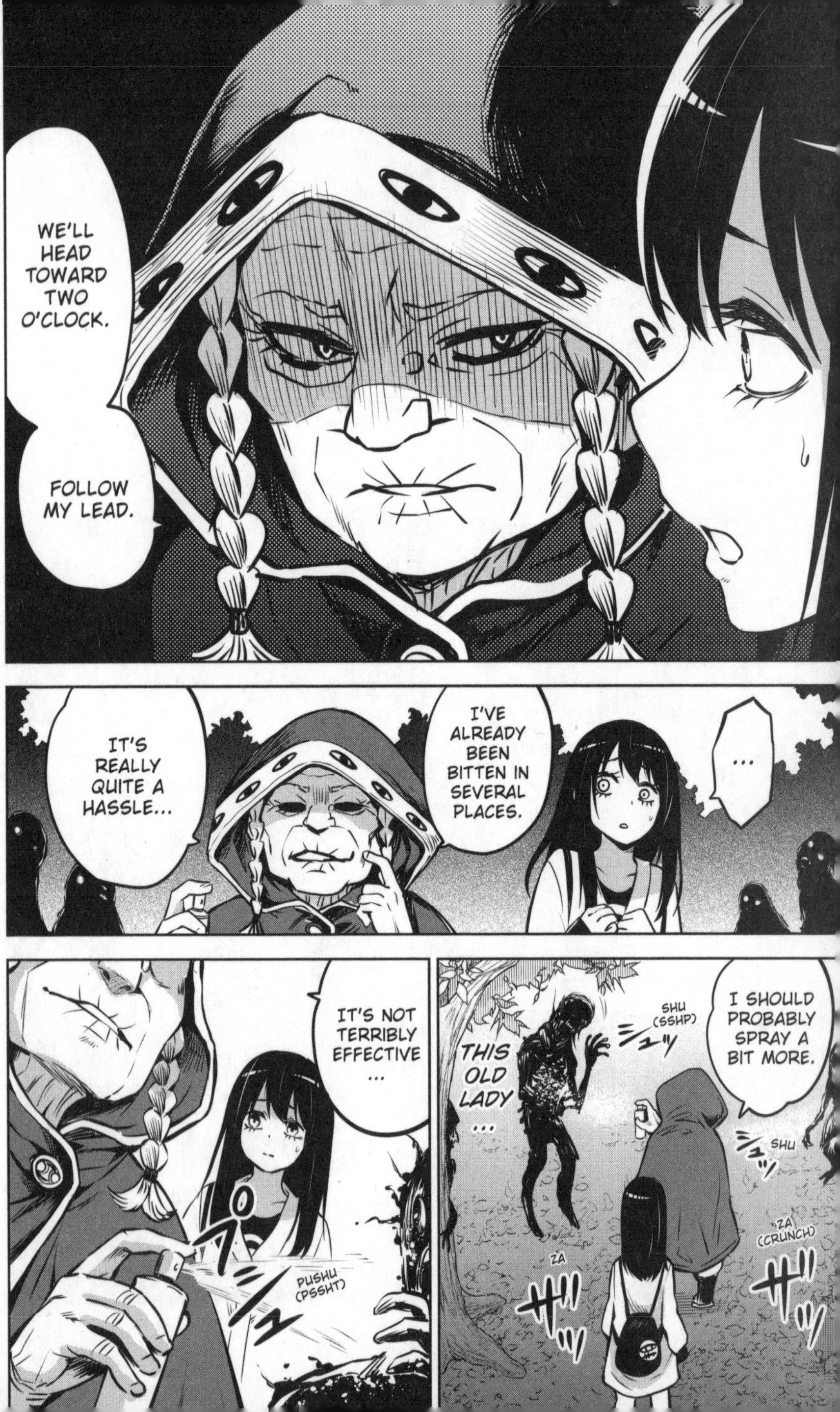
WE'LL HEAD TOWARD TWO O'CLOCK.
FOLLOW MY LEAD.
...
I'VE ALREADY BEEN BITTEN IN SEVERAL PLACES.
IT'S REALLY QUITE A HASSLE...
I SHOULD PROBABLY SPRAY A BIT MORE.
SHU (SSHP)
THIS OLD LADY...
SHU
ZA (CRUNCH)
ZA
IT'S NOT TERRIBLY EFFECTIVE...
PUSHU (PSSHT)

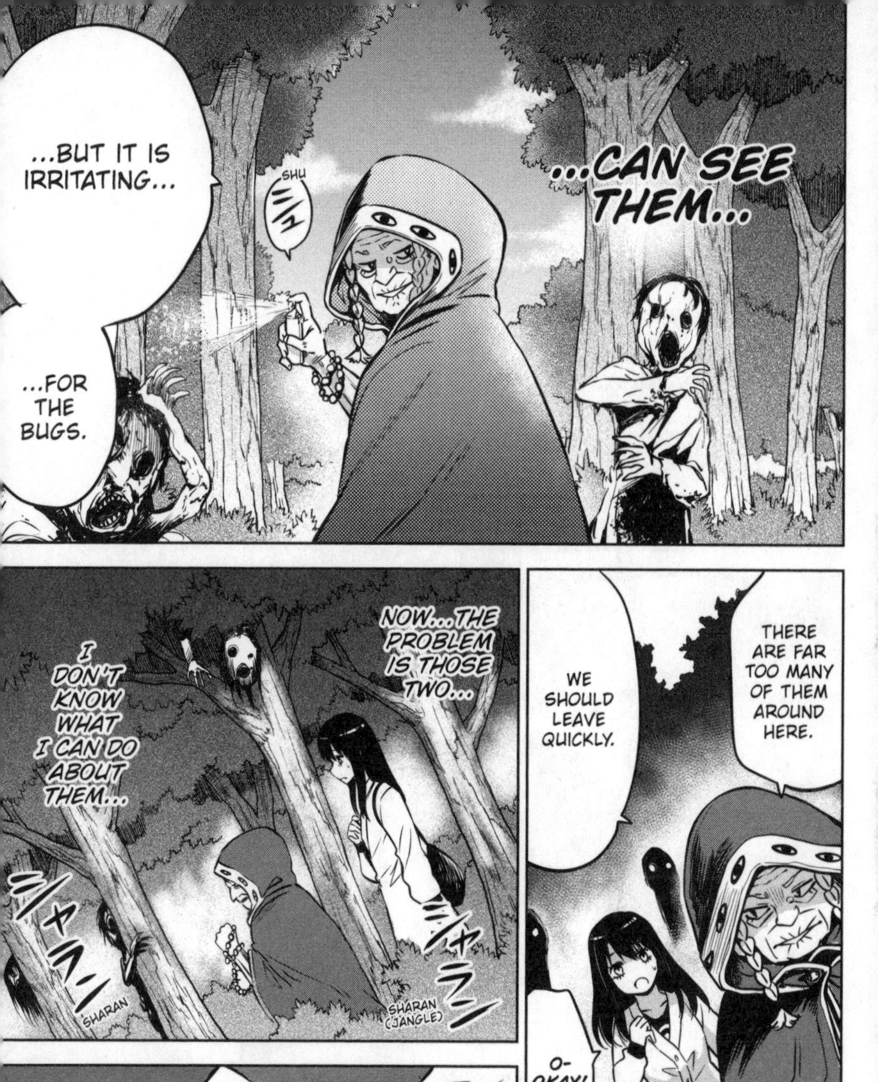
...CAN SEE THEM...
SHU
...BUT IT IS IRRITATING...
...FOR THE BUGS.
THERE ARE FAR TOO MANY OF THEM AROUND HERE.
WE SHOULD LEAVE QUICKLY.
O-OKAY!
SHU
NOW... THE PROBLEM IS THOSE TWO...
I DON'T KNOW WHAT I CAN DO ABOUT THEM...
SHARAN (JANGLE)
SHARAN
SHARAN
I'LL NEVER FORGET... THE SOUND OF THOSE BELLS.
GU (CLENCH)

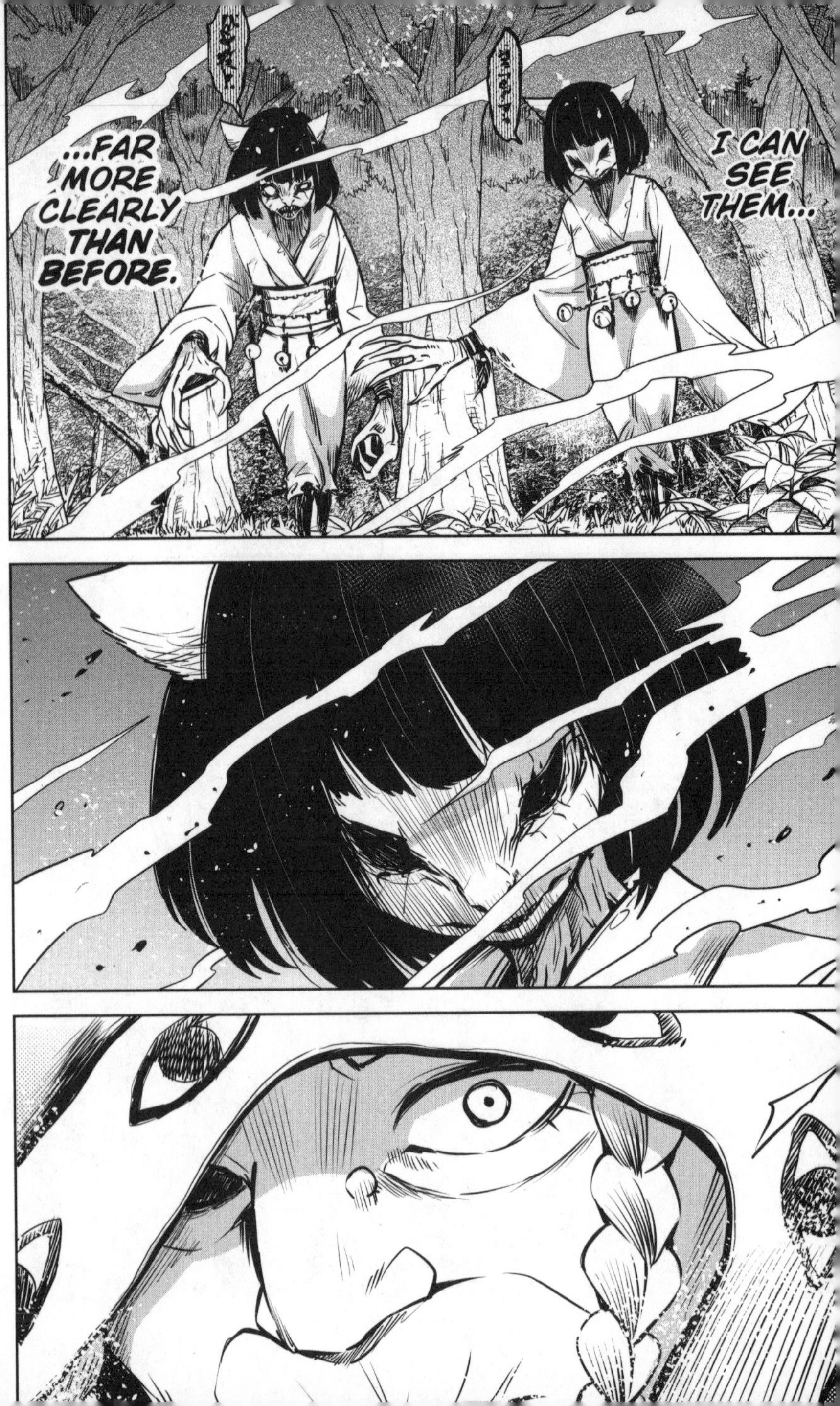
I CAN SEE THEM...
...FAR MORE CLEARLY THAN BEFORE.

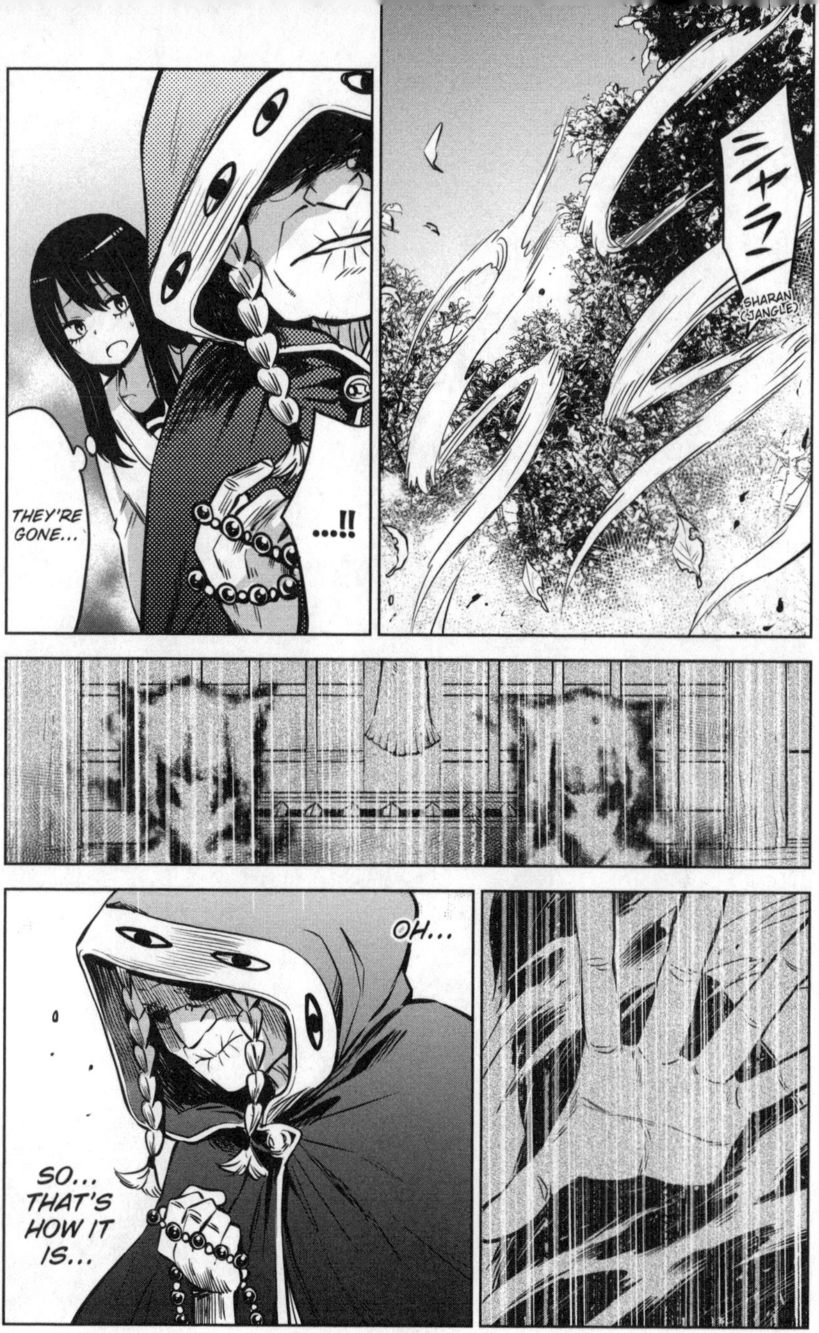
シャラン
SHARAN (JANGLE)
...!!
THEY'RE GONE...
OH...
SO... THAT'S HOW IT IS...

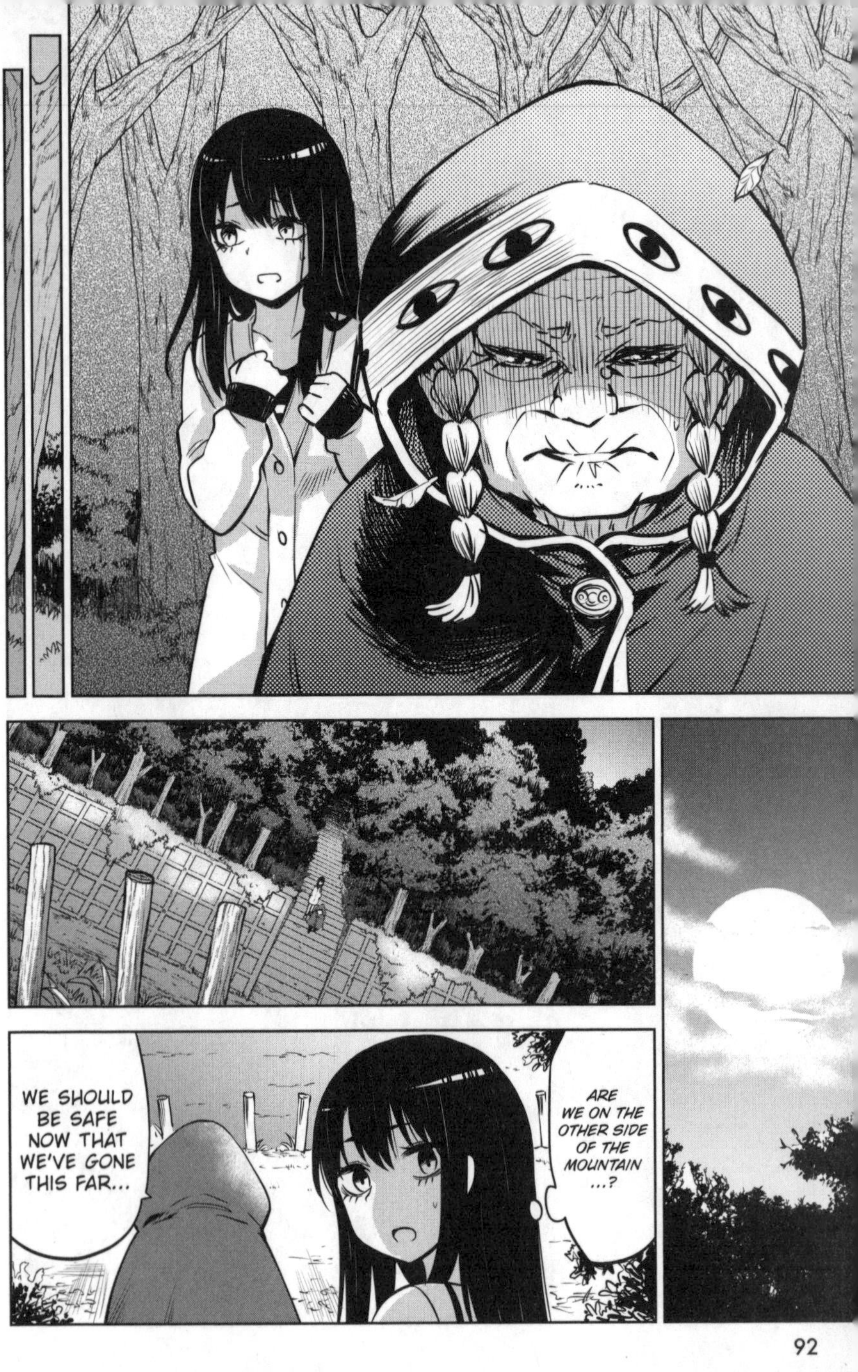
ARE WE ON THE OTHER SIDE OF THE MOUNTAIN ...?
WE SHOULD BE SAFE NOW THAT WE'VE GONE THIS FAR...

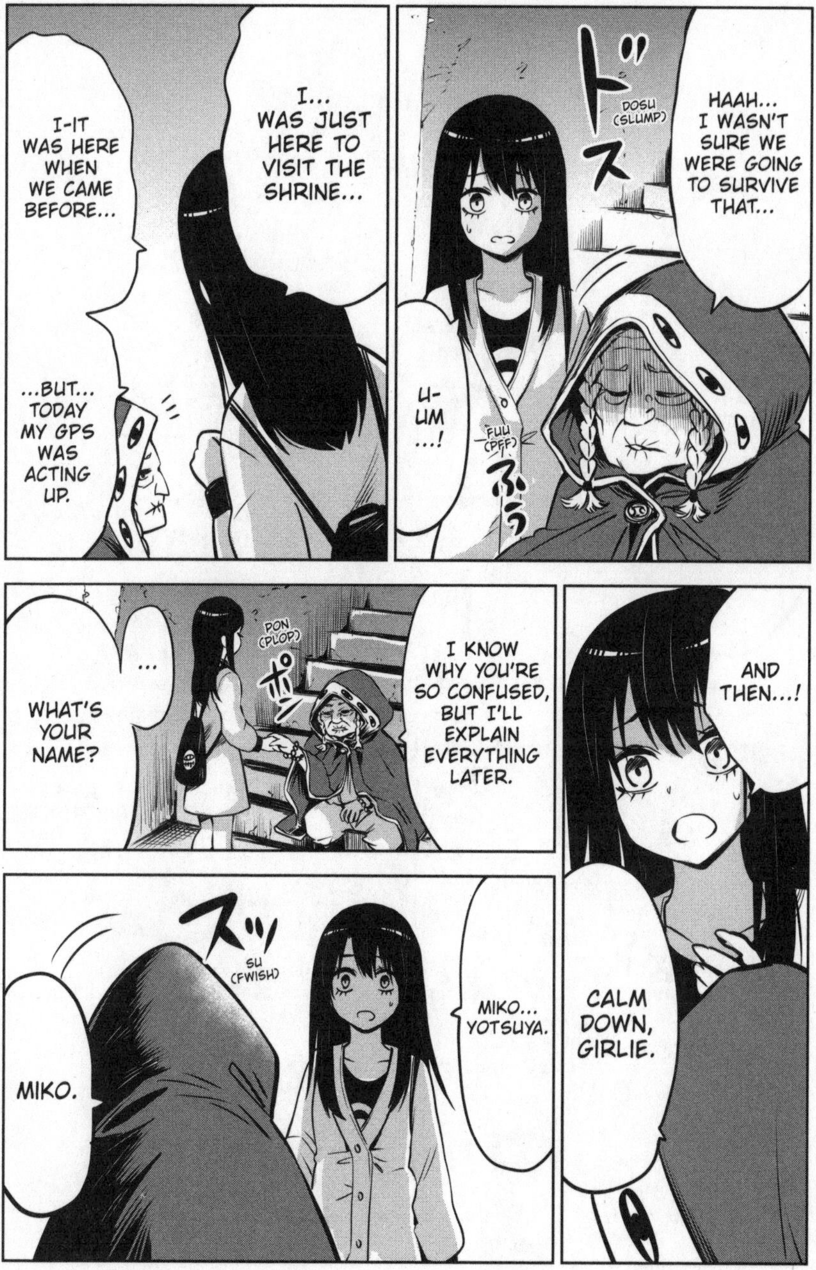
HAAH... I WASN'T SURE WE WERE GOING TO SURVIVE THAT...
ドス
DOSU (SLUMP)
U-UM...!
ふぅ
FUU (PFF)
I... WAS JUST HERE TO VISIT THE SHRINE...
I-IT WAS HERE WHEN WE CAME BEFORE...
...BUT... TODAY MY GPS WAS ACTING UP.
AND THEN...!
CALM DOWN, GIRLIE.
I KNOW WHY YOU'RE SO CONFUSED, BUT I'LL EXPLAIN EVERYTHING LATER.
ポン
PON (PLOP)
...
WHAT'S YOUR NAME?
MIKO... YOTSUYA.
スッ
SU (FWISH)
MIKO.

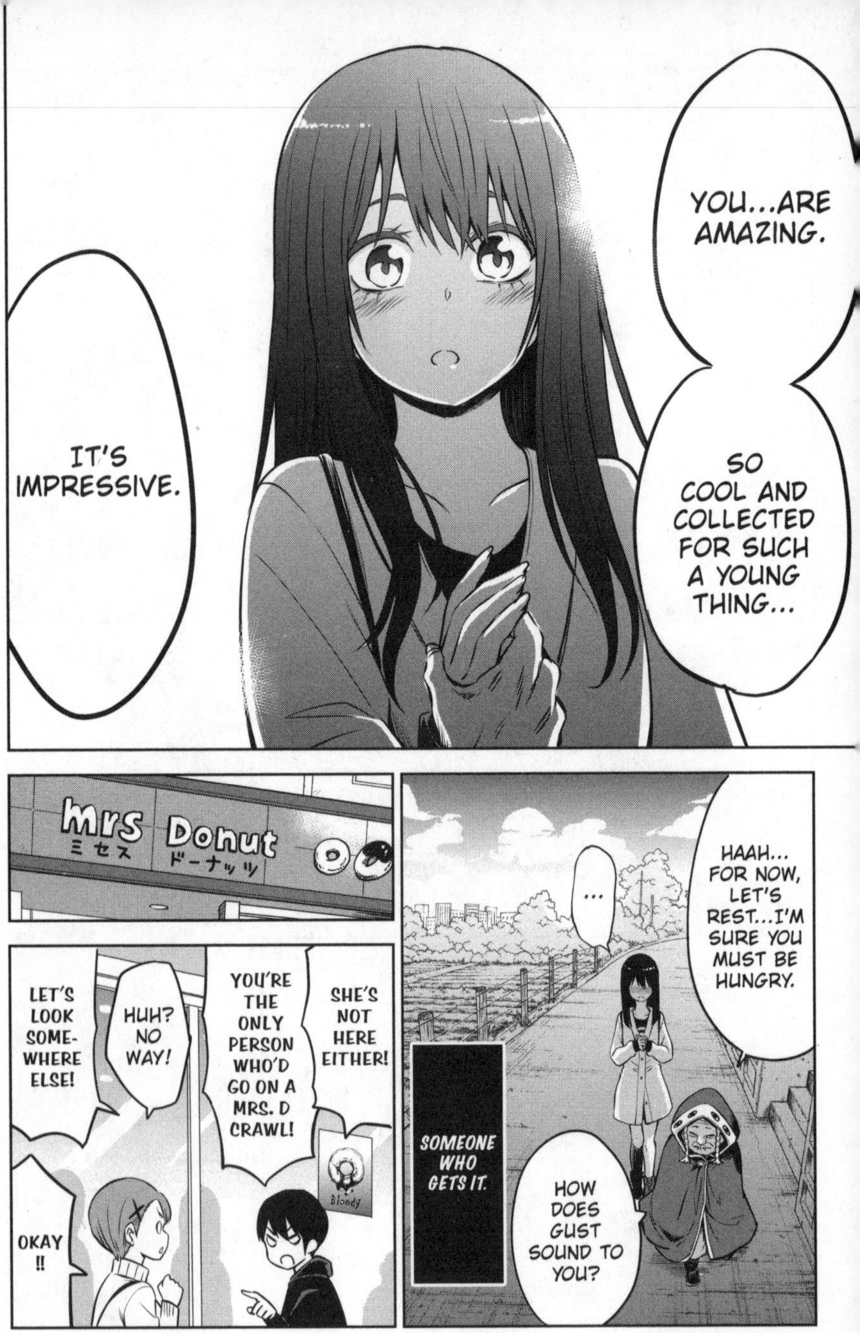
YOU...ARE AMAZING.
SO COOL AND COLLECTED FOR SUCH A YOUNG THING...
IT'S IMPRESSIVE.
HAAH... FOR NOW, LET'S REST...I'M SURE YOU MUST BE HUNGRY.
...
SOMEONE WHO GETS IT.
HOW DOES GUST SOUND TO YOU?
Mrs Donut
ミセス ドーナッツ
SHE'S NOT HERE EITHER!
YOU'RE THE ONLY PERSON WHO'D GO ON A MRS. D CRAWL!
HUH? NO WAY!
LET'S LOOK SOME-WHERE ELSE!
OKAY !!
Bloody

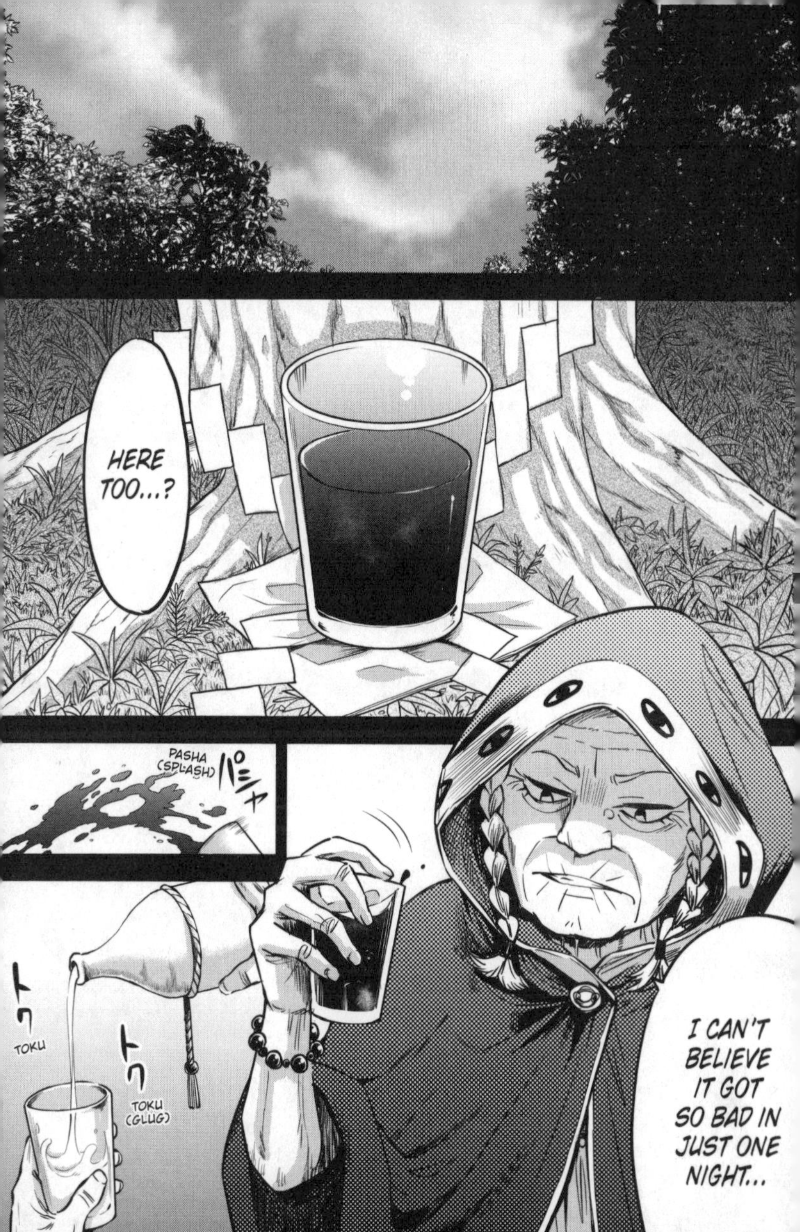
HERE TOO...?
I CAN'T BELIEVE IT GOT SO BAD IN JUST ONE NIGHT...
PASHA (SPLASH)
パシャ
トク
TOKU
トク
TOKU (GLUG)

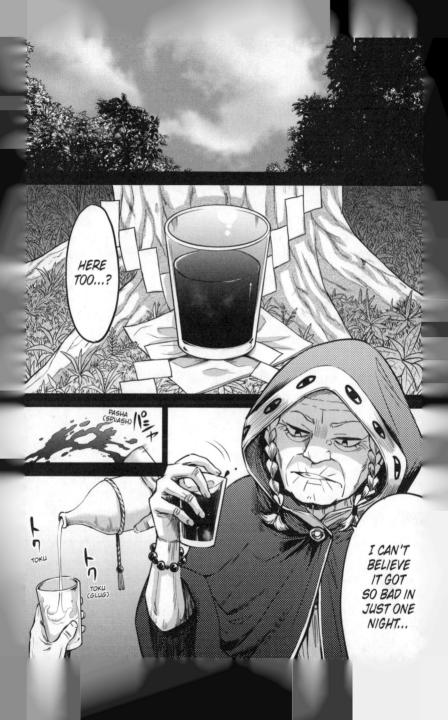

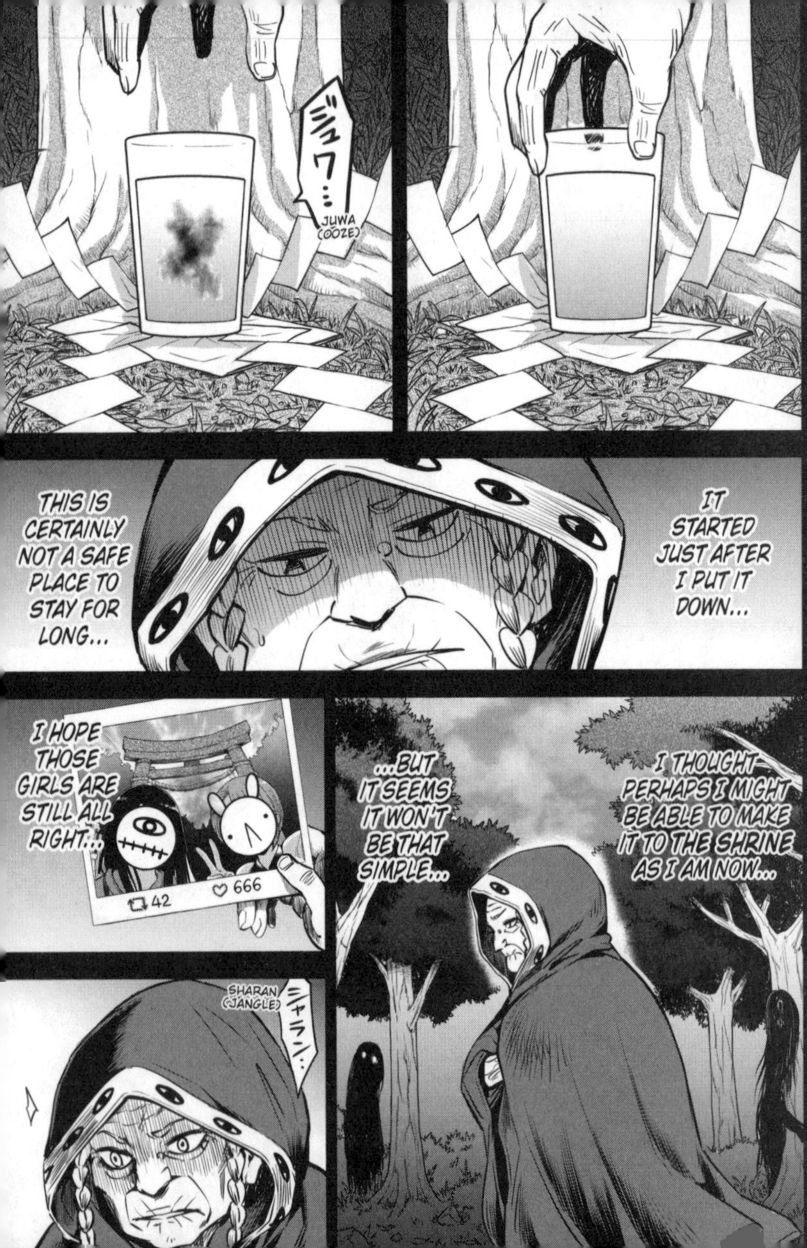
ジュワ…
JUWA (OOZE)
IT STARTED JUST AFTER I PUT IT DOWN…
THIS IS CERTAINLY NOT A SAFE PLACE TO STAY FOR LONG…
I THOUGHT PERHAPS I MIGHT BE ABLE TO MAKE IT TO THE SHRINE AS I AM NOW…
…BUT IT SEEMS IT WON'T BE THAT SIMPLE…
I HOPE THOSE GIRLS ARE STILL ALL RIGHT…
42
666
シャラン…
SHARAN (JANGLE)

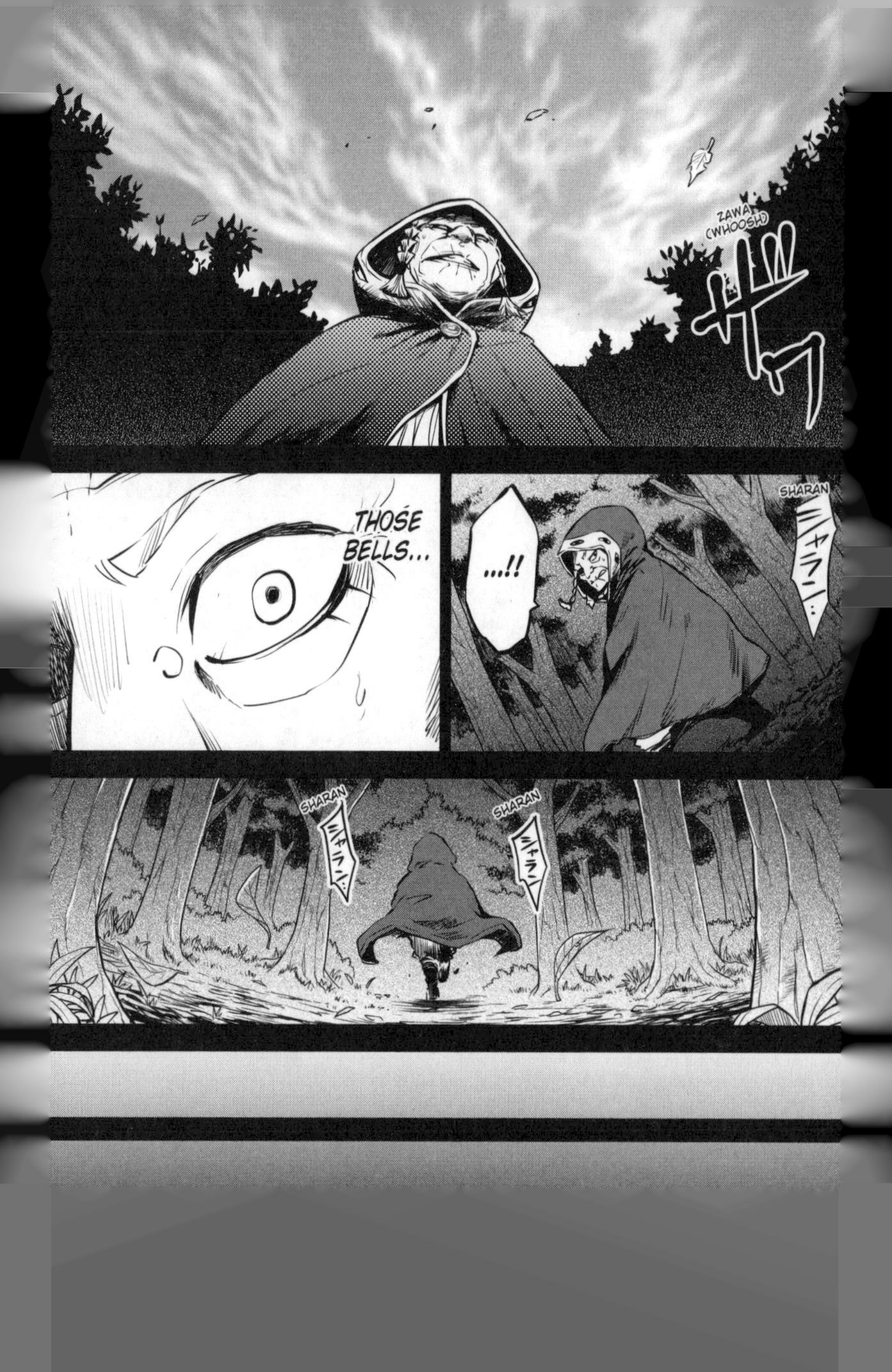
ZAWA (WHOOSH)
ザワ
...!!
SHARAN
シャラン…
THOSE BELLS...
SHARAN
シャラン…
SHARAN
シャラン…

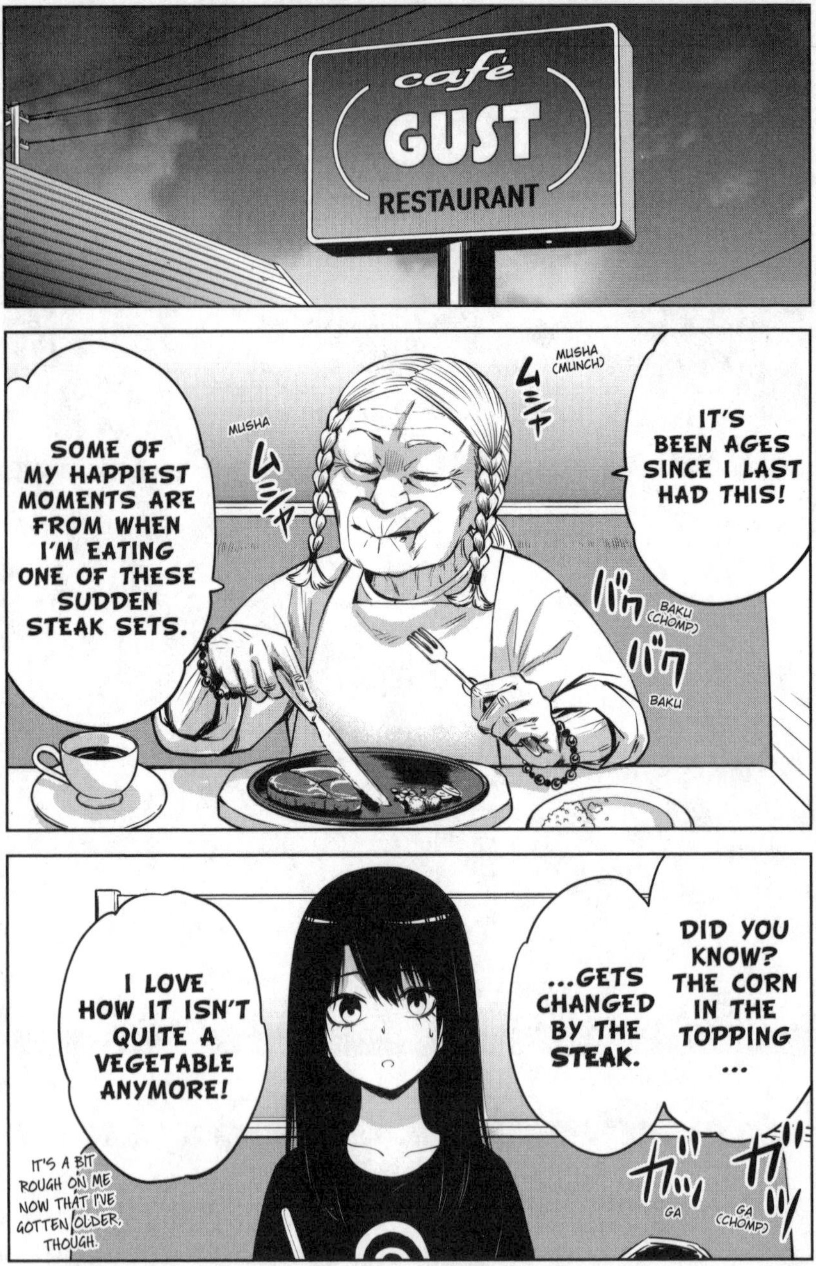
café
GUST
RESTAURANT
MUSHA (MUNCH)
IT'S BEEN AGES SINCE I LAST HAD THIS!
MUSHA
SOME OF MY HAPPIEST MOMENTS ARE FROM WHEN I'M EATING ONE OF THESE SUDDEN STEAK SETS.
BAKU (CHOMP)
BAKU
DID YOU KNOW? THE CORN IN THE TOPPING ...
...GETS CHANGED BY THE STEAK.
I LOVE HOW IT ISN'T QUITE A VEGETABLE ANYMORE!
GA (CHOMP)
GA
IT'S A BIT ROUGH ON ME NOW THAT I'VE GOTTEN OLDER, THOUGH.

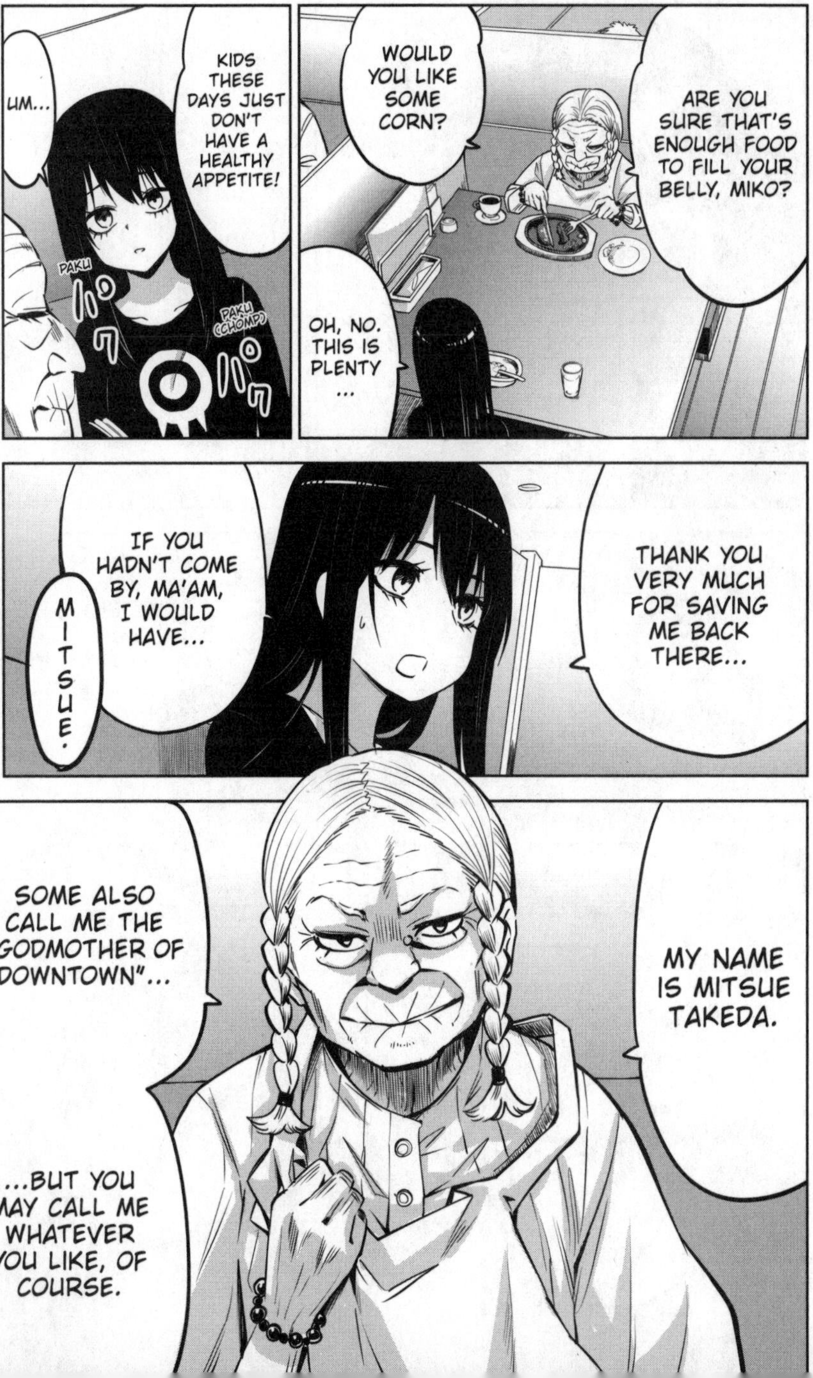
ARE YOU SURE THAT'S ENOUGH FOOD TO FILL YOUR BELLY, MIKO?
WOULD YOU LIKE SOME CORN?
OH, NO. THIS IS PLENTY ...
KIDS THESE DAYS JUST DON'T HAVE A HEALTHY APPETITE!
UM...
PAKU
PAKU (CHOMP)
THANK YOU VERY MUCH FOR SAVING ME BACK THERE...
IF YOU HADN'T COME BY, MA'AM, I WOULD HAVE...
MITSUE.
MY NAME IS MITSUE TAKEDA.
SOME ALSO CALL ME THE "GODMOTHER OF DOWNTOWN"...
...BUT YOU MAY CALL ME WHATEVER YOU LIKE, OF COURSE.

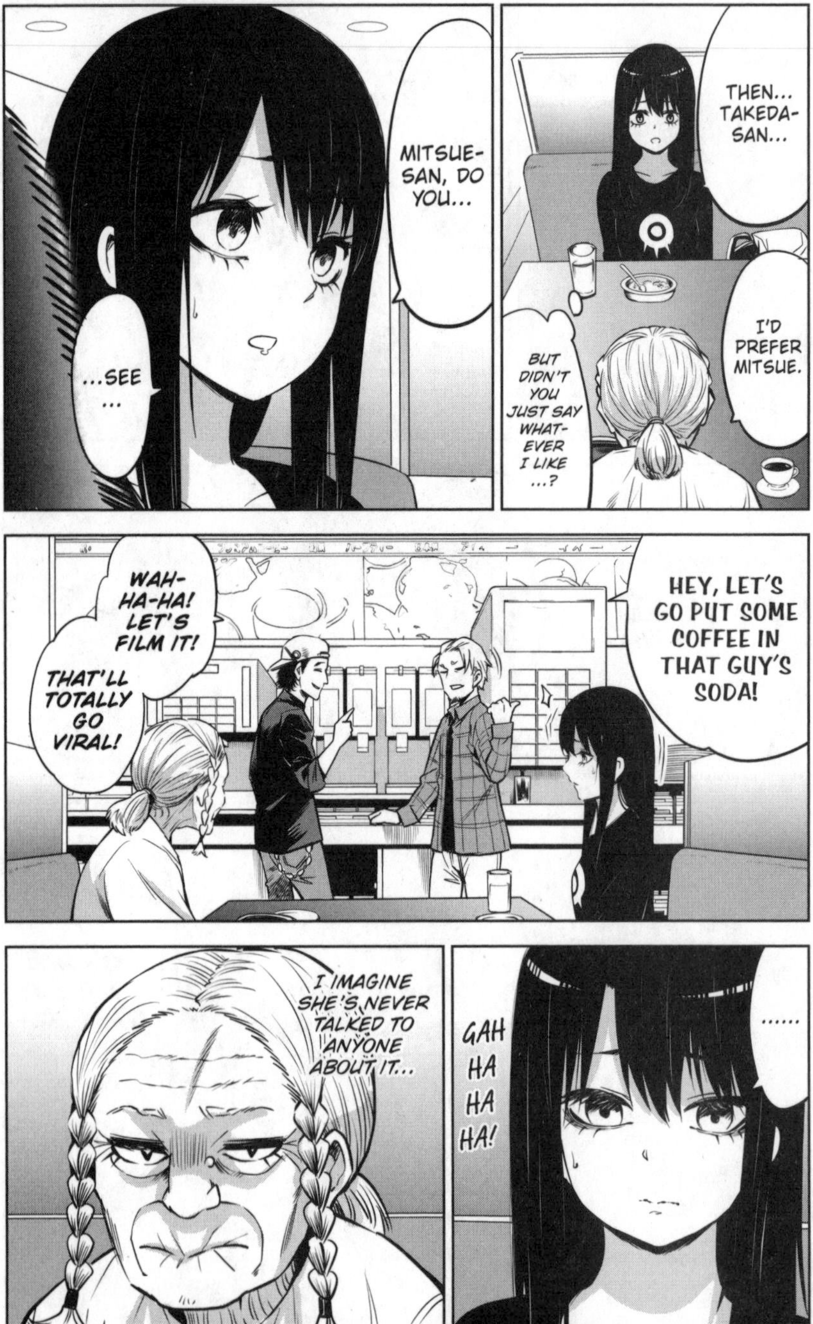
THEN... TAKEDA-SAN...
I'D PREFER MITSUE.
BUT DIDN'T YOU JUST SAY WHAT-EVER I LIKE ...?
MITSUE-SAN, DO YOU...
...SEE ...
HEY, LET'S GO PUT SOME COFFEE IN THAT GUY'S SODA!
WAH-HA-HA! LET'S FILM IT!
THAT'LL TOTALLY GO VIRAL!
......
GAH HA HA HA!
I IMAGINE SHE'S NEVER TALKED TO ANYONE ABOUT IT...

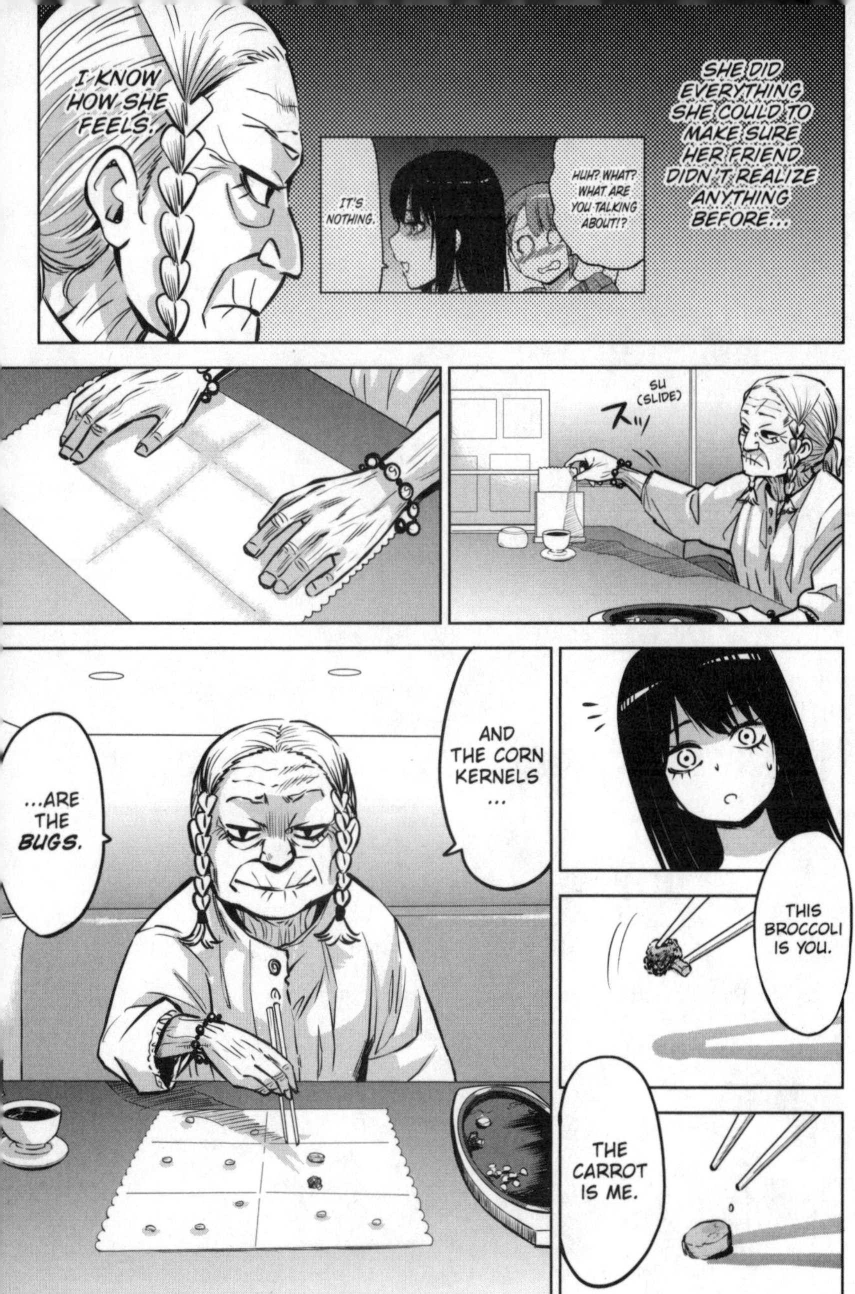
SHE DID EVERYTHING SHE COULD TO MAKE SURE HER FRIEND DIDN'T REALIZE ANYTHING BEFORE...
HUH? WHAT? WHAT ARE YOU TALKING ABOUT!?
IT'S NOTHING.
I KNOW HOW SHE FEELS.
SU (SLIDE)
ズッ
THIS BROCCOLI IS YOU.
THE CARROT IS ME.
AND THE CORN KERNELS ...
...ARE THE BUGS.

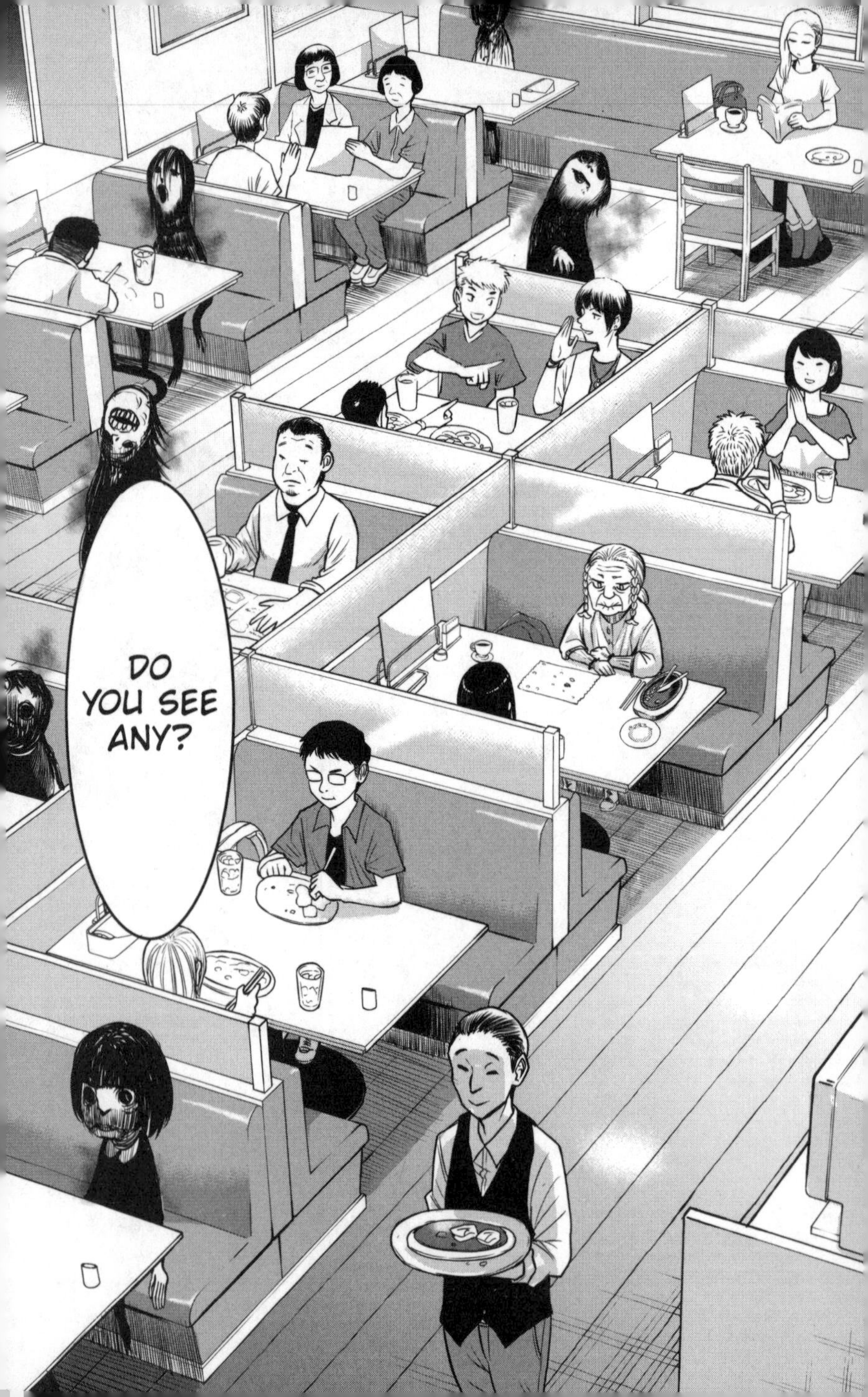
DO YOU SEE ANY?

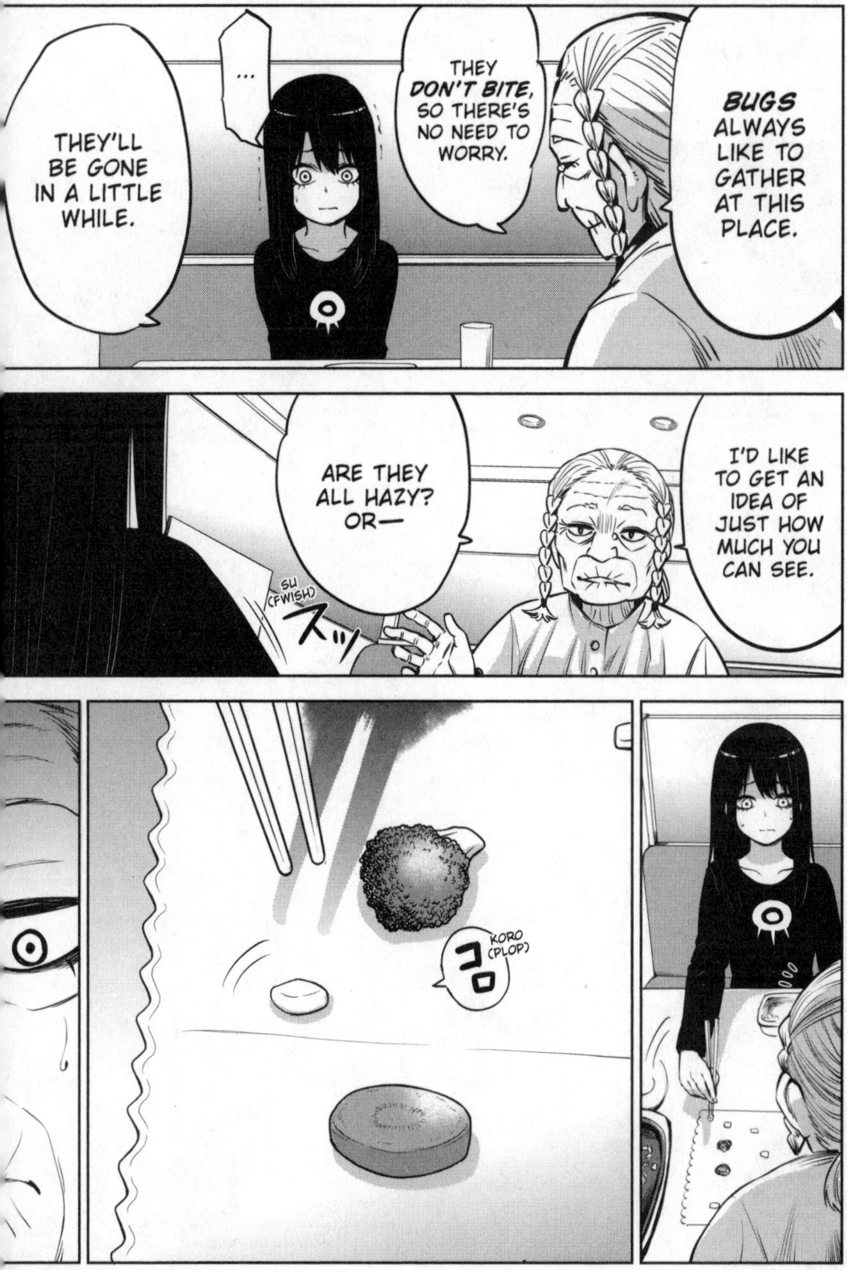
BUGS ALWAYS LIKE TO GATHER AT THIS PLACE.
THEY DON'T BITE, SO THERE'S NO NEED TO WORRY.
...
THEY'LL BE GONE IN A LITTLE WHILE.
I'D LIKE TO GET AN IDEA OF JUST HOW MUCH YOU CAN SEE.
ARE THEY ALL HAZY? OR—
SU (FWISH)
スッ
KORO (PLOP)
コロ

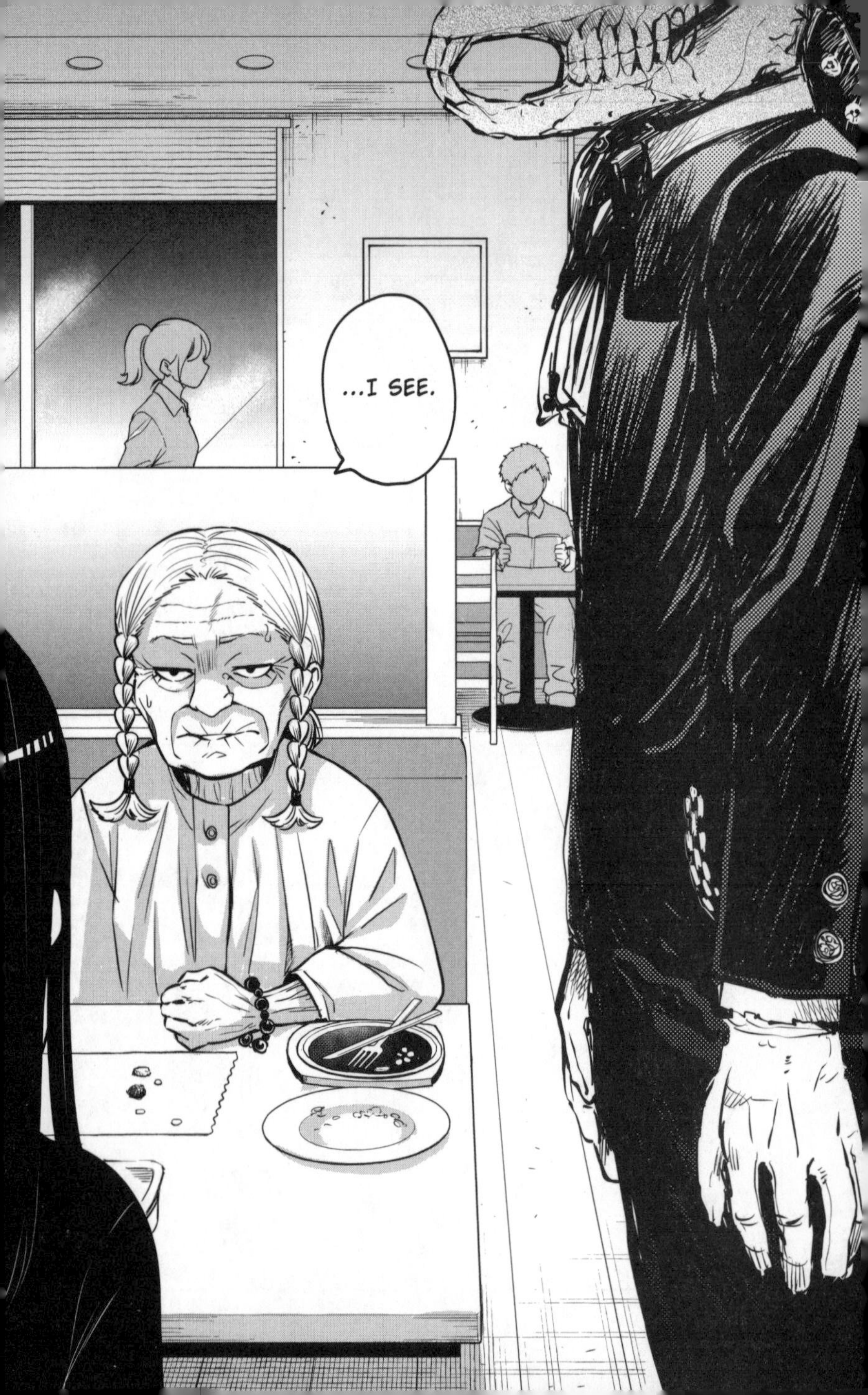
...I SEE.

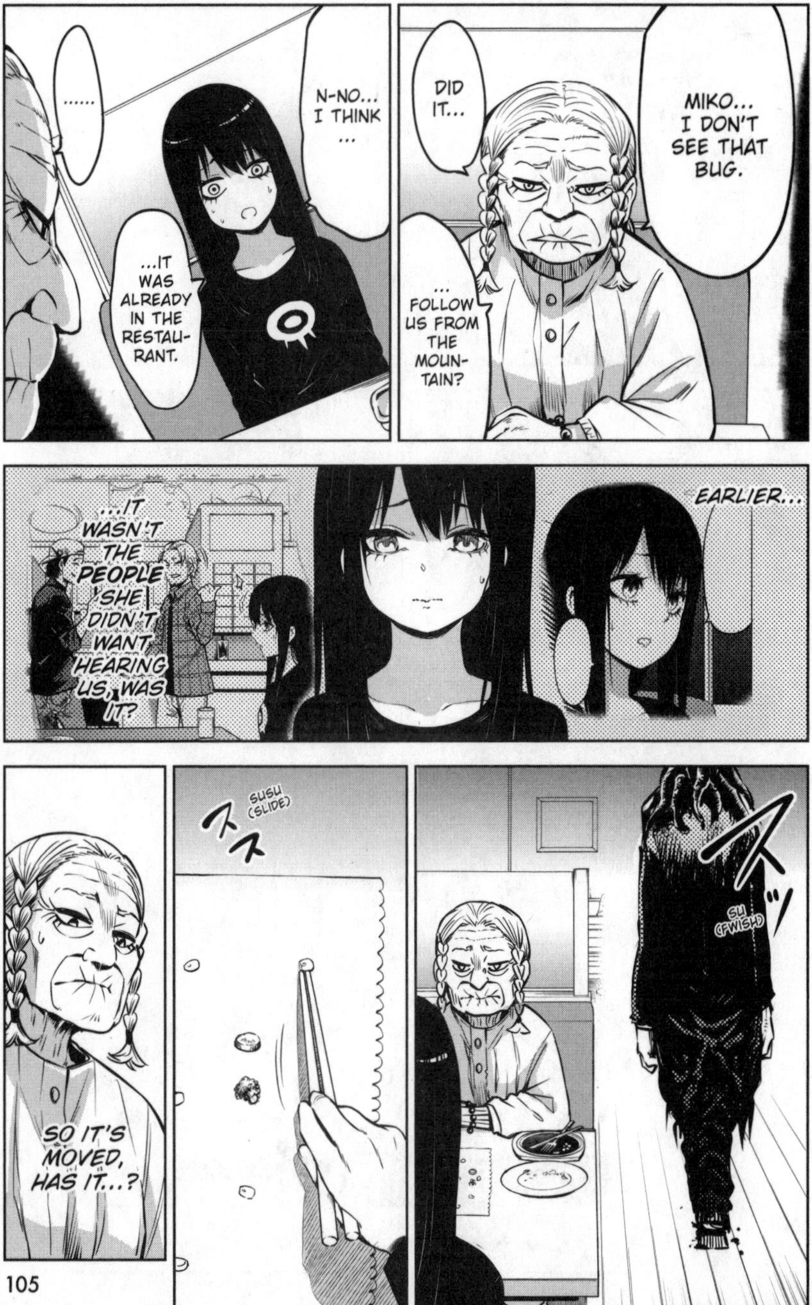
MIKO... I DON'T SEE THAT BUG.
DID IT...
...FOLLOW US FROM THE MOUNTAIN?
N-NO... I THINK...
......
...IT WAS ALREADY IN THE RESTAURANT.
EARLIER...
...IT WASN'T THE PEOPLE SHE DIDN'T WANT HEARING US, WAS IT?
SU (FWISH)
SUSU (SLIDE)
SO IT'S MOVED, HAS IT...?

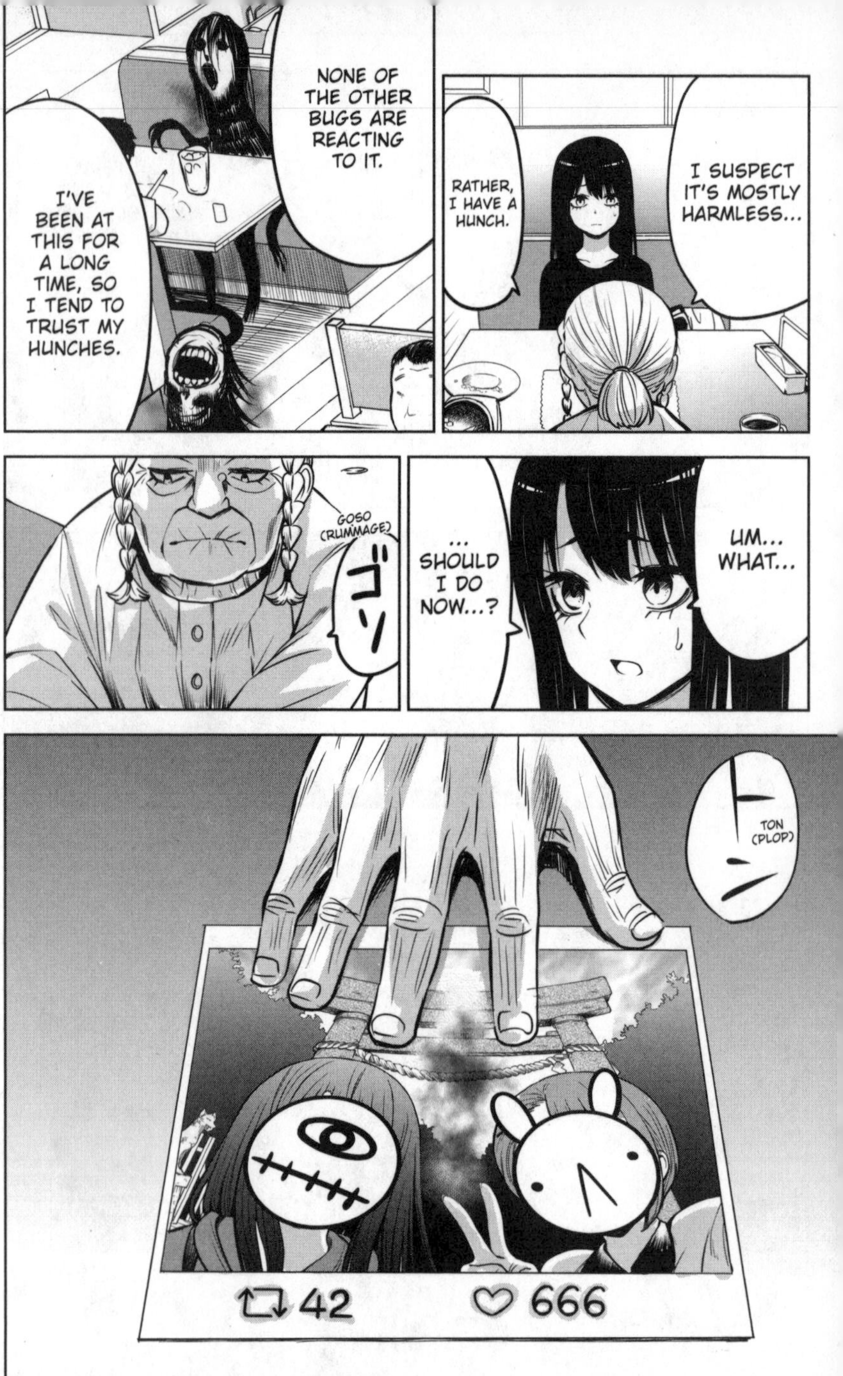
I SUSPECT IT'S MOSTLY HARMLESS...
RATHER, I HAVE A HUNCH.
NONE OF THE OTHER BUGS ARE REACTING TO IT.
I'VE BEEN AT THIS FOR A LONG TIME, SO I TEND TO TRUST MY HUNCHES.
UM... WHAT...
... SHOULD I DO NOW...?
ゴソ
GOSO (RUMMAGE)
トン
TON (PLOP)
42
666

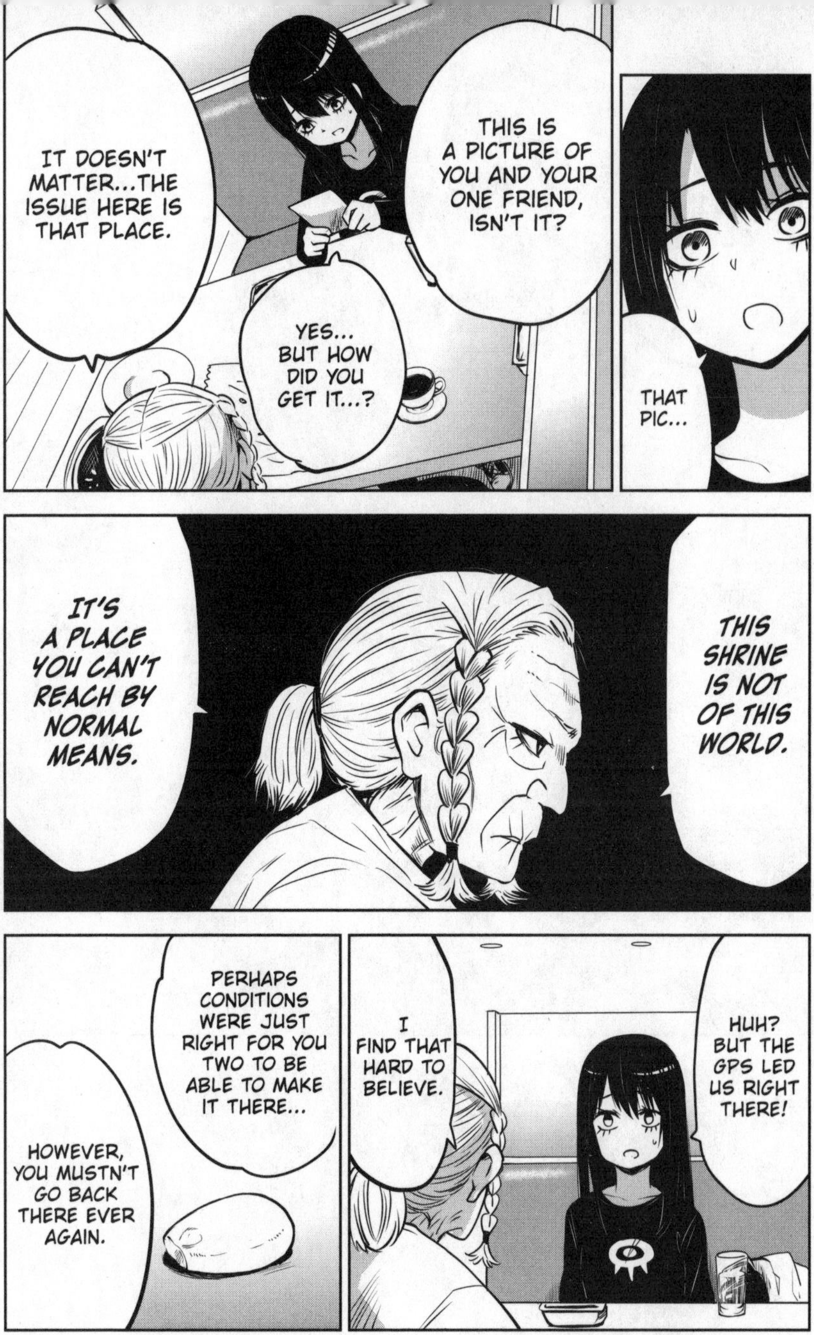
THAT PIC...
THIS IS A PICTURE OF YOU AND YOUR ONE FRIEND, ISN'T IT?
YES... BUT HOW DID YOU GET IT...?
IT DOESN'T MATTER...THE ISSUE HERE IS THAT PLACE.
THIS SHRINE IS NOT OF THIS WORLD.
IT'S A PLACE YOU CAN'T REACH BY NORMAL MEANS.
HUH? BUT THE GPS LED US RIGHT THERE!
I FIND THAT HARD TO BELIEVE.
PERHAPS CONDITIONS WERE JUST RIGHT FOR YOU TWO TO BE ABLE TO MAKE IT THERE...
HOWEVER, YOU MUSTN'T GO BACK THERE EVER AGAIN.

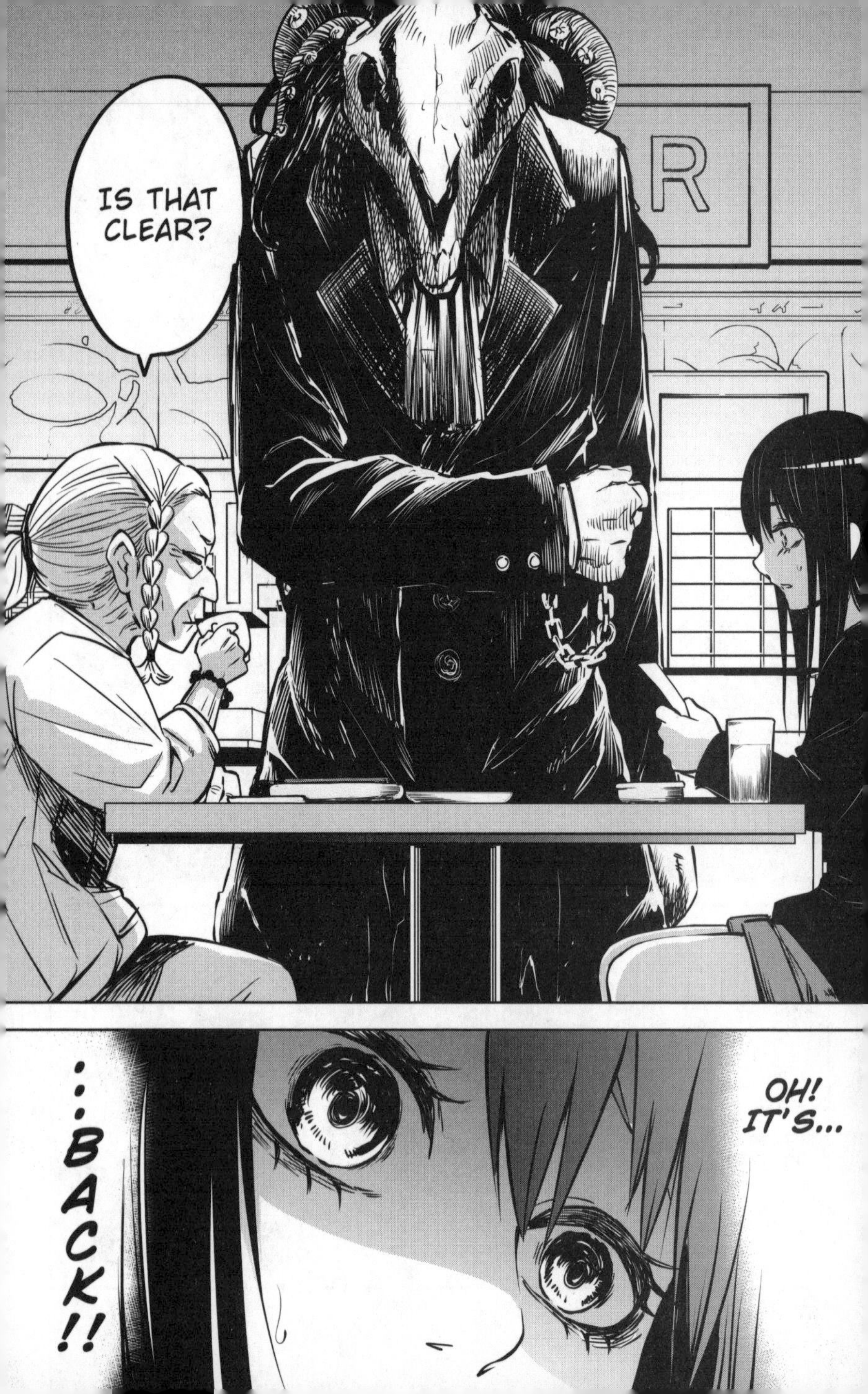
IS THAT CLEAR?
OH! IT'S...
...BACK!!

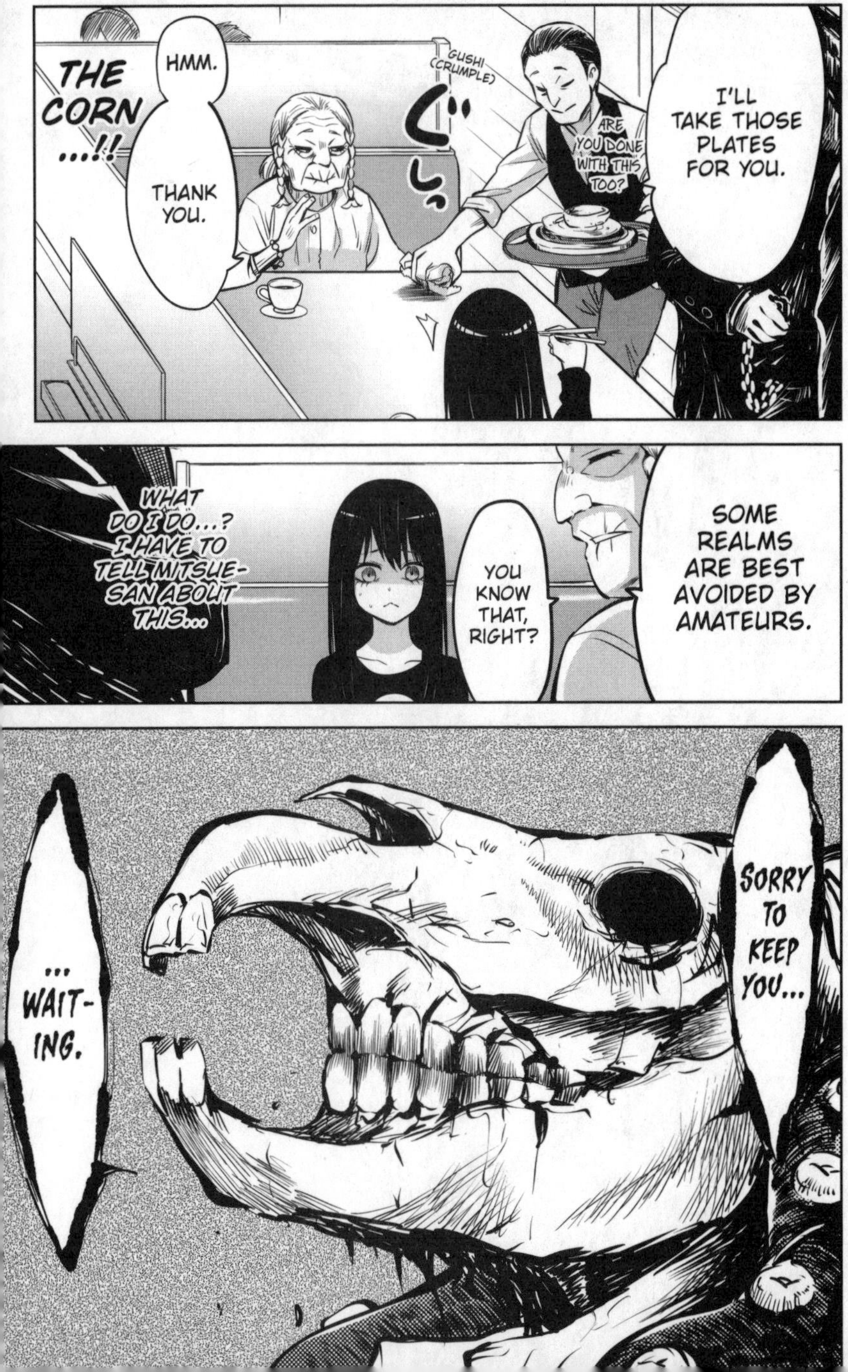

I'LL TAKE THOSE PLATES FOR YOU.
ARE YOU DONE WITH THIS TOO?
GUSHI (CRUMPLE)
HMM.
THANK YOU.
THE CORN ...!!
SOME REALMS ARE BEST AVOIDED BY AMATEURS.
YOU KNOW THAT, RIGHT?
WHAT DO I DO...? I HAVE TO TELL MITSUE-SAN ABOUT THIS...
SORRY TO KEEP YOU...
...WAIT-ING.

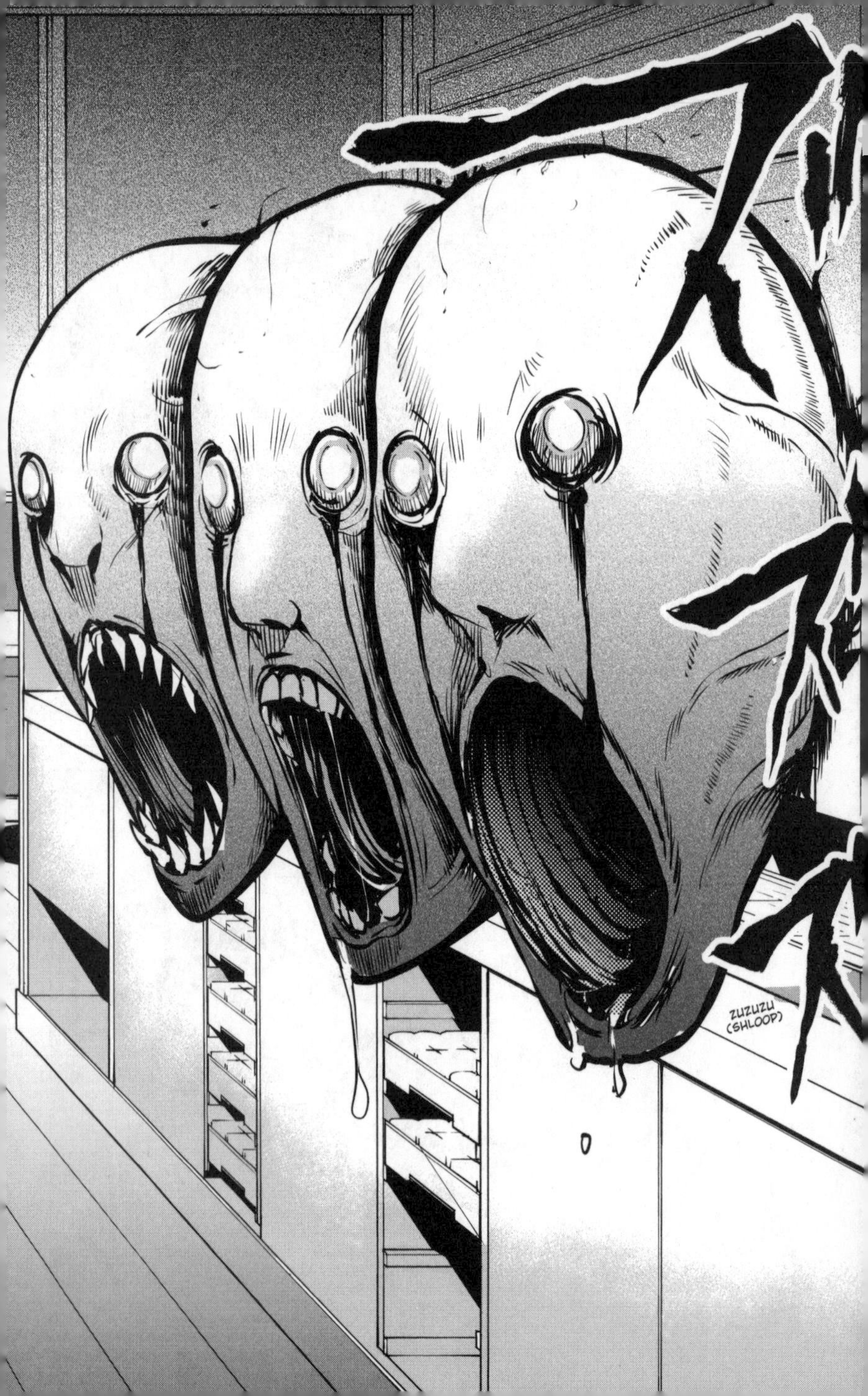
ZUZUZU
(SHLOOP)

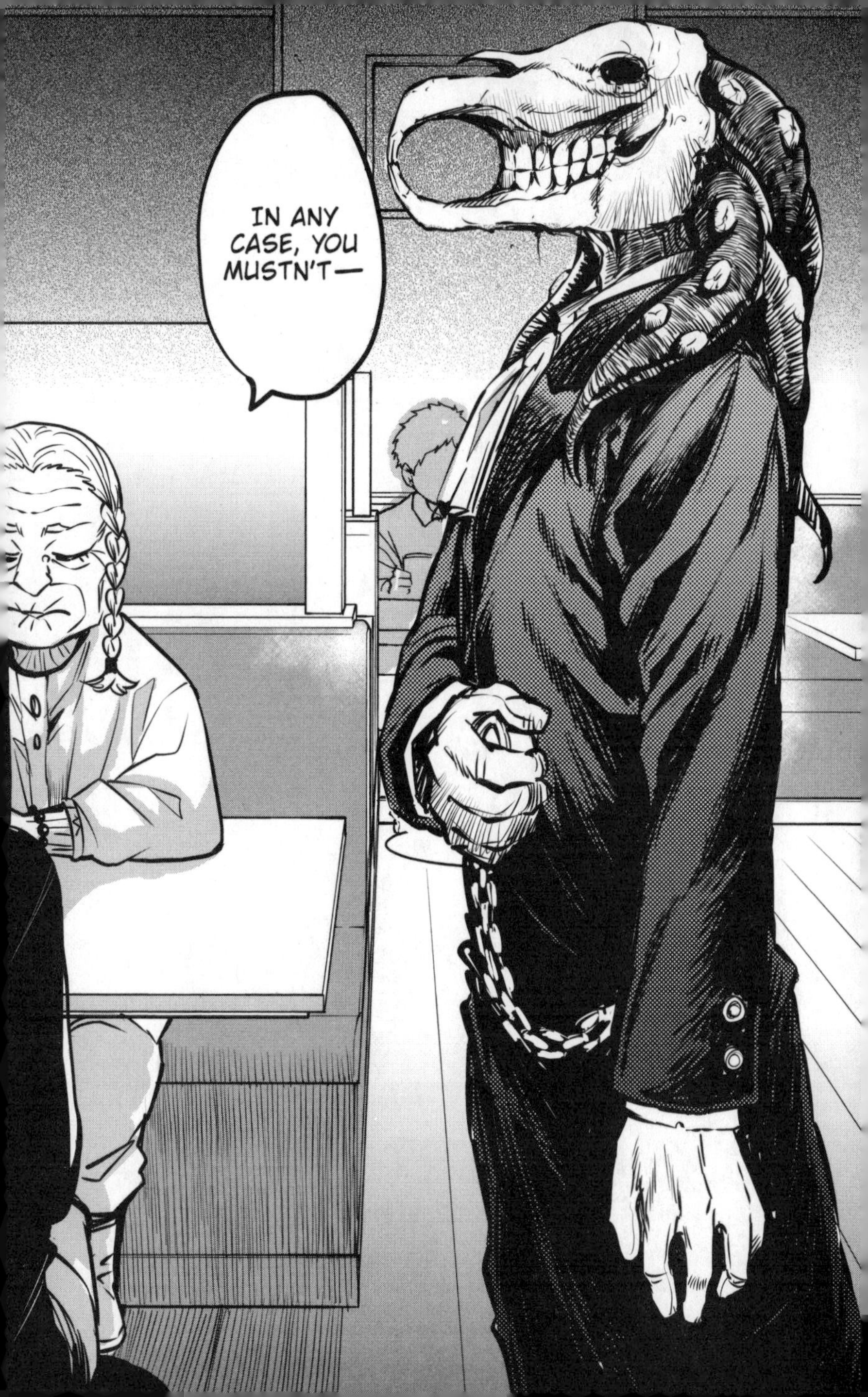
IN ANY CASE, YOU MUSTN'T—

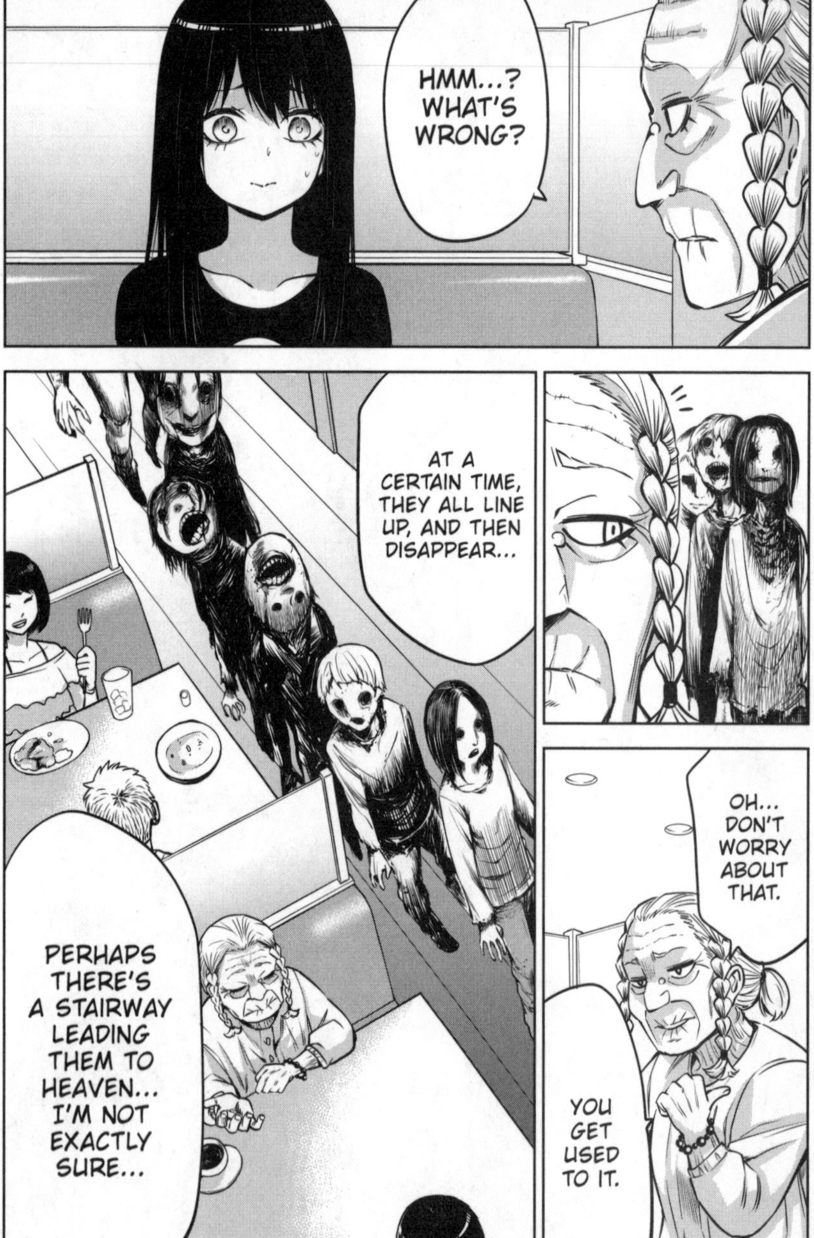
HMM...? WHAT'S WRONG?
OH... DON'T WORRY ABOUT THAT.
YOU GET USED TO IT.
AT A CERTAIN TIME, THEY ALL LINE UP, AND THEN DISAPPEAR...
PERHAPS THERE'S A STAIRWAY LEADING THEM TO HEAVEN... I'M NOT EXACTLY SURE...

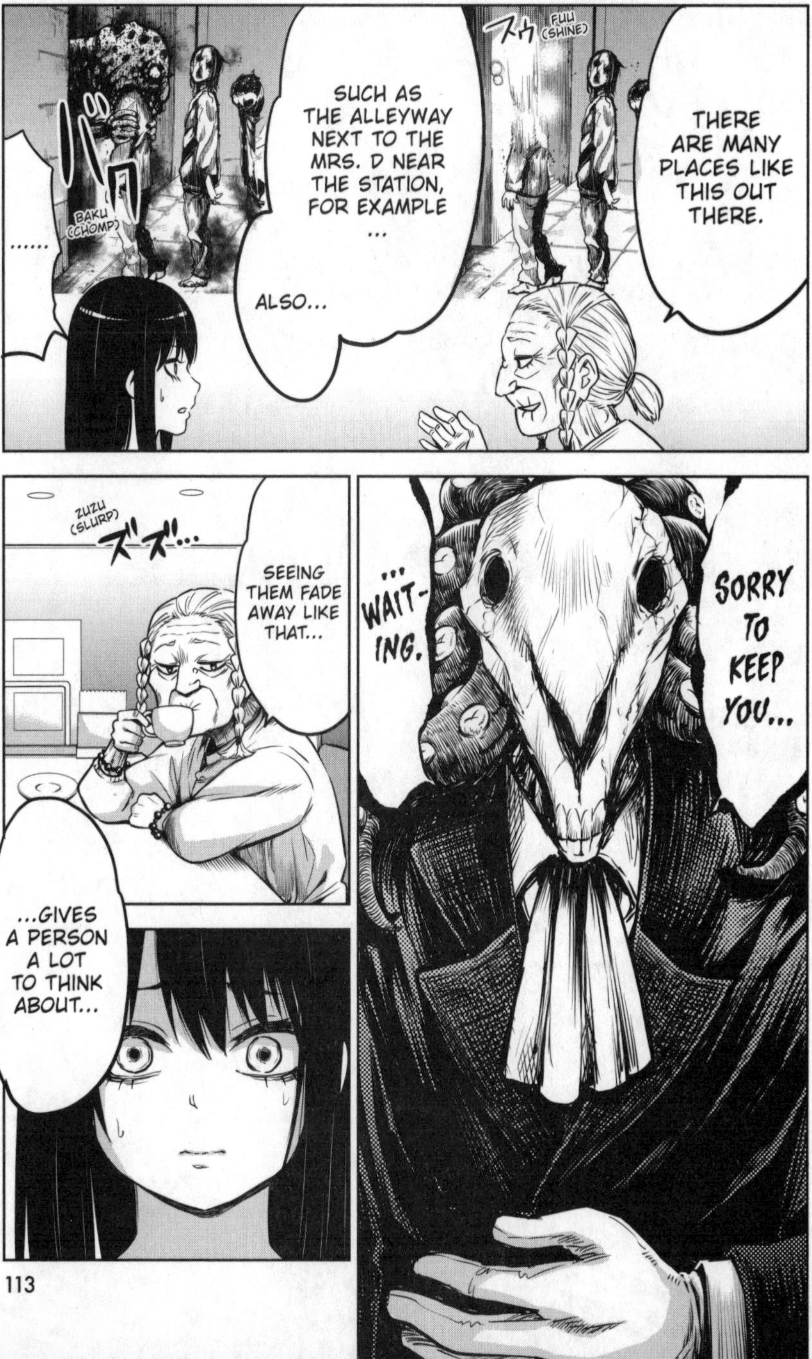
THERE ARE MANY PLACES LIKE THIS OUT THERE.
スゥ FUU (SHINE)
SUCH AS THE ALLEYWAY NEXT TO THE MRS. D NEAR THE STATION, FOR EXAMPLE ...
ALSO...
BAKU (CHOMP)
......
SORRY TO KEEP YOU...
...WAITING.
ズズ... ZUZU (SLURP)
SEEING THEM FADE AWAY LIKE THAT...
...GIVES A PERSON A LOT TO THINK ABOUT...

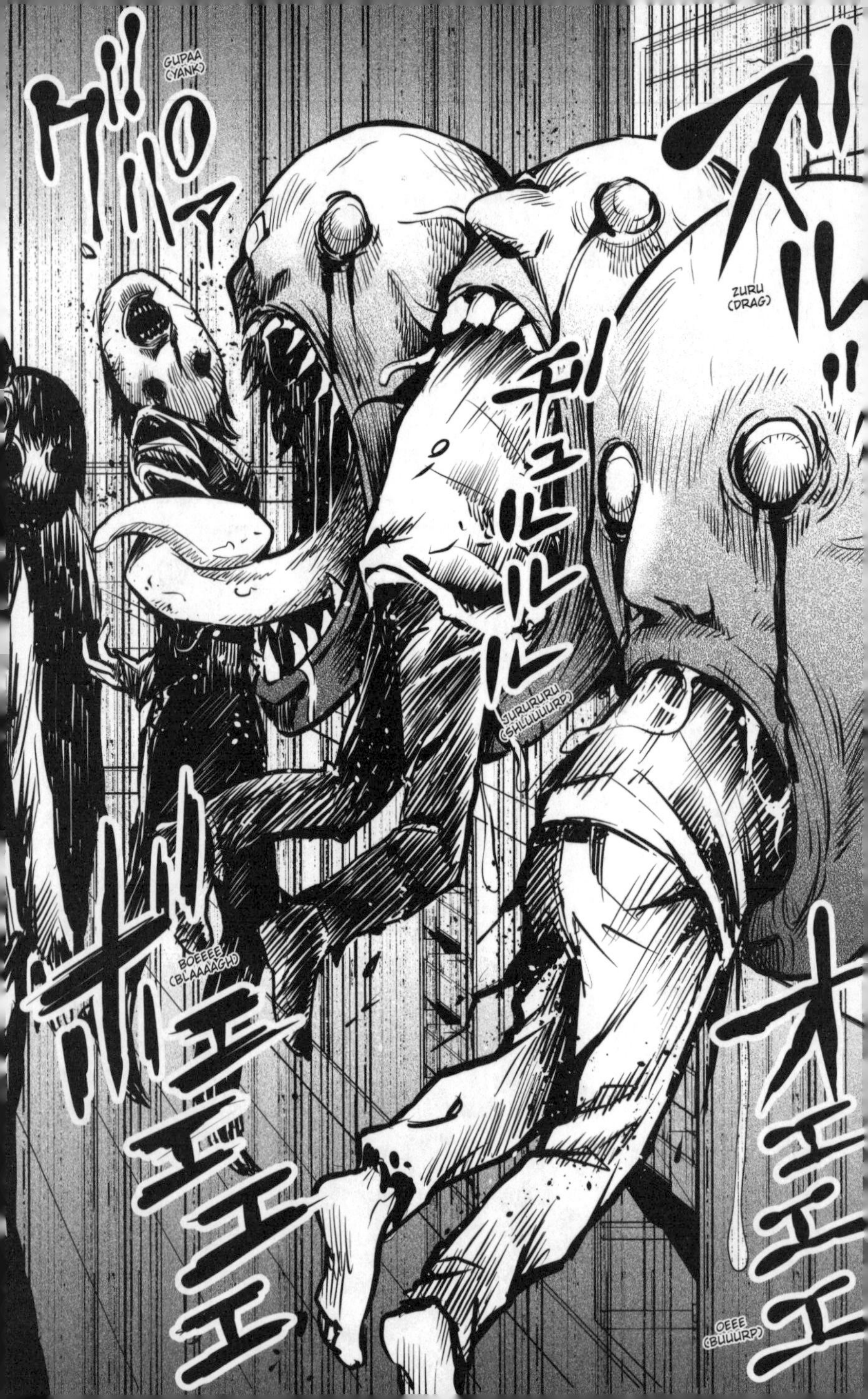
ZURU (DRAG)
GUPAA (YANK)
JURURURU (SHLUUUURP)
OEEE (BUUURP)
BOEEEE (BLAAAAGH)

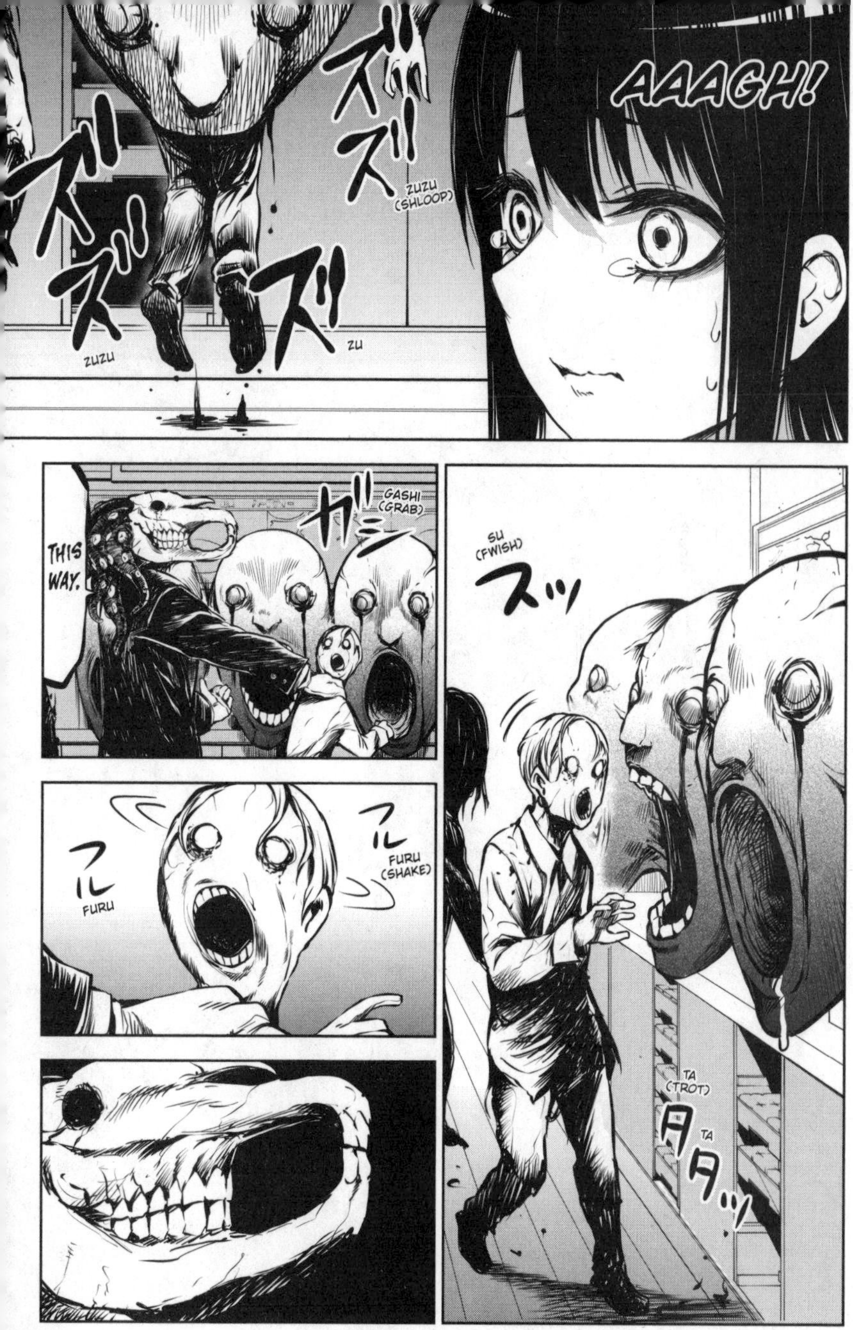
AAAGH!
ズズ
ZUZU (SHLOOP)
ズリ
ZU
ズズ
ZUZU
スッ
SU (FWISH)
TA (TROT)
タタッ
TA
ガシ
GASHI (GRAB)
THIS WAY.
フル
FURU (SHAKE)
フル
FURU

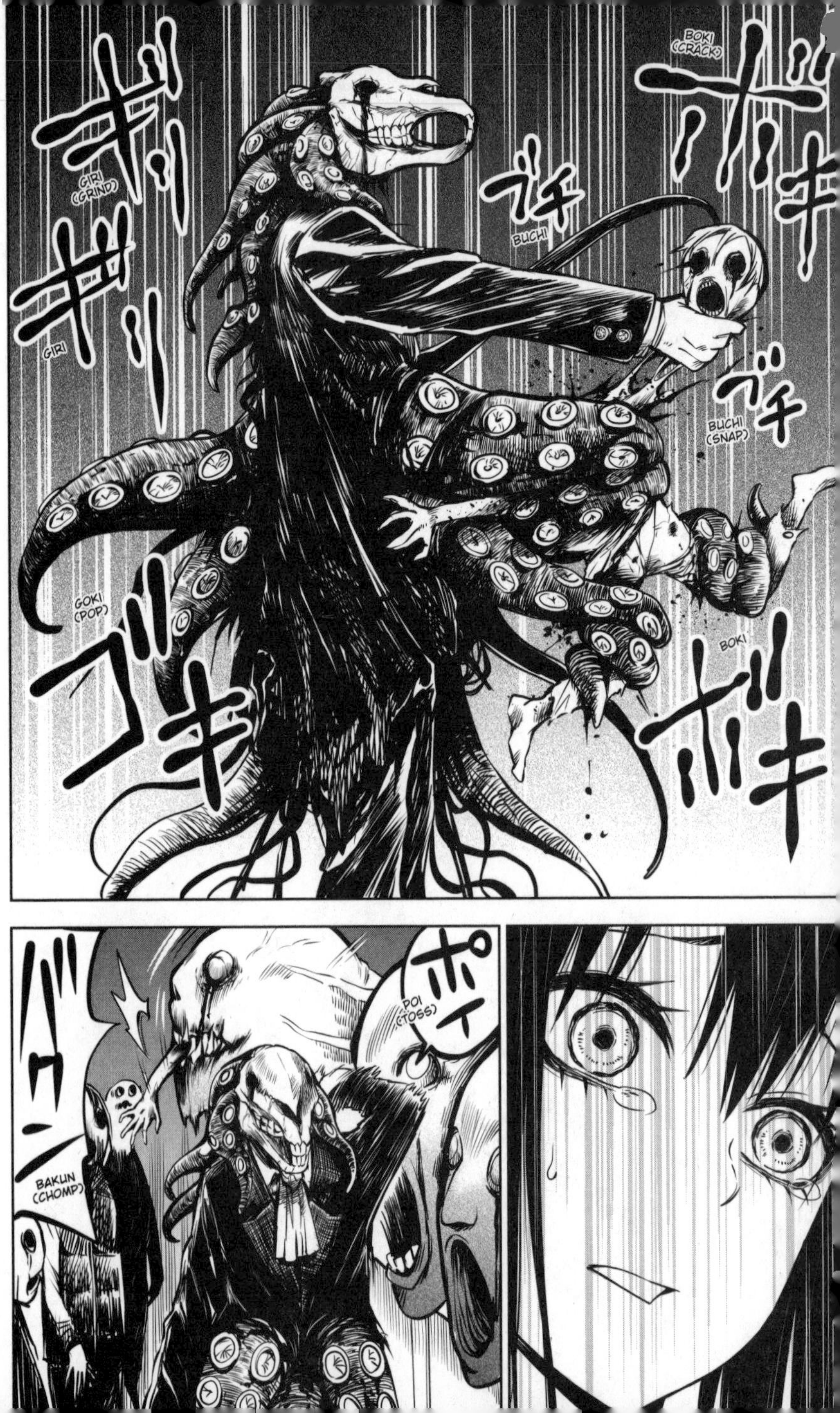
BOKI (CRACK)
BUCHI
GIRI (GRIND)
GIRI
BUCHI (SNAP)
BOKI
GOKI (POP)
POI (TOSS)
BAKUN (CHOMP)

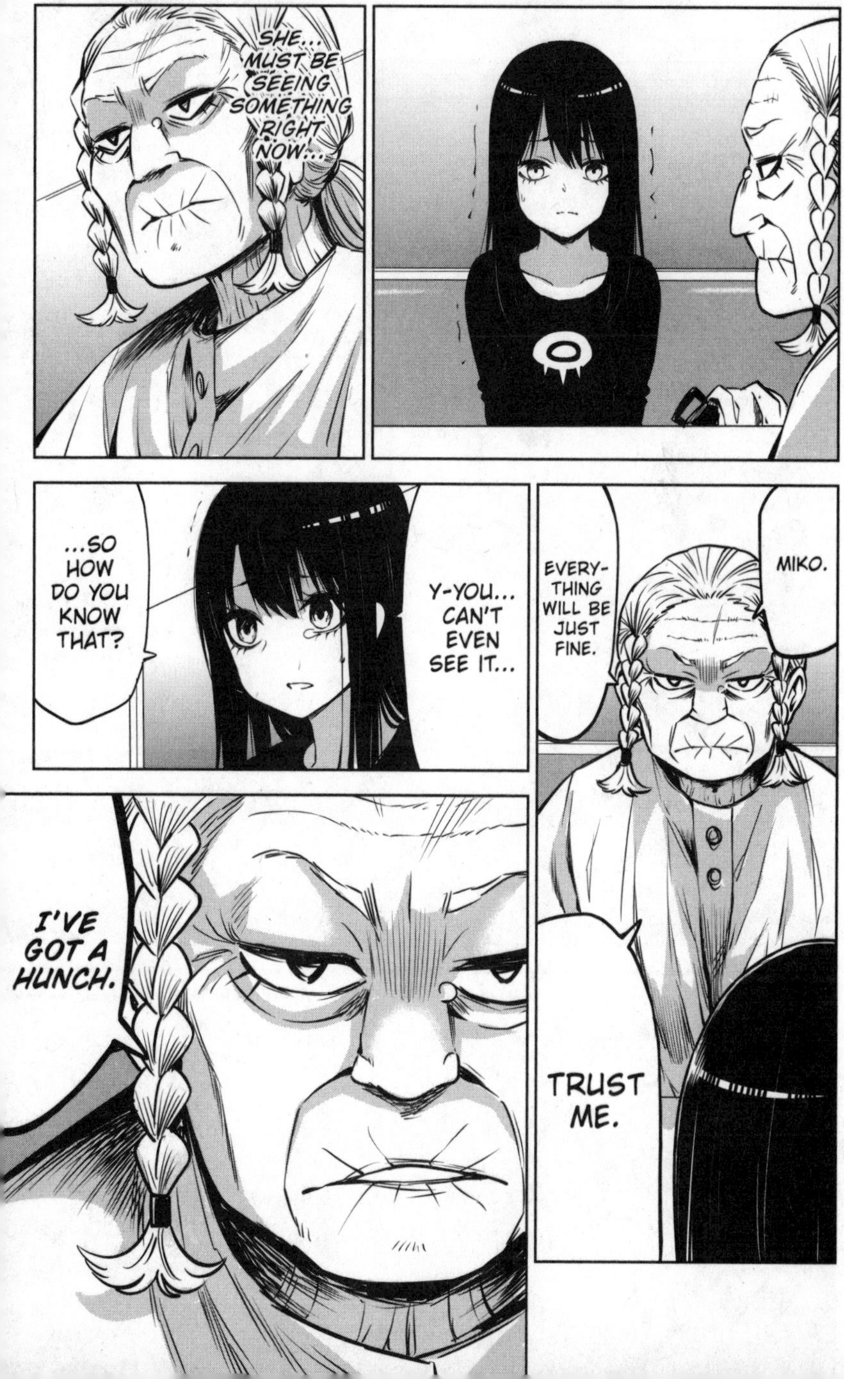
SHE... MUST BE SEEING SOMETHING RIGHT NOW...
MIKO.
EVERYTHING WILL BE JUST FINE.
TRUST ME.
Y-YOU... CAN'T EVEN SEE IT...
...SO HOW DO YOU KNOW THAT?
I'VE GOT A HUNCH.

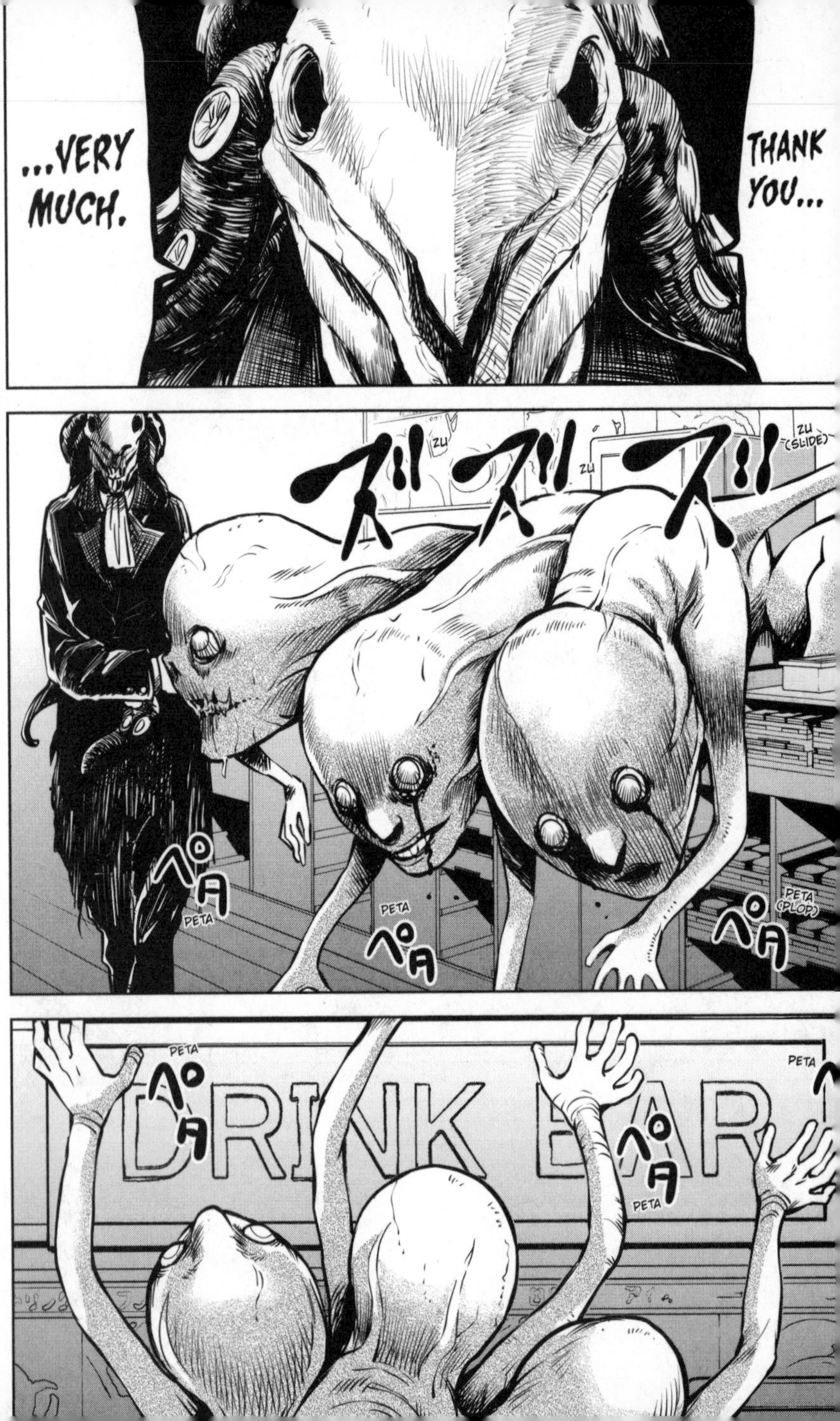
THANK YOU...
...VERY MUCH.
ZU (SLIDE)
ZU
ZU
PETA (PLOP)
PETA
PETA
PETA
PETA
DRINK BAR
PETA

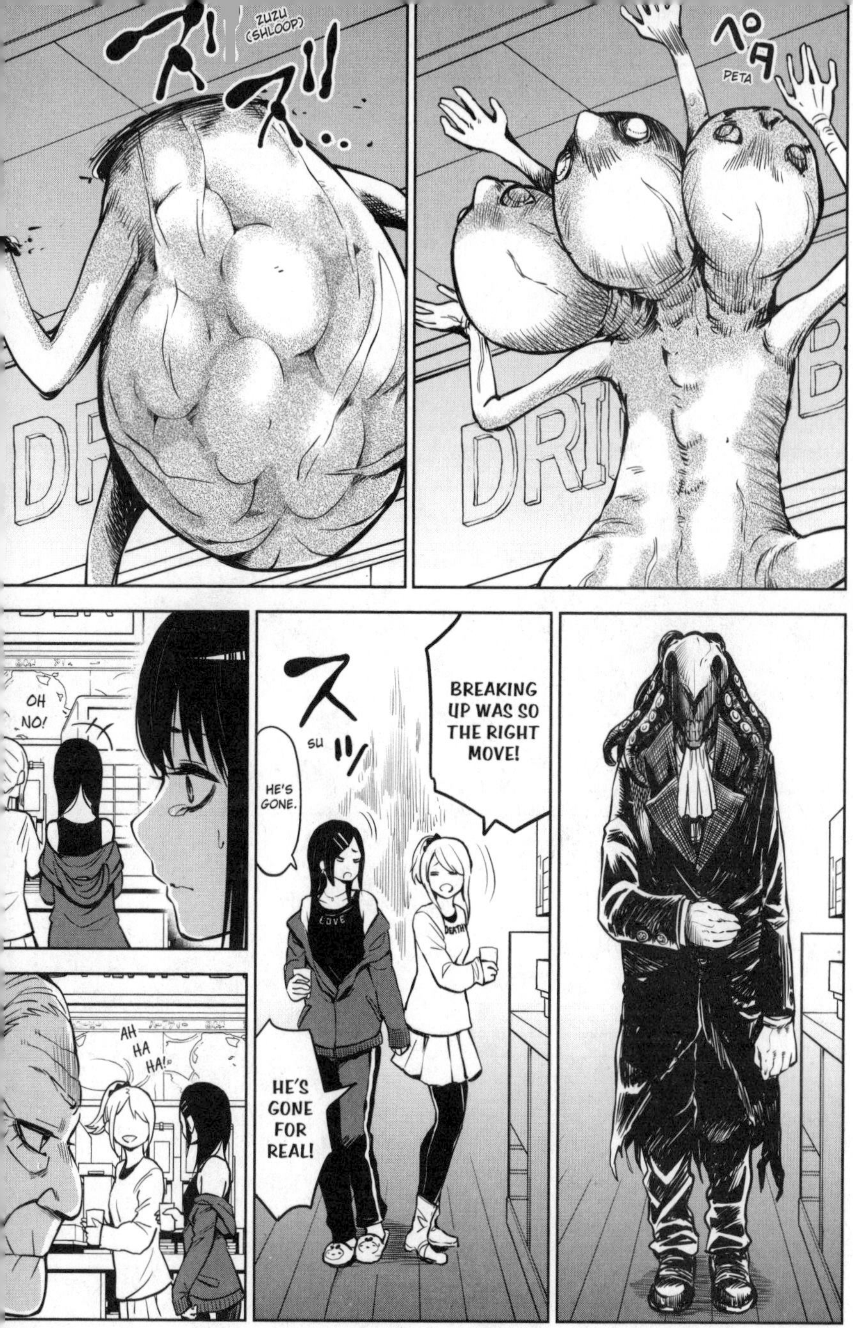

ペタ
PETA
ズリ ズリ
ZUZU (SHLOOP)
BREAKING UP WAS SO THE RIGHT MOVE!
スッ
SU
HE'S GONE.
HE'S GONE FOR REAL!
OH NO!
AH HA HA!

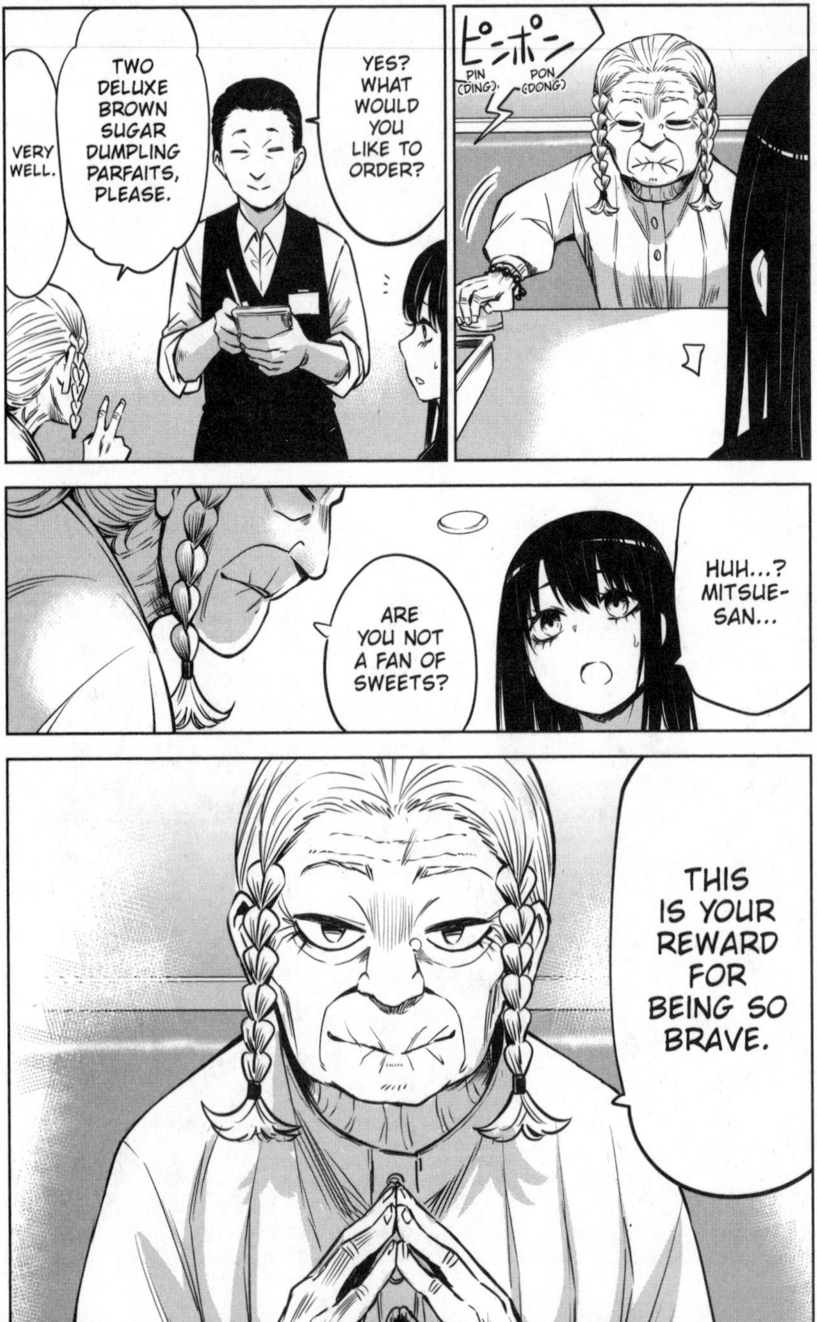
ピンポン
PIN (DING), PON (DONG)
YES? WHAT WOULD YOU LIKE TO ORDER?
TWO DELUXE BROWN SUGAR DUMPLING PARFAITS, PLEASE.
VERY WELL.
HUH...? MITSUE-SAN...
ARE YOU NOT A FAN OF SWEETS?
THIS IS YOUR REWARD FOR BEING SO BRAVE.

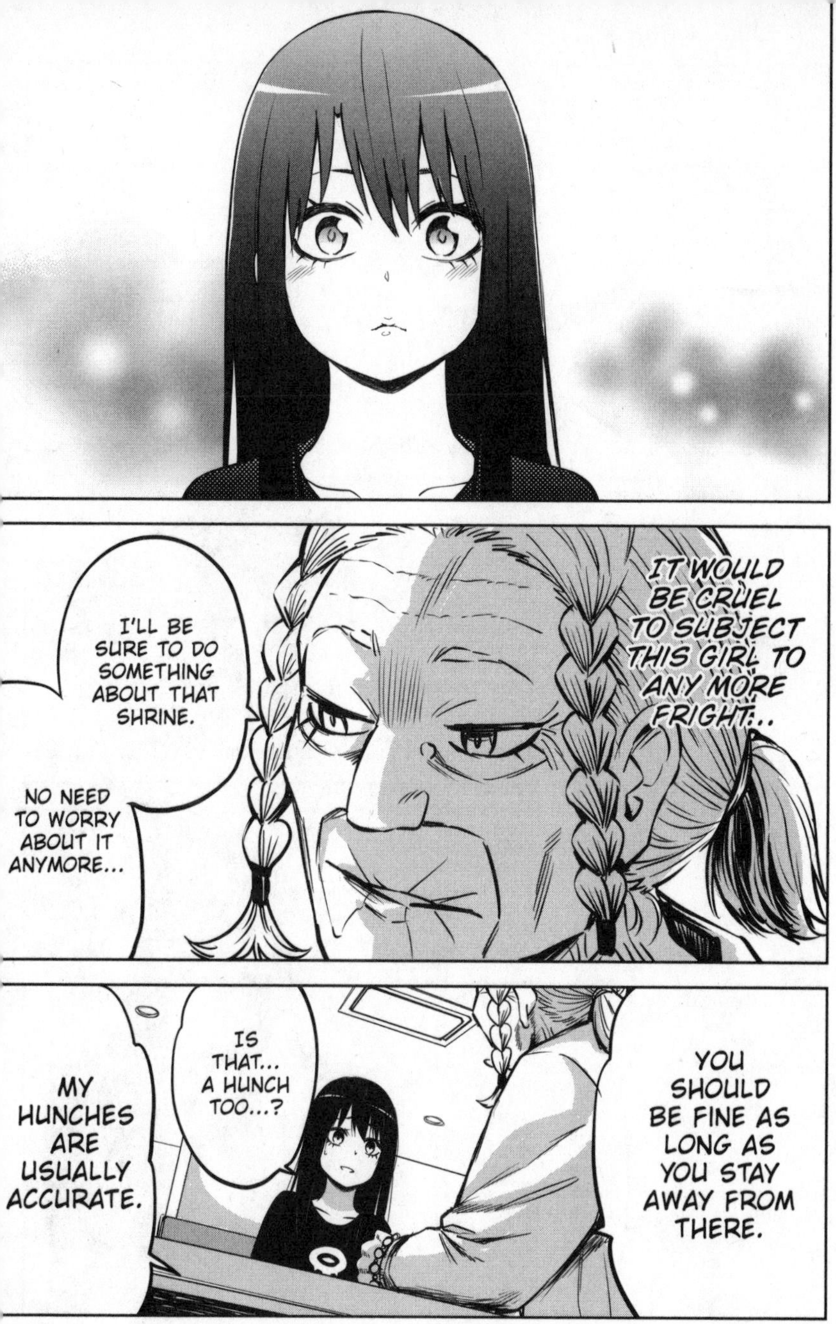
IT WOULD BE CRUEL TO SUBJECT THIS GIRL TO ANY MORE FRIGHT...
I'LL BE SURE TO DO SOMETHING ABOUT THAT SHRINE.
NO NEED TO WORRY ABOUT IT ANYMORE...
YOU SHOULD BE FINE AS LONG AS YOU STAY AWAY FROM THERE.
IS THAT... A HUNCH TOO...?
MY HUNCHES ARE USUALLY ACCURATE.

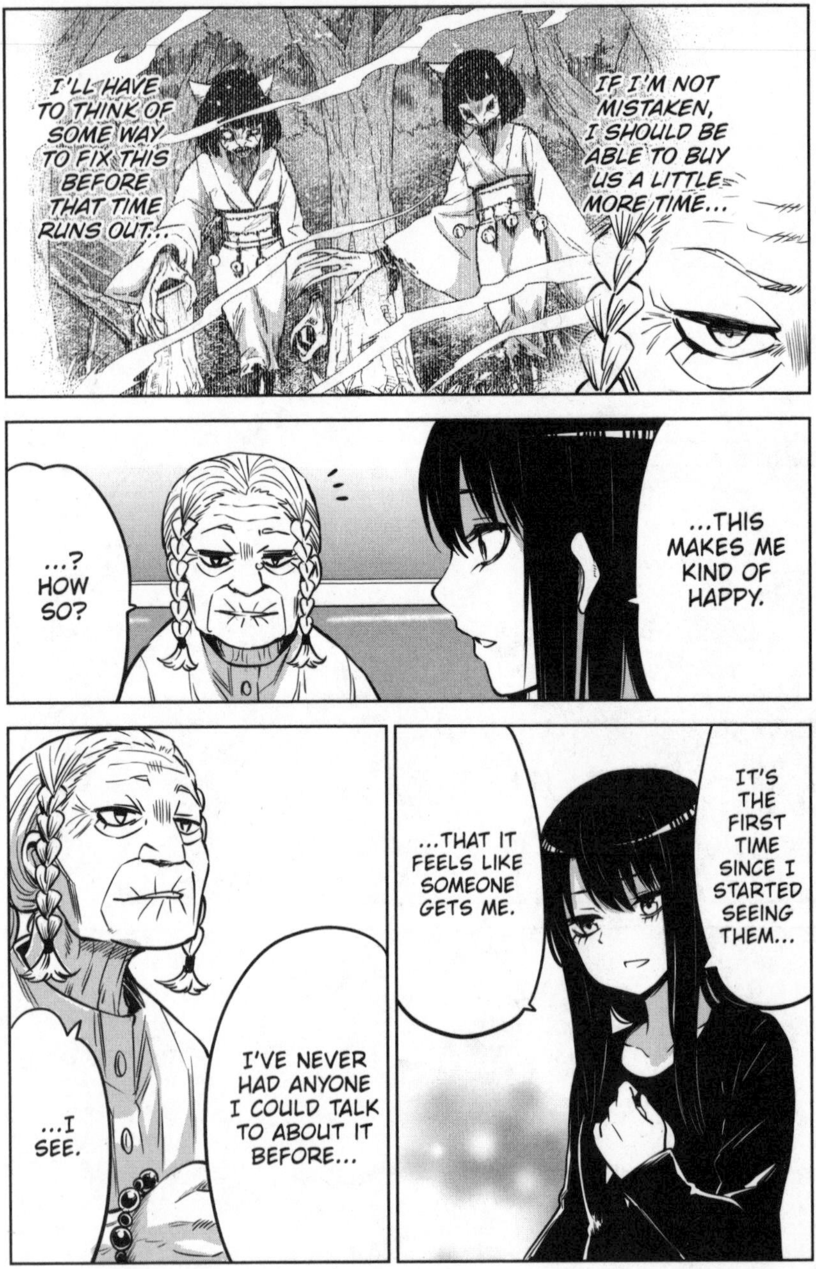
IF I'M NOT MISTAKEN, I SHOULD BE ABLE TO BUY US A LITTLE MORE TIME...
I'LL HAVE TO THINK OF SOME WAY TO FIX THIS BEFORE THAT TIME RUNS OUT...
...THIS MAKES ME KIND OF HAPPY.
...? HOW SO?
IT'S THE FIRST TIME SINCE I STARTED SEEING THEM...
...THAT IT FEELS LIKE SOMEONE GETS ME.
I'VE NEVER HAD ANYONE I COULD TALK TO ABOUT IT BEFORE...
...I SEE.

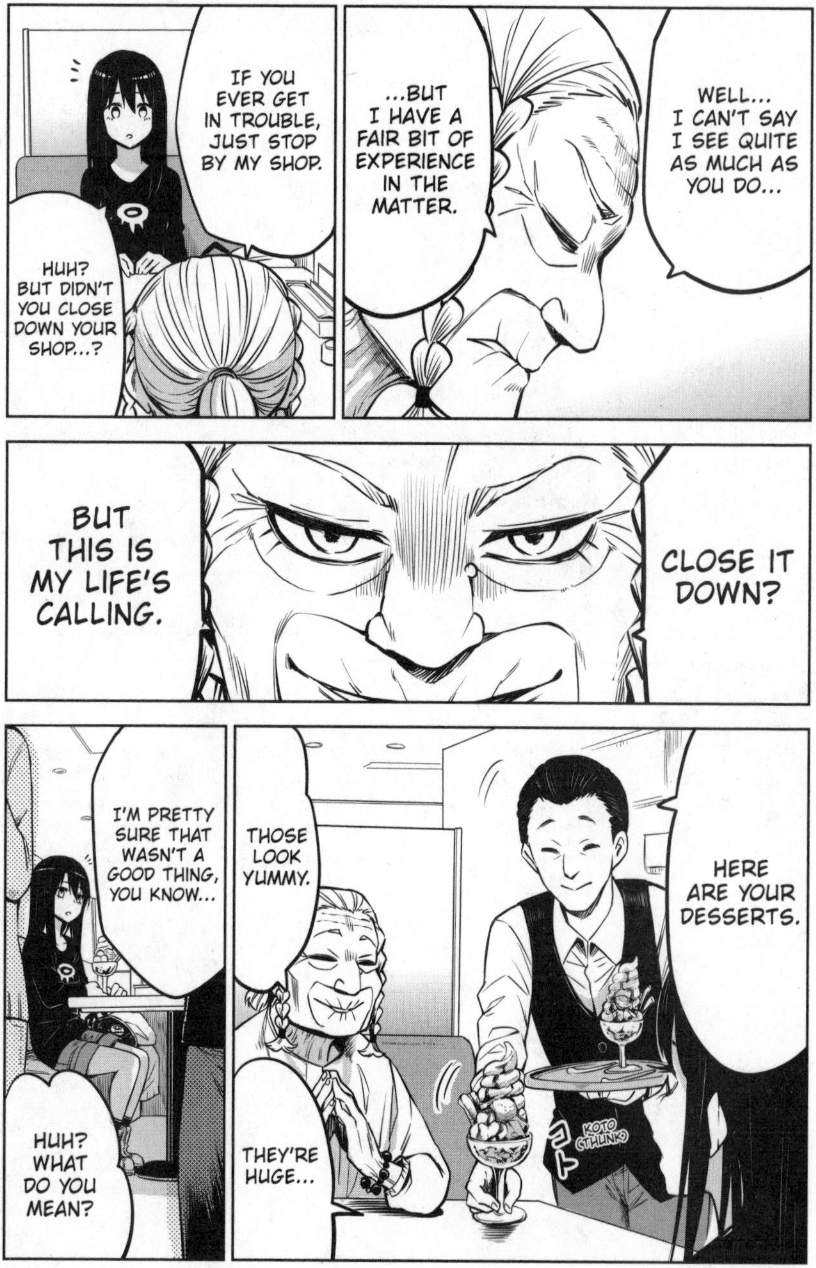
WELL... I CAN'T SAY I SEE QUITE AS MUCH AS YOU DO...
...BUT I HAVE A FAIR BIT OF EXPERIENCE IN THE MATTER.
IF YOU EVER GET IN TROUBLE, JUST STOP BY MY SHOP.
HUH? BUT DIDN'T YOU CLOSE DOWN YOUR SHOP...?
CLOSE IT DOWN?
BUT THIS IS MY LIFE'S CALLING.
HERE ARE YOUR DESSERTS.
KOTO (THUNK)
THOSE LOOK YUMMY.
THEY'RE HUGE...
I'M PRETTY SURE THAT WASN'T A GOOD THING, YOU KNOW...
HUH? WHAT DO YOU MEAN?

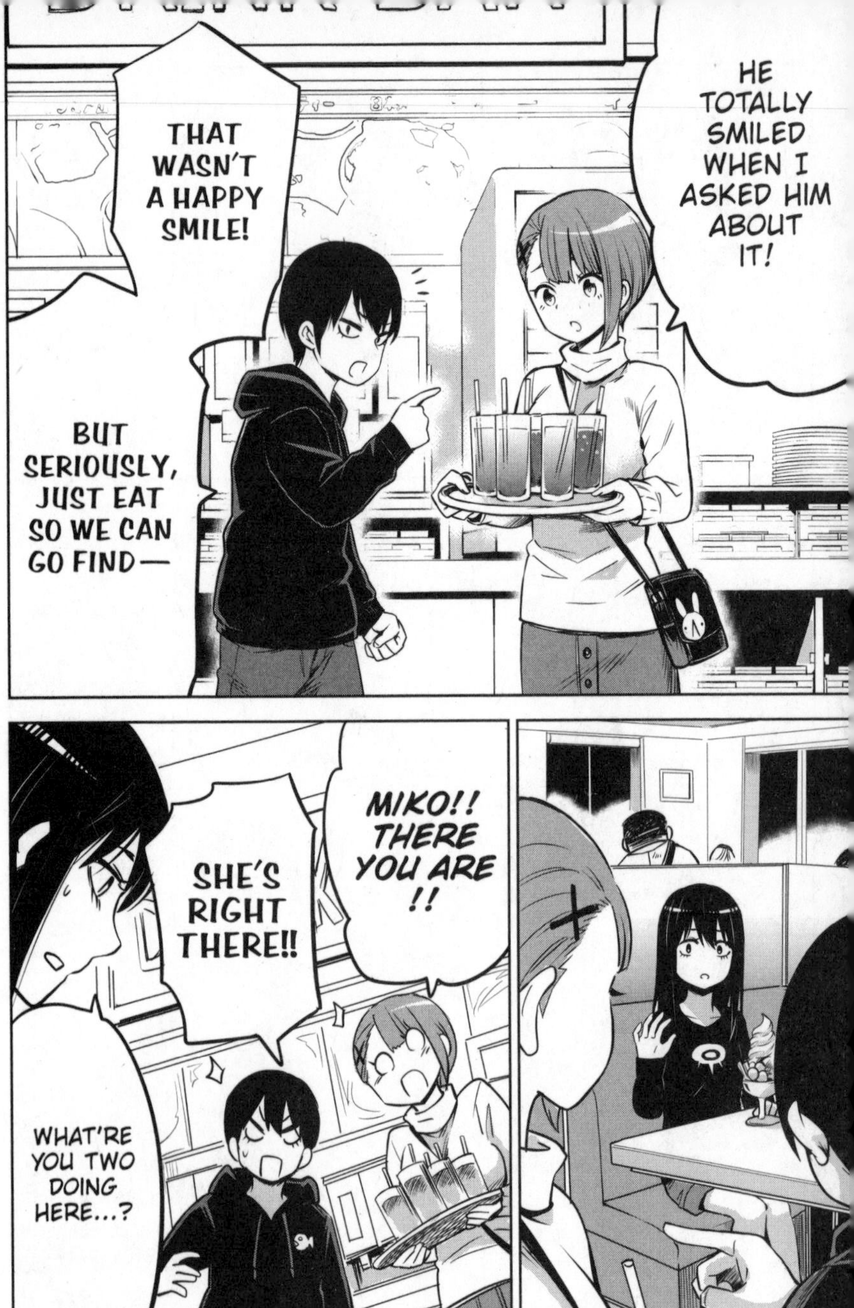
HE TOTALLY SMILED WHEN I ASKED HIM ABOUT IT!
THAT WASN'T A HAPPY SMILE!
BUT SERIOUSLY, JUST EAT SO WE CAN GO FIND—
MIKO!! THERE YOU ARE!!
SHE'S RIGHT THERE!!
WHAT'RE YOU TWO DOING HERE...?

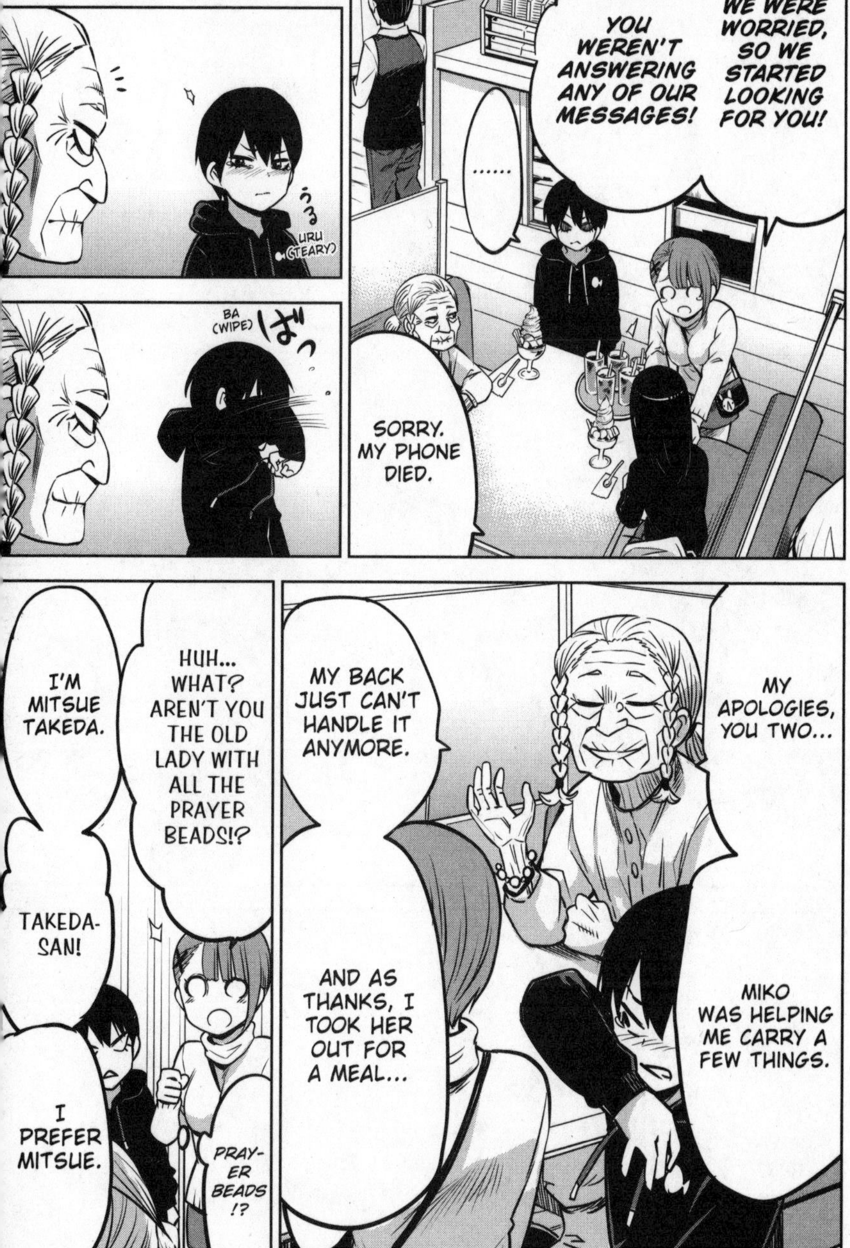
WE WERE WORRIED, SO WE STARTED LOOKING FOR YOU!
YOU WEREN'T ANSWERING ANY OF OUR MESSAGES!
......
SORRY. MY PHONE DIED.
うる
URU (TEARY)
ばっ
BA (WIPE)
MY APOLOGIES, YOU TWO...
MY BACK JUST CAN'T HANDLE IT ANYMORE.
MIKO WAS HELPING ME CARRY A FEW THINGS.
AND AS THANKS, I TOOK HER OUT FOR A MEAL...
HUH... WHAT? AREN'T YOU THE OLD LADY WITH ALL THE PRAYER BEADS!?
I'M MITSUE TAKEDA.
TAKEDA-SAN!
PRAYER BEADS!?
I PREFER MITSUE.

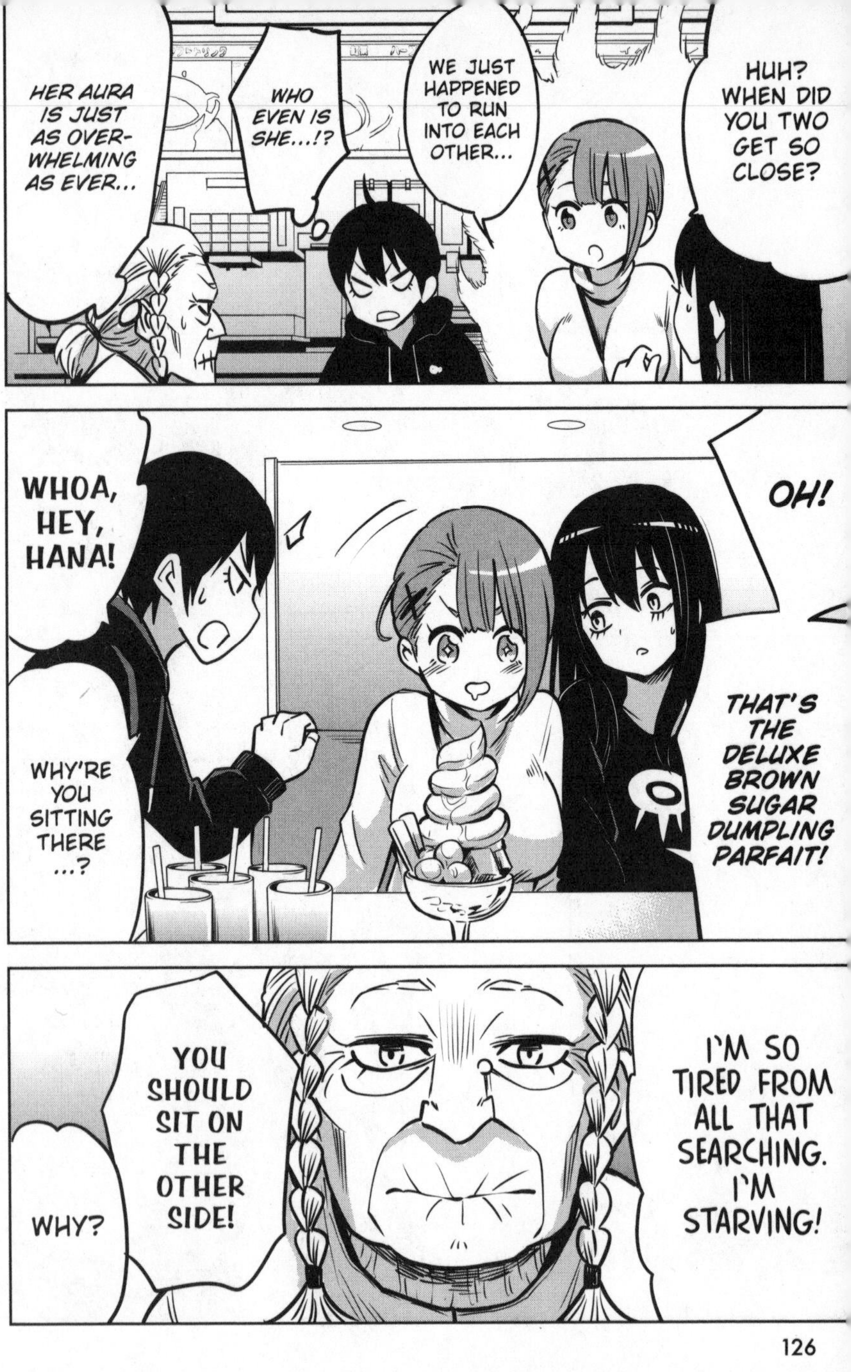
HUH? WHEN DID YOU TWO GET SO CLOSE?
WE JUST HAPPENED TO RUN INTO EACH OTHER...
WHO EVEN IS SHE...!?
HER AURA IS JUST AS OVER-WHELMING AS EVER...
OH!
THAT'S THE DELUXE BROWN SUGAR DUMPLING PARFAIT!
WHOA, HEY, HANA!
WHY'RE YOU SITTING THERE ...?
I'M SO TIRED FROM ALL THAT SEARCHING. I'M STARVING!
YOU SHOULD SIT ON THE OTHER SIDE!
WHY?

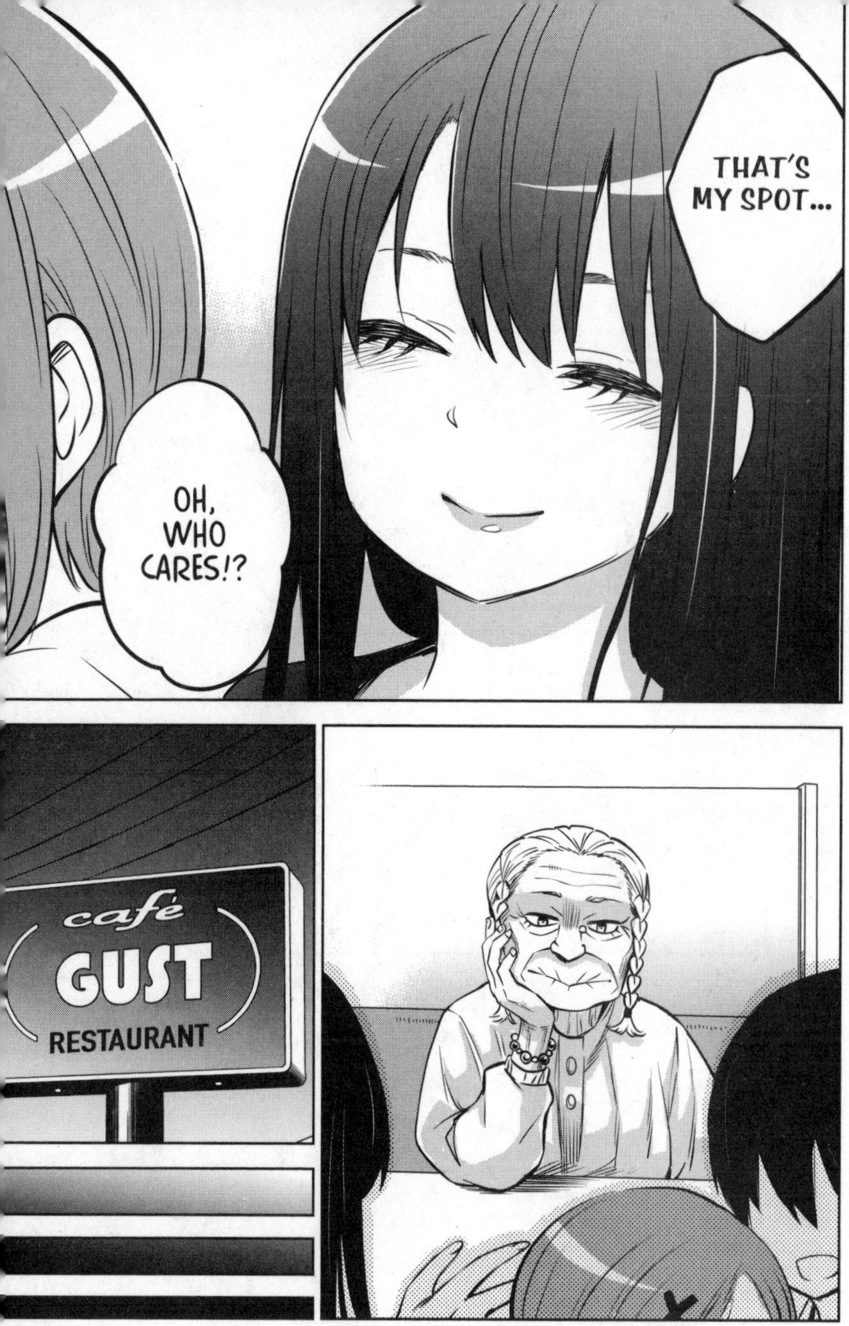
THAT'S MY SPOT...
OH, WHO CARES!?
café GUST RESTAURANT

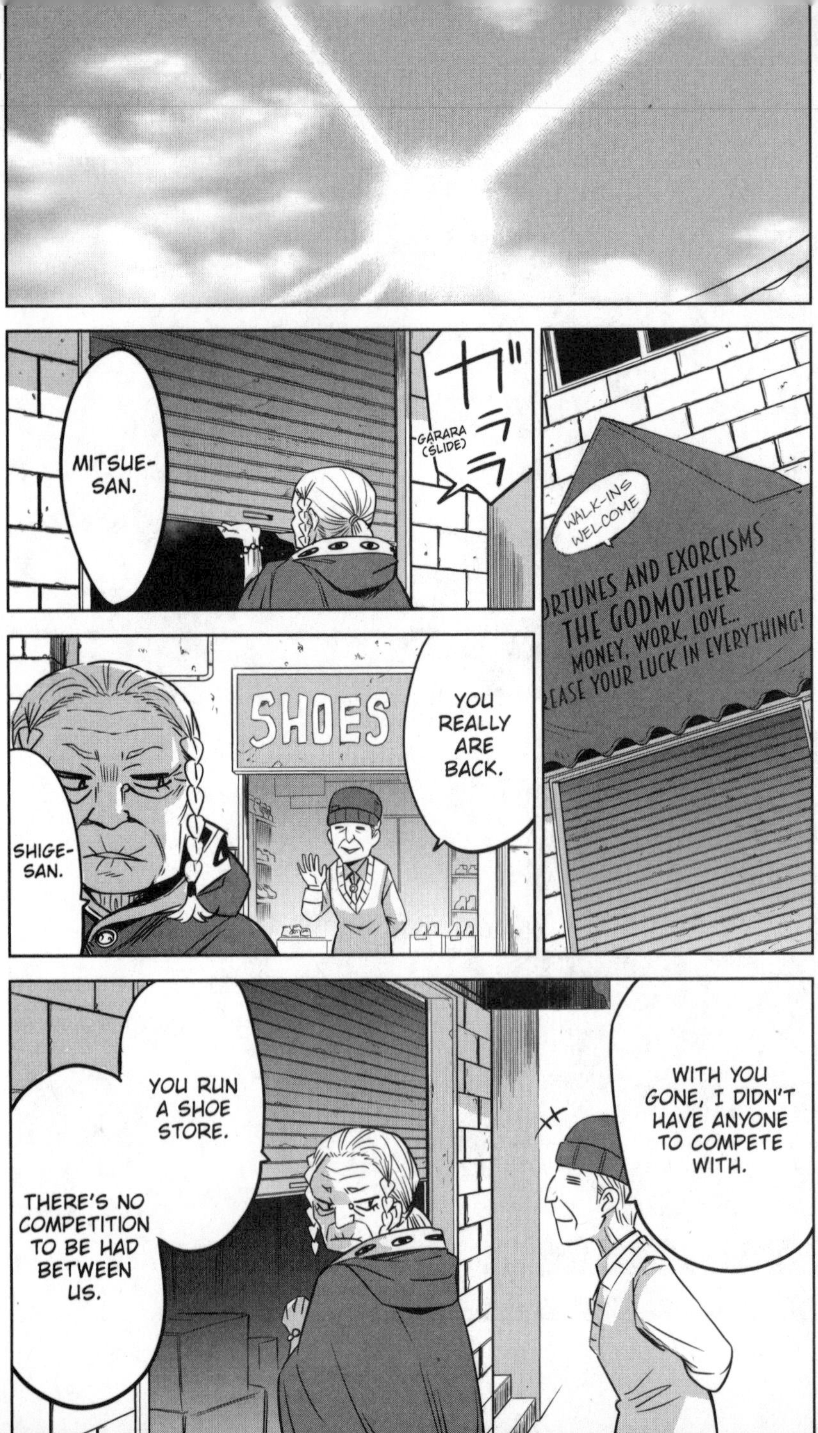
WALK-INS WELCOME
ORTUNES AND EXORCISMS
THE GODMOTHER
MONEY, WORK, LOVE...
REASE YOUR LUCK IN EVERYTHING!
ガララ
GARARA (SLIDE)
MITSUE-SAN.
SHOES
YOU REALLY ARE BACK.
SHIGE-SAN.
WITH YOU GONE, I DIDN'T HAVE ANYONE TO COMPETE WITH.
YOU RUN A SHOE STORE.
THERE'S NO COMPETITION TO BE HAD BETWEEN US.

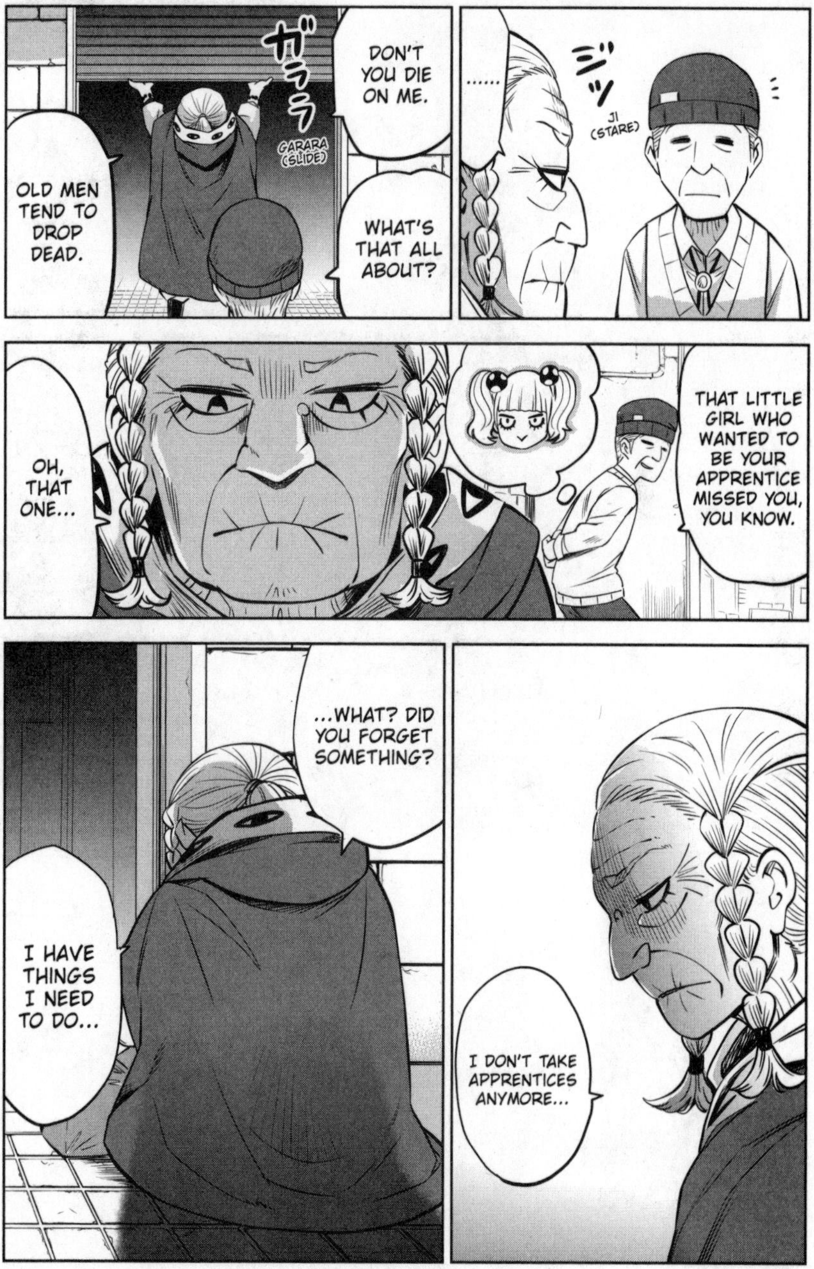
......
ジッ
JI (STARE)
DON'T YOU DIE ON ME.
ガラララ
GARARA (SLIDE)
WHAT'S THAT ALL ABOUT?
OLD MEN TEND TO DROP DEAD.
THAT LITTLE GIRL WHO WANTED TO BE YOUR APPRENTICE MISSED YOU, YOU KNOW.
OH, THAT ONE...
I DON'T TAKE APPRENTICES ANYMORE...
...WHAT? DID YOU FORGET SOMETHING?
I HAVE THINGS I NEED TO DO...

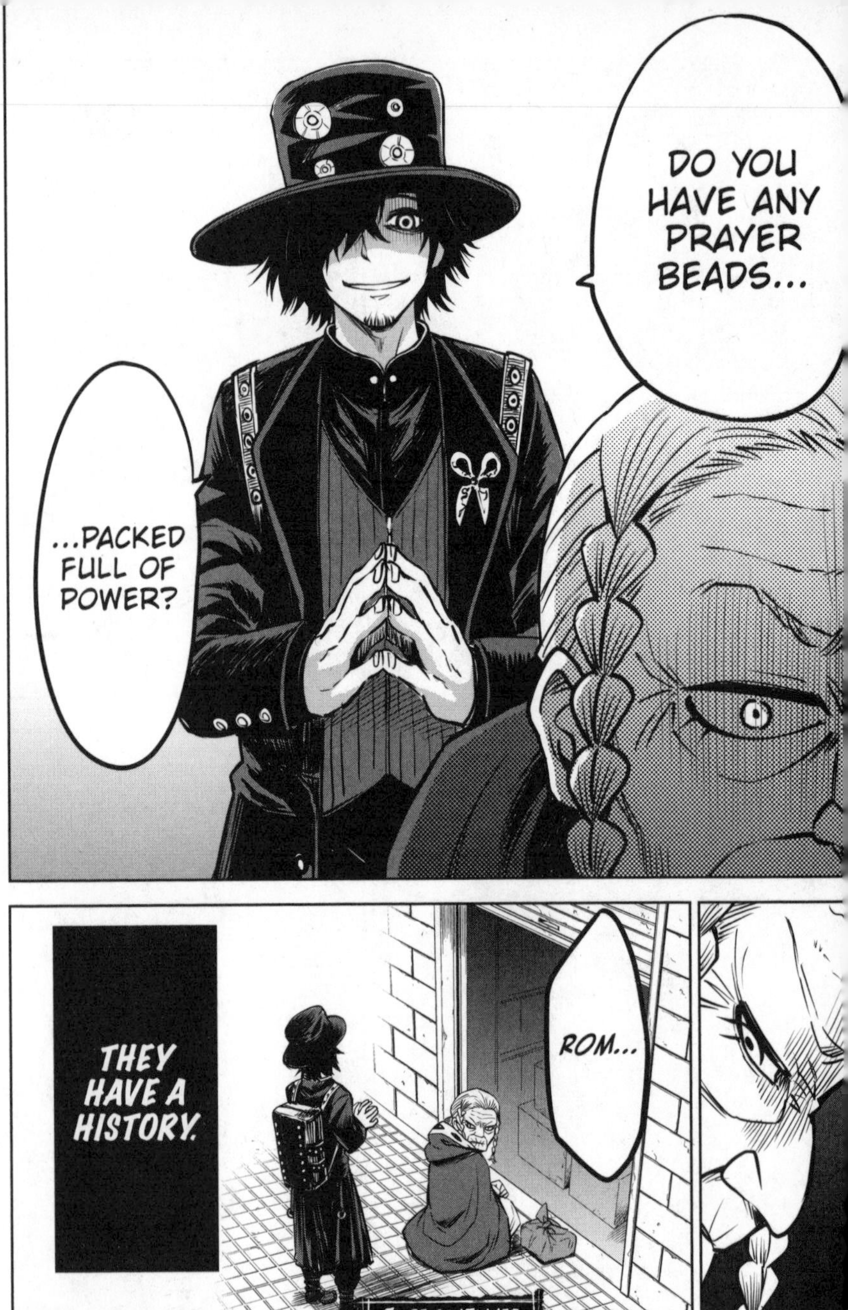
DO YOU HAVE ANY PRAYER BEADS...
...PACKED FULL OF POWER?
ROM...
THEY HAVE A HISTORY.
TO BE CONTINUED

MIERUKO-CHAN

HONORIFICS

-SAN:
The Japanese equivalent of Mr./Mrs./
Miss. If a situation calls for politeness,
this is the fail-safe honorific.

-KUN:
Used most often when referring to boys, this indicates
affection or familiarity. Occasionally, it is used by
older men among their peers, but it may also be used
by anyone referring to a person of lower standing.

-CHAN:
An affectionate honorific indicating familiarity used
mostly in reference to girls; also used in reference
to cute persons or animals of either gender.

-SENSEI:
A respectful term for teachers, artists,
or high-level professionals.

TRANSLATION NOTES

TITLE:
The title *Mieruko-chan* comes from the main character's name, Miko, and the term *mieru*. *Mieru* literally
translates to "can see" but has a deeper connotation related to invisible things becoming visible and understandable.
Ko means "child" but is also used colloquially as an equivalent for "girl" and as a popular ending for
female names in Japanese. So the literal translation is "girl who can see (invisible things)," which also sounds like
her name, especially with the *-chan* suffix attached.

PAGE 16:
My Nearby Troll 2 by **Studio Mibli** is a reference to another famous movie studio in Japan. Some of Studio
Mibli's other famous movies include *Demons Away*, *Princess Oboroge*, and *The Dog Returns*.

PAGE 30:
Miko's words reveal her belief that the two spiritual beings who protected her several times already
are actually some type of guardian deity, and so should be treated as such. In keeping with Shinto
religious traditions, Miko decides to present them with an offering. Since Shinto deities are often
based on nature spirits and the like, they usually do not have a human sense of morality, and as such,
offerings are meant as both an expression of gratitude and an attempt to appease the deity.

PAGE 46:
Five hundred yen is approximately $4.56.

PAGE 48:
Donki is a nickname for Don Quijote, one of the biggest discount chains in Japan, totaling over 160 stores.
The products inside range from basic groceries to electronics and clothing.

PAGE 77:
Mon de Ring is a play on the Pon de Ring donut from Mister Donut, made of a circle of connected dough balls.
The name supposedly comes from the Portuguese dish *pão de queijo*, which is a small, baked cheese roll.

Namandabu is a word that originates from the practice of *nenbutsu* in the Buddhist Pure Land sect (Namu Amida
Buddhism). *Nenbutsu* is the art of meditation—specifically when thinking on or contemplating the Buddha. Practitioners
of *nenbutsu* quickly chanting sutras praising the Buddha sometimes sound like they are saying "namandabu" instead.

Amanita muffins are Mrs. D muffins shaped like amanita mushrooms. The mushrooms are red with white spots,
and look very similar to Yuria's hair decorations.

PAGE 94:
Gust refers to a popular restaurant chain in Japan that is known for both its Western and Japanese cuisine.

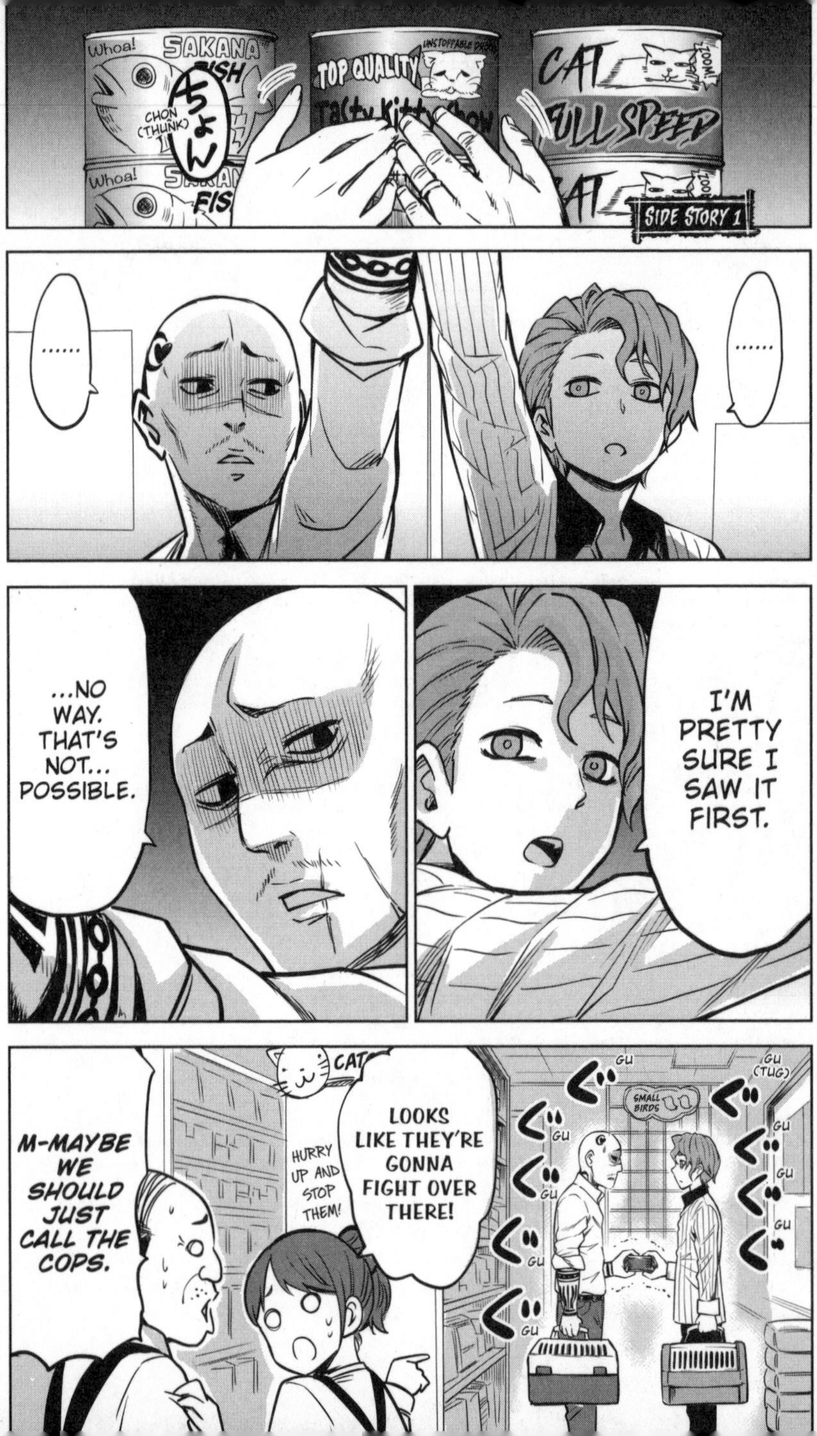
CAT FULL SPEED
ZOOM!
TOP QUALITY
Tasty Kitty Chow
Whoa! SAKANA FISH
ちょん
CHON (THUNK)
SIDE STORY 1
......
......
I'M PRETTY SURE I SAW IT FIRST.
...NO WAY. THAT'S NOT... POSSIBLE.
ぐっ GU (TUG)
GU
SMALL BIRDS
CAT
LOOKS LIKE THEY'RE GONNA FIGHT OVER THERE!
HURRY UP AND STOP THEM!
M-MAYBE WE SHOULD JUST CALL THE COPS.

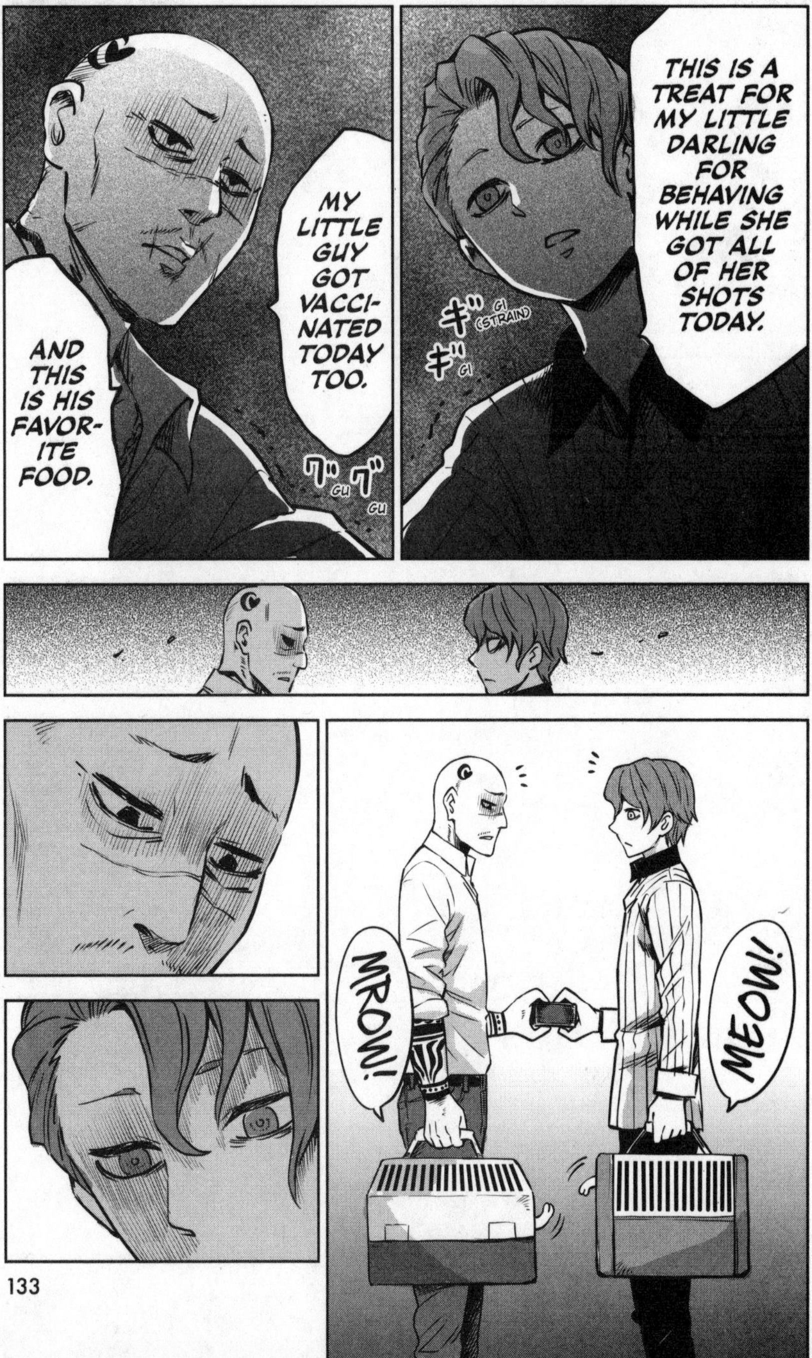
THIS IS A TREAT FOR MY LITTLE DARLING FOR BEHAVING WHILE SHE GOT ALL OF HER SHOTS TODAY.
ギ GI (STRAIN) ギ GI
MY LITTLE GUY GOT VACCINATED TODAY TOO.
AND THIS IS HIS FAVORITE FOOD.
グ GU グ GU
MEOW!
MROW!

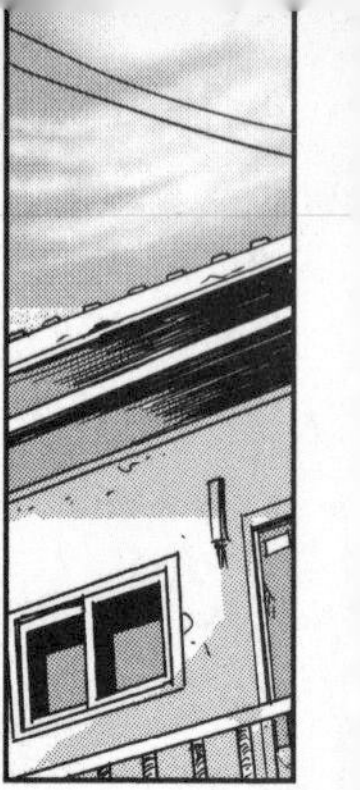
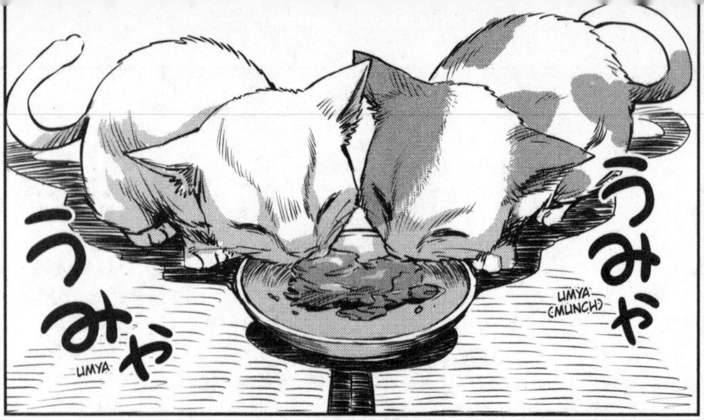
うみゃ
UMYA (MUNCH)
うみゃ
UMYA
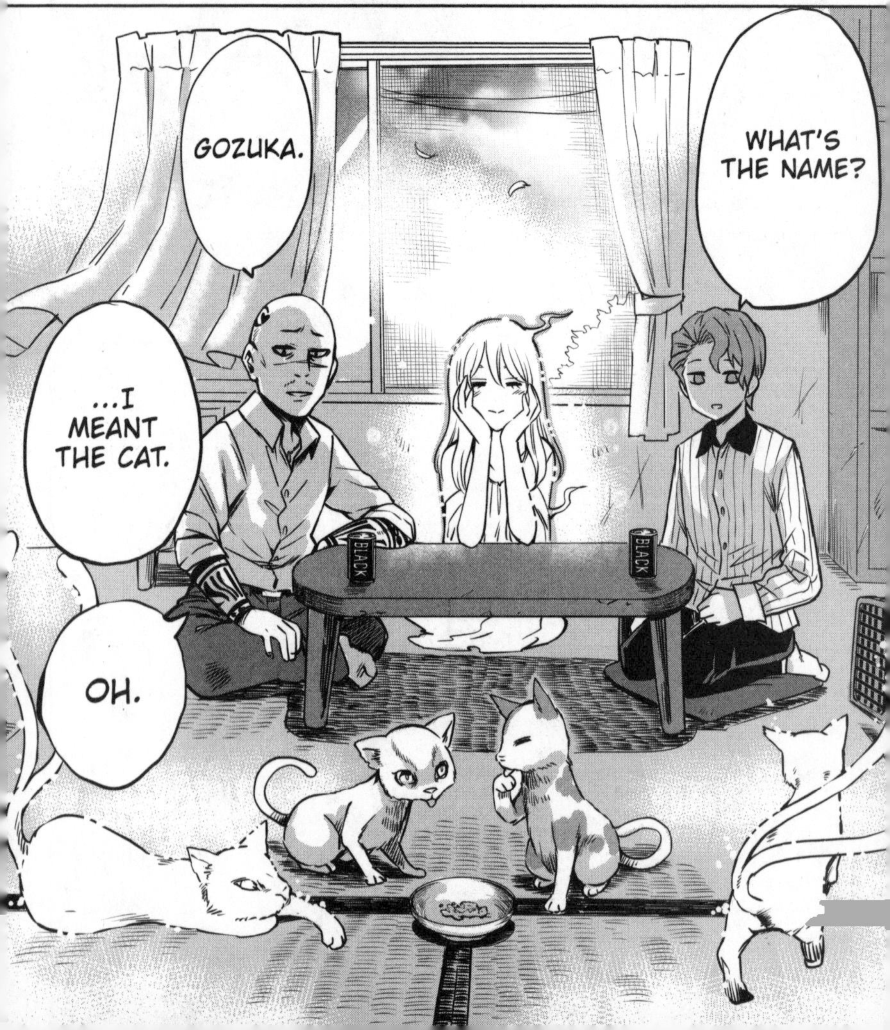
WHAT'S THE NAME?
GOZUKA.
...I MEANT THE CAT.
OH.
BLACK
BLACK

SHOPPING FOR SWIMSUITS (SIGHT VER.)

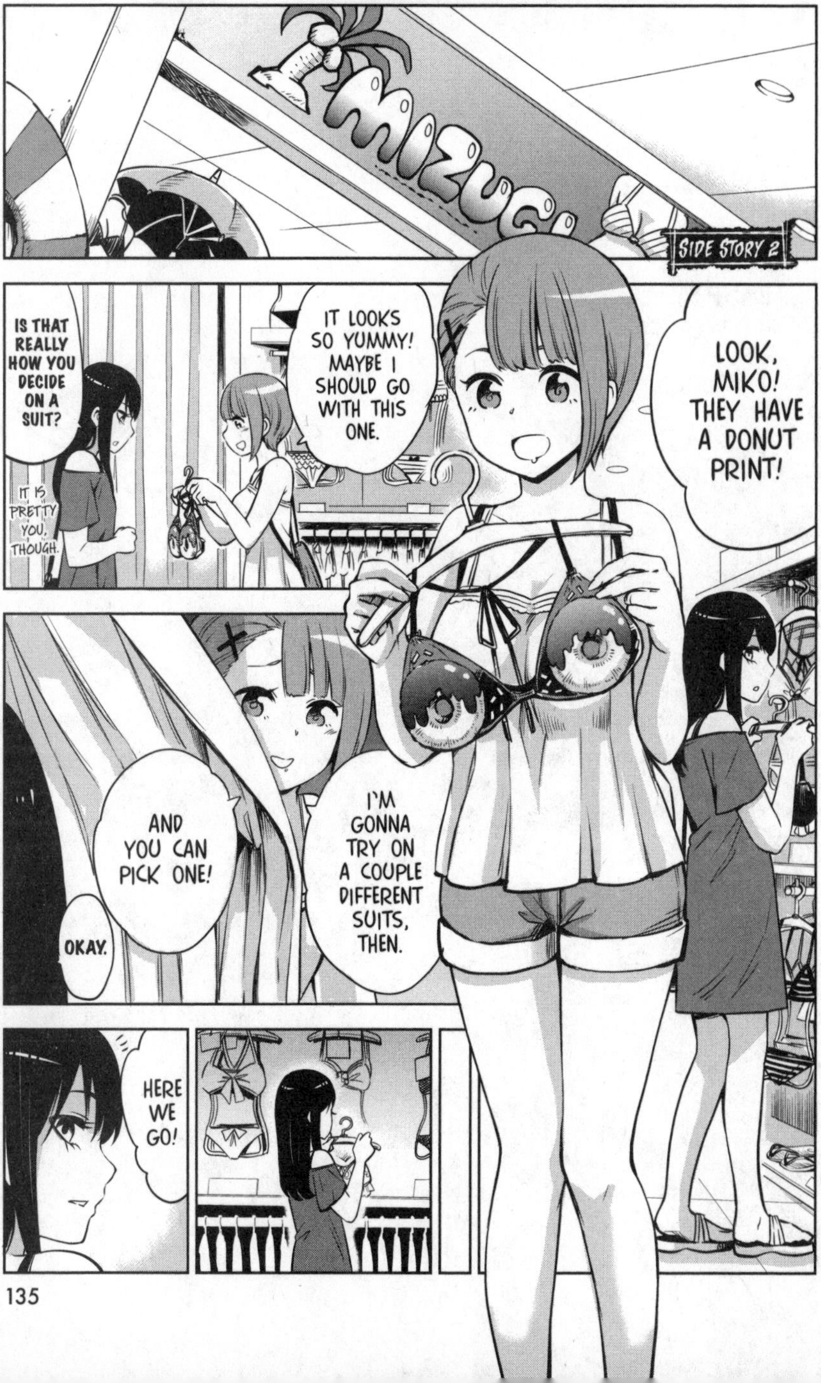
MIZUGI
SIDE STORY 2
LOOK, MIKO! THEY HAVE A DONUT PRINT!
IT LOOKS SO YUMMY! MAYBE I SHOULD GO WITH THIS ONE.
IS THAT REALLY HOW YOU DECIDE ON A SUIT?
IT IS PRETTY YOU, THOUGH.
I'M GONNA TRY ON A COUPLE DIFFERENT SUITS, THEN.
AND YOU CAN PICK ONE!
OKAY.
HERE WE GO!

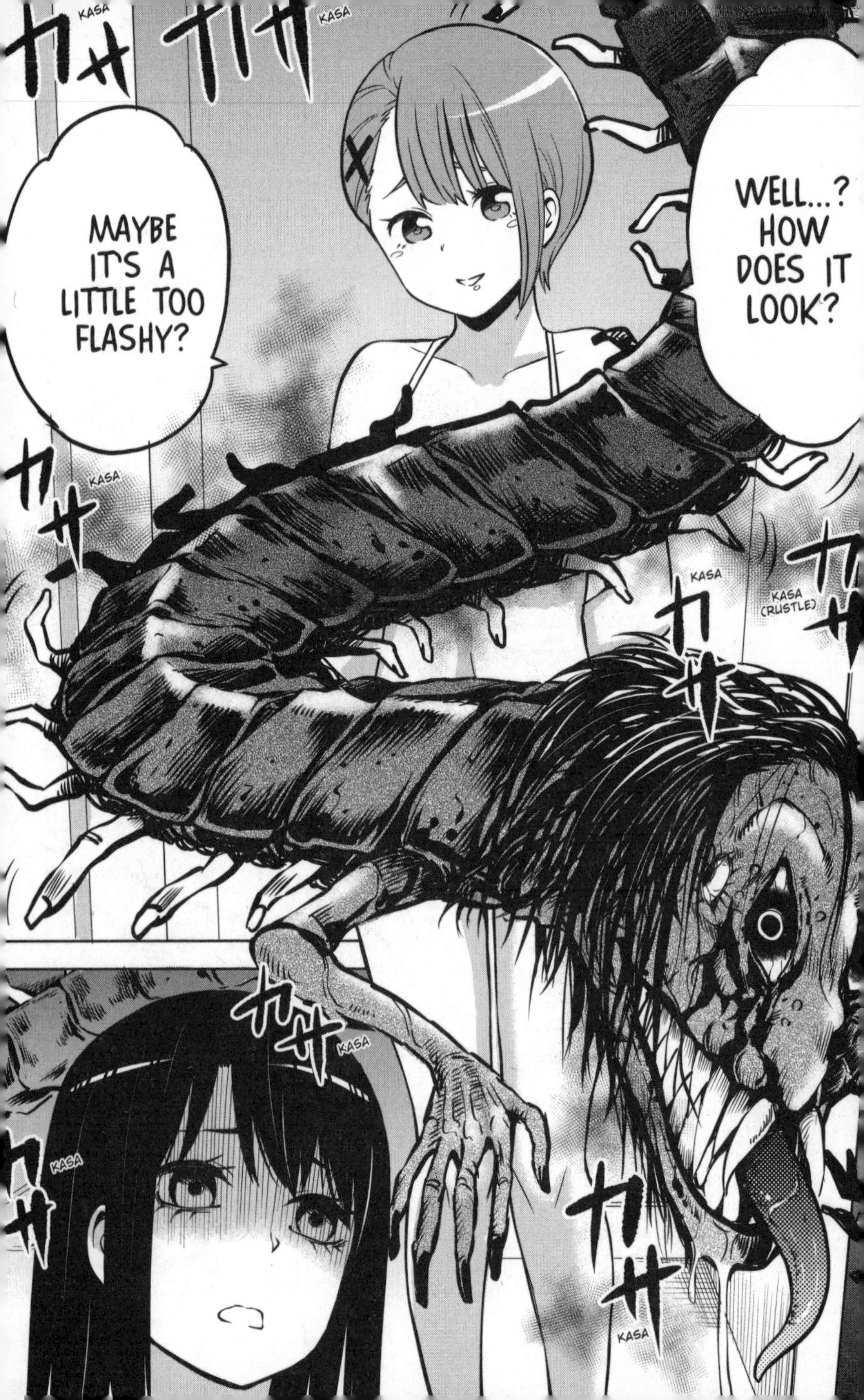

KASA
KASA
WELL...? HOW DOES IT LOOK?
MAYBE IT'S A LITTLE TOO FLASHY?
KASA (RUSTLE)
KASA
KASA
KASA
KASA
KASA

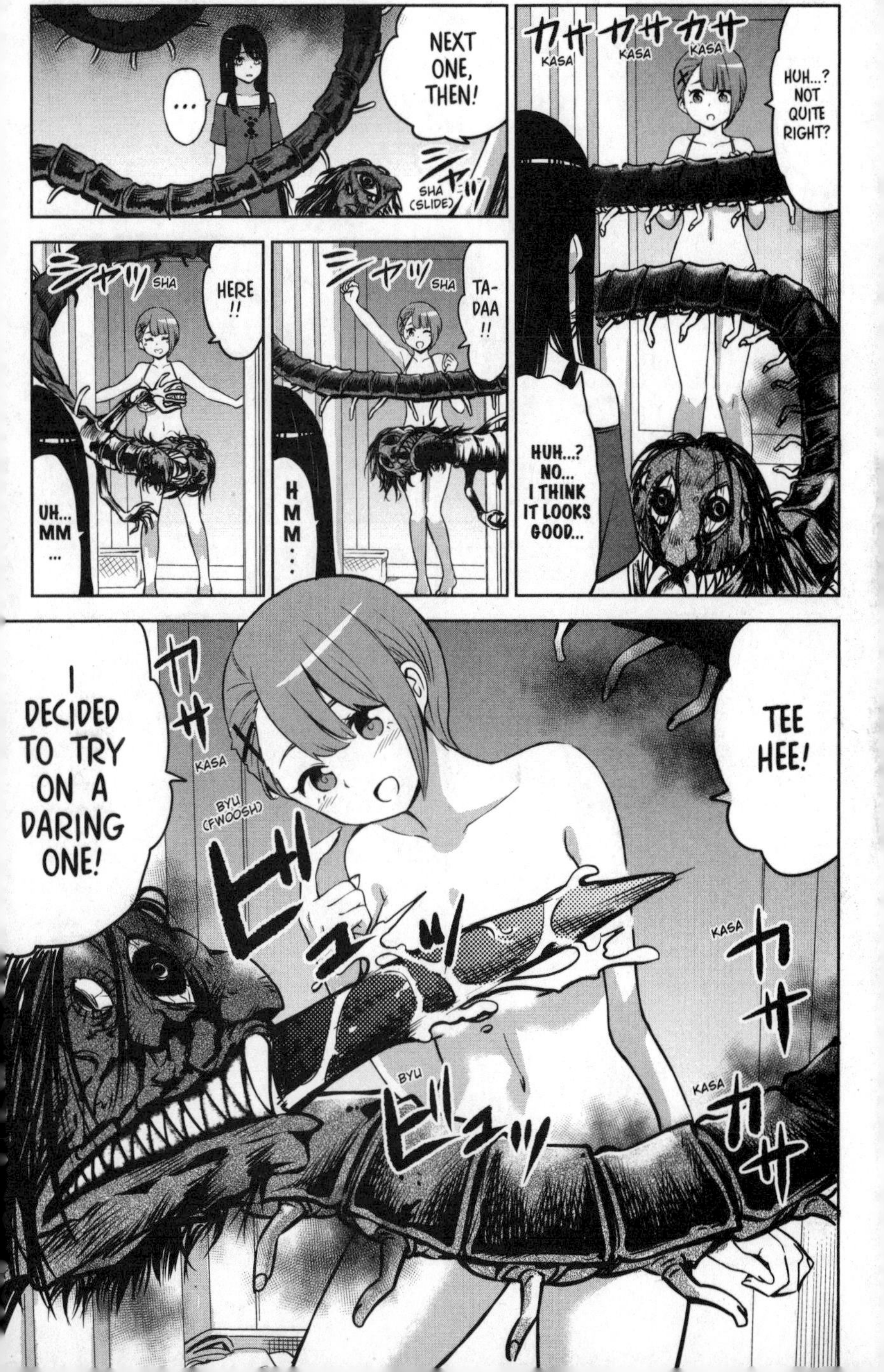
カサカサカサ
KASA KASA KASA
HUH...? NOT QUITE RIGHT?
HUH...? NO... I THINK IT LOOKS GOOD...
NEXT ONE, THEN!
...
SHA (SLIDE)
SHA
TA-DAA!!
HMM...
SHA
HERE!!
UH... MM...
TEE HEE!
I DECIDED TO TRY ON A DARING ONE!
KASA
BYU (FWOOSH)
KASA
BYU
KASA

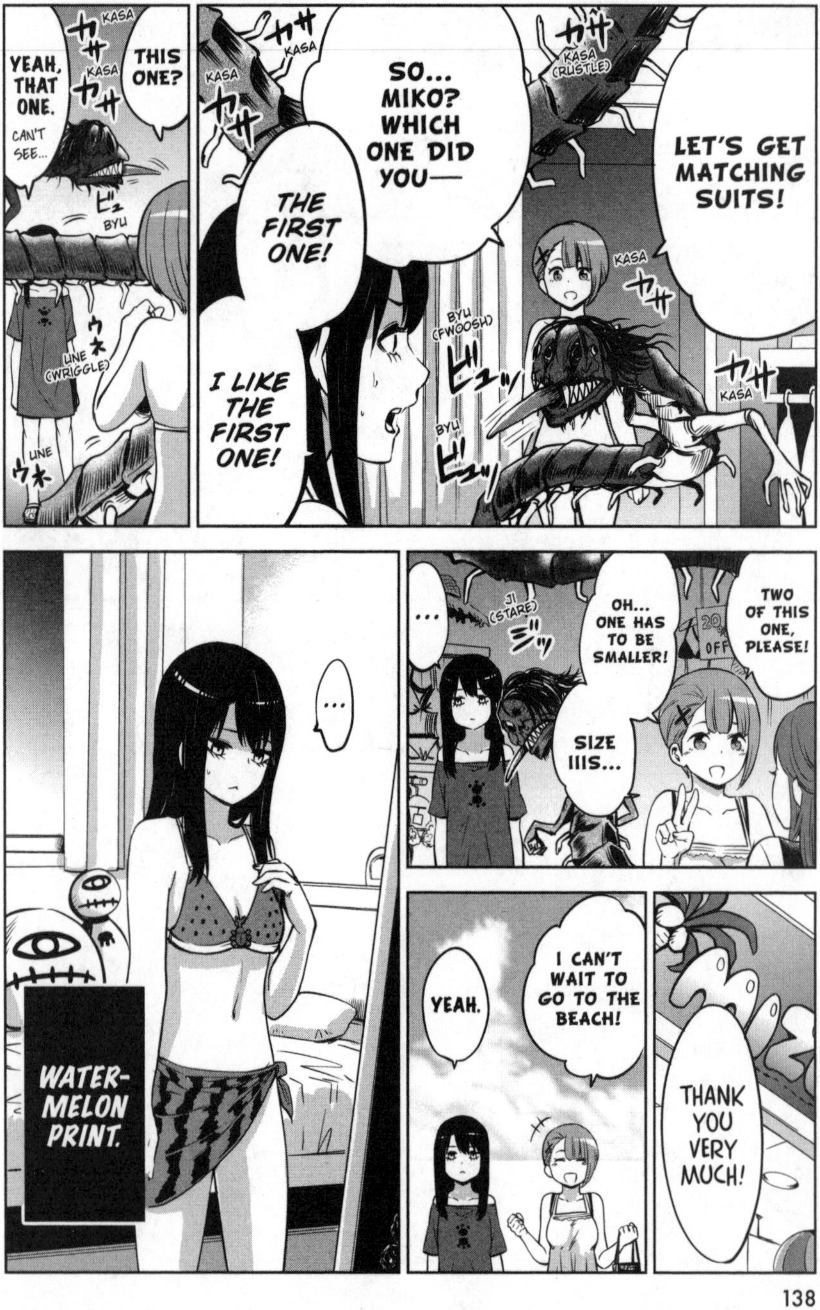
KASA (RUSTLE)
LET'S GET MATCHING SUITS!
KASA
KASA
SO... MIKO? WHICH ONE DID YOU—
KASA
KASA
THE FIRST ONE!
BYU (FWOOSH)
BYU
I LIKE THE FIRST ONE!
KASA
THIS ONE?
KASA
YEAH, THAT ONE.
CAN'T SEE...
BYU
UNE (WRIGGLE)
UNE
TWO OF THIS ONE, PLEASE!
OH... ONE HAS TO BE SMALLER!
JI (STARE)
...
SIZE IIIS...
THANK YOU VERY MUCH!
I CAN'T WAIT TO GO TO THE BEACH!
YEAH.
...
WATER-MELON PRINT.

139

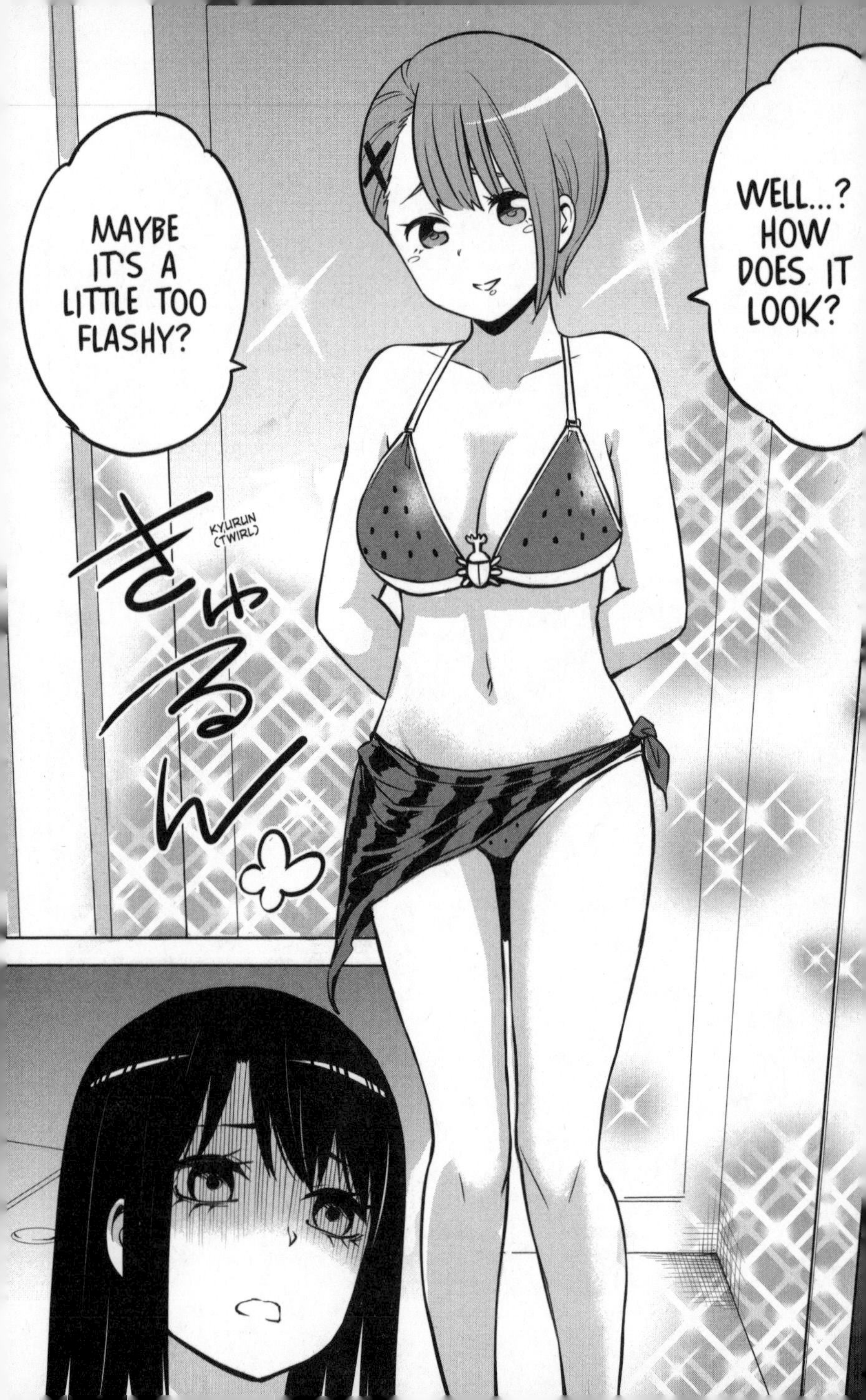
WELL...? HOW DOES IT LOOK?
MAYBE IT'S A LITTLE TOO FLASHY?
きゅるん
KYURUN (TWIRL)

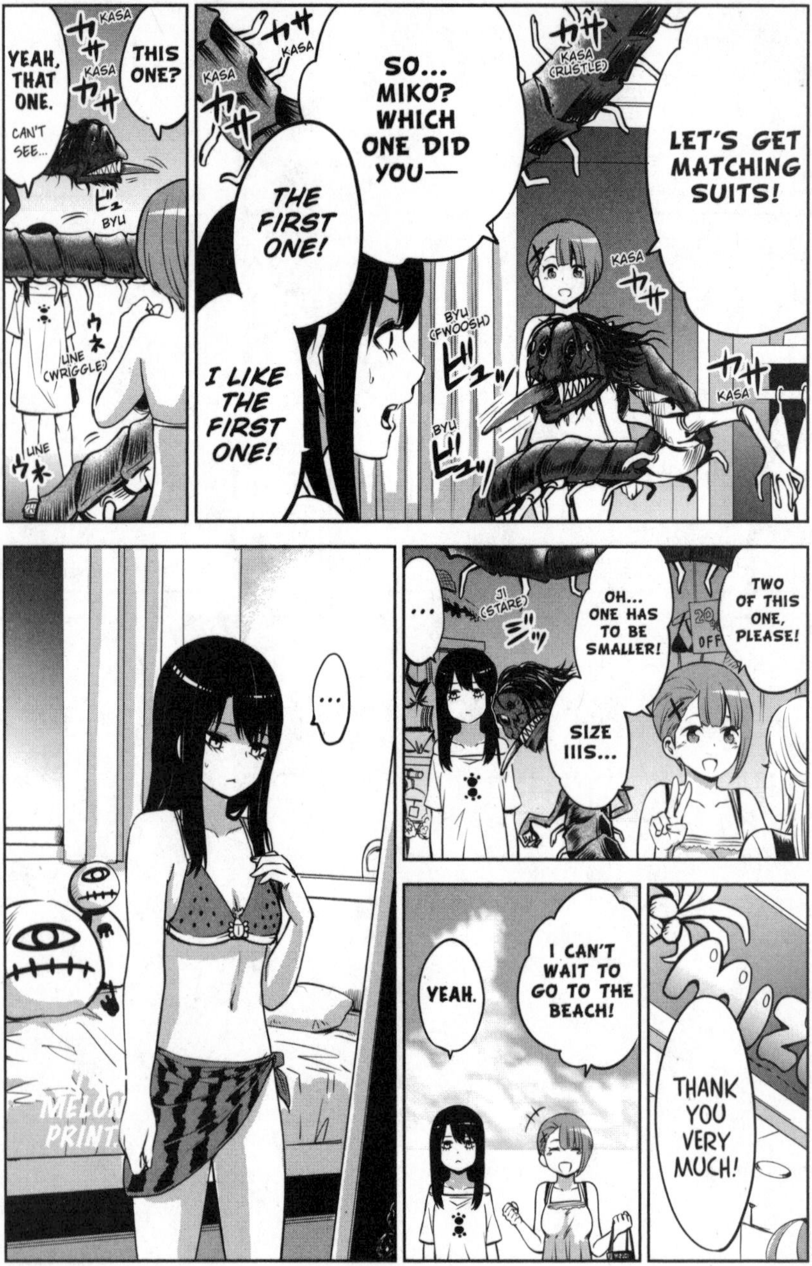
LET'S GET MATCHING SUITS!
カサ
KASA (RUSTLE)
SO... MIKO? WHICH ONE DID YOU—
カサ
KASA
カサ
KASA
カサ
KASA
カサ
KASA
BYU (FWOOSH)
ビュッ
BYU
ビュッ
THE FIRST ONE!
I LIKE THE FIRST ONE!
THIS ONE?
カサ
KASA
カサ
KASA
YEAH, THAT ONE.
CAN'T SEE...
ビュ
BYU
ウネ
UNE (WRIGGLE)
UNE
ウネ
TWO OF THIS ONE, PLEASE!
20% OFF
OH... ONE HAS TO BE SMALLER!
JI (STARE)
ジッ
SIZE IIIS...
...
THANK YOU VERY MUCH!
I CAN'T WAIT TO GO TO THE BEACH!
YEAH.
...
MELON PRINT.

AFTERWORD

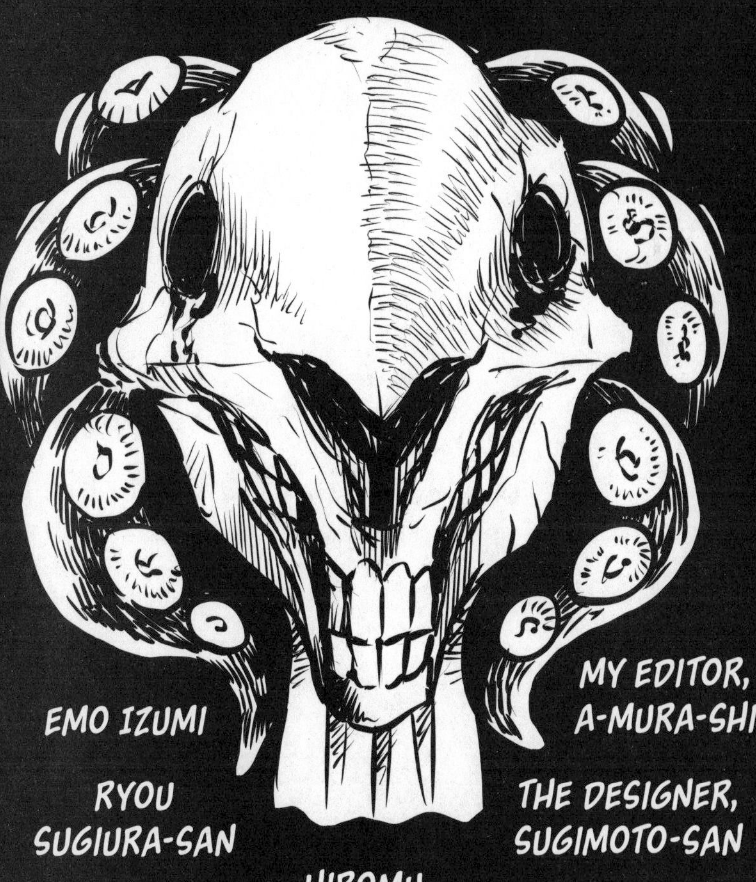

EMO IZUMI

RYOU SUGIURA-SAN

HIROMU NAGASE-SAN

MY EDITOR, A-MURA-SHI

THE DESIGNER, SUGIMOTO-SAN

SEE YOU NEXT VOLUME!

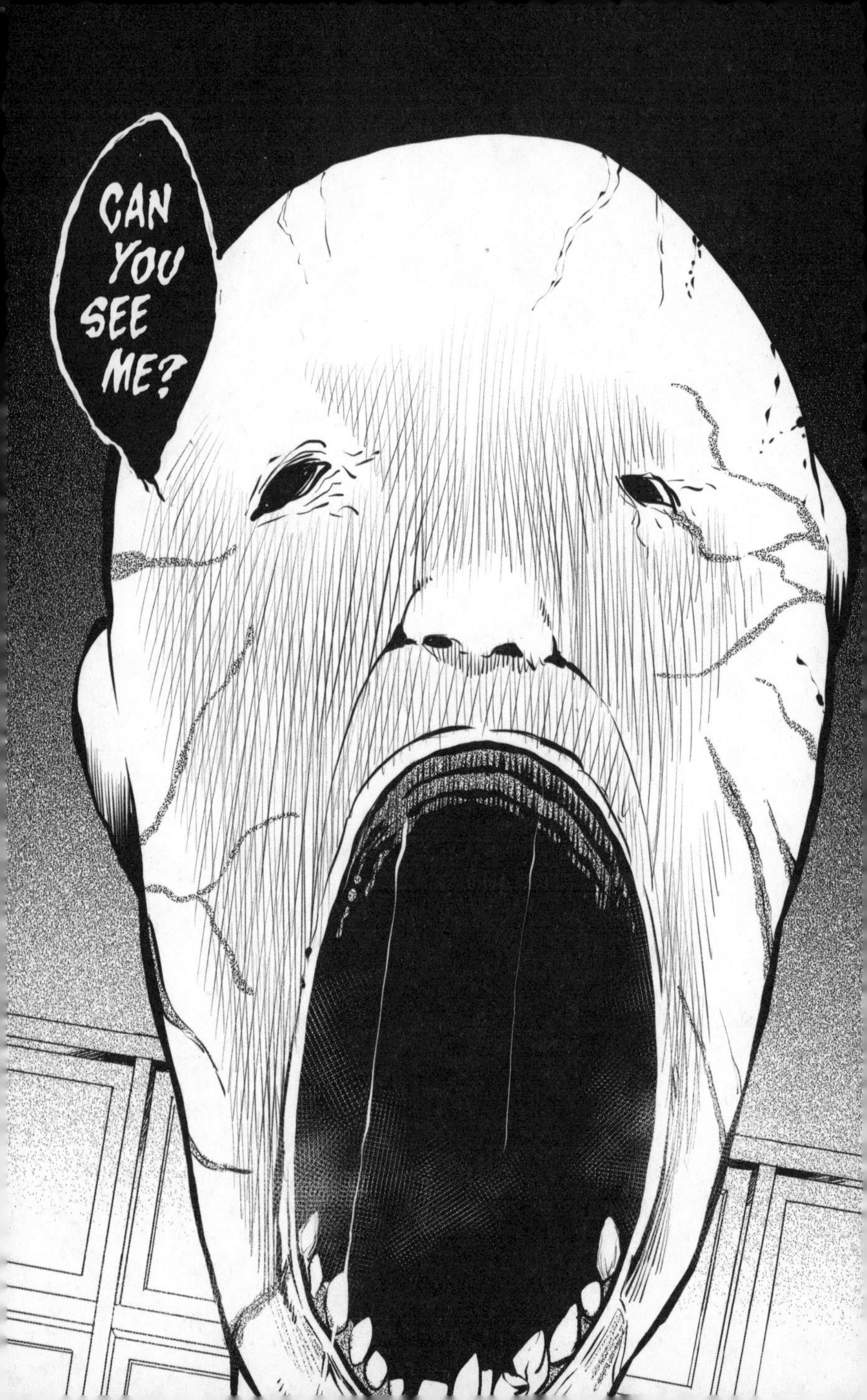
CAN YOU SEE ME?

MIERUKO-CHAN 4

Tomoki Izumi

Translation: LEIGHANN HARVEY   Lettering: ALEXIS ECKERMAN

MIERUKO-CHAN vol. 4
© Tomoki Izumi 2020
First published in Japan in 2020 by KADOKAWA CORPORATION, Tokyo.
English translation rights arranged with KADOKAWA CORPORATION, Tokyo, and Yen Press, LLC through Tuttle-Mori Agency, Inc.

English translation © 2021 by Yen Press, LLC

Yen Press
150 West 30th Street, 19th Floor
New York, NY 10001

Visit us at yenpress.com • facebook.com/yenpress • twitter.com/yenpress • yenpress.tumblr.com

First Yen Press Edition: November 2021

Yen Press is an imprint of Yen Press, LLC.
The Yen Press name and logo are trademarks of Yen Press, LLC.

The publisher is not responsible for websites (or their content) that are not owned by the publisher.

Library of Congress Control Number: 2020944845

ISBNs: 978-1-9753-2569-5 (paperback)
        978-1-9753-2570-1 (ebook)

10 9 8 7 6 5 4 3 2 1

WOR

Printed in the United States of America